"Paul Coughlin delivers a jolt of pure adrenaline! This is not bedtime reading—it is reveille for the Christian man. I loved it!"

—**Nate Larkin,** founder of The Samson Society,
author of *Samson and the Pirate Monks*

"You're going to love this book! If you're a man, it will be revolutionary. It was for me. If you're a woman, give it to the men you care about. They will rise up and call you blessed . . . and you'll care about them even more. Either way, get this book. And, oh yes, you'll owe me for having recommended it to you."

—**Steve Brown,** columnist for *Plain Truth,*
author, seminary professor, and teacher
for *Key Life,* a syndicated radio program

"Powerful and provocative, *Unleashing Courageous Faith* is impossible to put down. It immediately grabbed my attention, stirred my soul, and challenged my ideas about men and spirituality. As a female reader, I wanted to get out my pompons and cheer on the men in my life after reading this book."

—**Jennifer D. Degler,** PhD, clinical psychologist,
Interfaith Counseling Center

"This book is such a refreshing break from the norm. Needs are not met and lives are not transformed by a faith community sitting in pews. We must engage our God-given thumos to get out of our seats and into the street. Embrace the full character of Christ and let Him guide you to a new life of courage and impact."

—**Todd Dickerson,** regional director, Pacific
Northwest Fellowship of Christian Athletes

PAUL COUGHLIN

UNLEASHING COURAGEOUS FAITH

THE HIDDEN POWER
OF A MAN'S SOUL

Published by Bethany House Publishers
11400 Hampshire Avenue South
Bloomington, Minnesota 55438

Bethany House Publishers is a division of
Baker Publishing Group, Grand Rapids, Michigan.

Printed in the United States of America

ISBN 978-0-7642-0647 (International Trade Paper)

Library of Congress Cataloging-in-Publication Data

Coughlin, Paul T.
    Unleashing courageous faith : the hidden power of a man's soul / Paul Coughlin.
        p. cm.
    Includes bibliographical references.
    Summary: "Paul Coughlin exhorts men to take action and exercise manly courage shown in the Bible: the power, purpose and integrity that will make them better leaders, disciples, husbands, and fathers"—Provided by publisher.
    ISBN 978-0-7642-0577-4 (hardcover : alk. paper)
    1. Men (Christian theology). 2. Christian men—Religious life. I. Title.

BT703.5.C68   2009
248.8'.42—dc22

                                                                2008045786

To those who are "too good for a world like this,"
who do not "shrink back and are lost,"
who "have the faith to make life their own,"
and have the thumos to put the joke where
it belongs and dance with the ugly one
in the corner, now touched and loved.

[HEBREWS 11:38; 10:38–39]

ACKNOWLEDGMENTS

Thank you to the team that's becoming an army:

Sandy Coughlin, Reggie and Anni Jones, Barbara Wiedenbeck, Larry D'Apice, Kortland Foqua, Jeff Anderson, Jason Atkinson, Jeff Smith, Janet Grant, Tom Cheshire, Christopher Soderstrom, Jeff Rush, Brian Doyle, R. Dennis Hughett Jr., Rhett Lafleur, and the many more to come.

CONTENTS

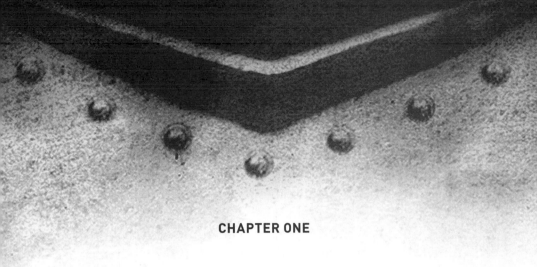

CHAPTER ONE

WHEN A DOG IS MORE MANLY

Heaven goes by favor.
If it went by merit, you would stay out
and your dog would go in.
(MARK TWAIN)

When I joke during men's conferences that my cairn terrier, Haggis McStitch, has taught me more about what it means to be a man than most men's gatherings, I'm not really joking.

Haggis is the most popular being in our home. He's the same breed as Toto in *The Wizard of Oz*, though I shudder to point this out because Toto didn't represent the breed well. Like most terriers, Haggis is a mountain of a dog inside a compact body.

When we went to pick him up in Redding, California, the first dog we saw looked robust, winsome, and cuddly.

"Is this *Haggis*?!" my daughter screamed with delight. "He's so cuuuuuute!"

"No," said Richard, the breeder. "That's his brother, Barley. This," he said, pointing, "is Haggis."

I looked at Haggis and decided Richard had pointed at the most expensive rat in all of history. Haggis was ugly. His coarse hair was pressed down, revealing his scrawny frame. He didn't have his brother's round healthiness, or becoming face, or attractive coloring. I wanted to leave right then and there.

Rip-off, I thought. But thankfully we would find that there's far more to Haggis than meets the eye.

"He's the feistiest dog I've ever bred," Richard added. Nearly four years later, I can only say amen.

A *cairn* is what the Scottish call a pile of stones. Cairn terriers have been bred to kill whatever is lurking between or underneath those stones: rats, mice, weasels, ferrets. It takes a lot of guts—that's a blue-collar word for "courage"—to go into lightless holes and instantly fight whatever you ambush.

Once, after our family returned from a trip, we found small poop droppings on our living room windowsill. Then we noticed that Haggis would not leave a certain broken TV outlet alone. Then he didn't sleep for days, which etched haggard exhaustion onto his face. (This happens when a dog—or a man—is kept from what he was designed to be and do.) We finally put two and two together and lowered him into the nearby crawl space.

He immediately kicked into action, his brindled coat bristling. Within seconds he found the intruder: a foot-long rat hiding behind the paper backing of fiberglass insulation. He shook it, breaking its neck, and brought it to me.

A family has never been prouder of a four-legged beast. Haggis had rid our home of a troubling invader. We paraded him around the house on our shoulders like Alexander the Great after the Battle of the Hydaspes. Haggis ate what we ate that night. We toasted him with wine, milk, and tap water. I considered having the rat stuffed and mounted for posterity's sake.

Actually, we think it was his third rat that year. Sometimes Sandy, my wife, makes the squishy discovery in the morning with her bare toes. Her screech could set off car alarms as she leaps through the morning air like an epileptic River Dancer. On the bright side, this is an opportunity to teach our children biology.

They also learn criminology as we form a crude circle around the little carcass that's always lying on its side. We proceed to analyze the whole scene—like on *CSI*, but without HD-grade makeup, flaming egos, or withering sarcasm.

Me: "Not a house rat. It's too skinny. And look at the coarse hair. This one's wild."

We savor the word *wild*. . . .

Garrett, my thirteen-year-old: "There's no blood. Haggis must have got him and snapped his neck."

Elliot, my fifteen-year-old: "Yeah, Filly usually chews the heads off. You can hear it at night if your door's open." (Filly is our American shorthair cat, a beautiful, natural-born hunter, but one whose tougher nature is unemployable for noble means.)

Abby, my eleven-year-old, with her hands still over her eyes, provides a two-tiered alibi for our other cat. "Hobbes slept in my room last night. Besides, she's a weenie. I love her, but it's true. She can't kill anything." (Somehow, in Hobbes's puny brain, wires are crossed. Instead of bringing us vermin, she delivers leaves, twigs, rubber frogs, and at her best, crunchy dragonflies.)

Hardwired Courage

A dog's courage can be a real pain. For example, we have to sneak into our own backyard, soundlessly, or else Haggis bursts forth, on Secret-Service-level alert, sniffing every molecule of air for any whiff of evil and, often, barking on a rampage from border to border, warding off imaginary foes. Though he's doing his job with bravado and gusto, sometimes we wish he'd take a chill pill.

Sometimes a boy's burgeoning courage can be a real pain as well. I have coached boys for nearly fifteen years. I've written before about the times when it's tempting to kill their manly fire—to squash it, to "break its neck" in order to sidestep disruption and achieve the highly popular state of "compliant comfort." We neuter them early nowadays.

Once I inherited a courageous player from a fellow coach who didn't want him, who didn't see what his born leadership could do, could become. This was the age-old ruse of painting the courageous one as the black sheep.

"He's a dangerous player," the coach told other coaches. But what he and most of our culture consider dangerous, people of eras less obsessed with status-quo comfort have lauded as spirited and vigorous. Though this player was being labeled a "hothead," I noticed that he had never been thrown out of a game (unlike other "more respectable" players).

This boy who was once slandered and reviled became part of the backbone of my team. His spirit and his will didn't need breaking, but direction. Let me tell you this: He's the kind of young man who someday will have the guts, unlike his cattle-herd peers, to stand up and, like a prophet, say NO! on behalf of the oppressed and the weak. He's the white knight our society pegs wrongly as the black sheep because we've forgotten that it takes inner heat—not a big toothy grin—to do the right thing.

When I say things like this in church, it's usually only the oddballs, sadly, who give an amen. In today's timid culture, our average neighborhood church is largely made up of mild people searching for Bible verses to sanctify mildness. Courage as a liability? It *is*, in our commonly distorted understanding of why we're here, of how we were made, of what we're charged to do.

We were preparing for a *700 Club* interview in our home one morning when Haggis somehow slipped out the front door unnoticed. We couldn't find him, and immediately it was hard to keep my mind on anything else. All I could really think about was Haggis, out there by himself. *What if he gets hit by a car? What if he's attacked by bigger dogs?* . . .

That evening, Elliot and I sat on our front porch, weeping.

Elliot: "He's such a friendly dog. What if someone takes advantage of him?"

Me: "I hope he's not hurt."

Elliot, with heat in his eyes: "If someone hurts him, I'll kill 'em!"

My evangelical Protestant upbringing has had me well trained in what it thinks an ideal Christian, especially a man, should be. I'm still a regular Pavlov's dog sometimes, and I hate it. Right there, instinctively, like an old biddy with perfectly coiffed blue-gray hair, with shame-dripping lips ready to pounce on any infraction, I almost launched into a *tsk, tsk, tsk* lecture of disapproval against my son. I would have corrected his strong language, admonished him that "anger will get you nowhere," and dropped any number of blah-blah-blah warnings a Christian man is supposed to pass on to his sons.

Sometimes we evangelical men are good in the worst sense, when our virtues become so excessive that they become vices. We may not sleep around like the younger brother in Jesus' preposterous story of the prodigal son (Luke 15:11), a revealing of God's grace that is so extravagant and illogical by human standards that God the Father comes off as a seemingly crazy old fool with white and tangled mad-scientist hair that flails in the wind as he runs half-robed down the dirt lane to embrace a son whose decision to return contains not one edifying quality. He's the heartbreaker, the broke and selfish druggy in the family whose God is his appetite and who turns to God, not because He is good and worthy of honor, but because all other options of filling his churlish belly are gone. Prayer, wrote Twain, is the last bastion of a scoundrel, and we need to look no further than the prodigal son for proof. And if we're honest, ourselves.

Unlike the prodigal, we evangelical men are often too dutiful and rule-bound to be so spirited and uninhibited. We're too governed—but by what? Does our goodness come from a love of truth, or from the fear of living, of exposure? Do we refuse to chase after skirts, not because we love our wives and fear our Lord, but because we don't have enough guts to walk on the wild side? Some of us avoid adultery, not because we're gallant and committed, but because we're afraid to.

Do we come home after work, not because we long to fervently know our wife and kids, but because home is where the comfort is, where our bread is buttered? If so, then men who have never darkened the doorstep of a church do that as well.

I fear our "goodness" has a lot more to do with Pavlov's slavish behavior modification than soulful transformation. We're the dutiful older brother, who isn't enslaved by a host of deadly sins, but by a collection of virtues gone deadly. We're the ones who refuse to take part in the party even when God pleads for us to [Luke 15:32]. Instead of gluttony, we killjoys have our "principles" and our practice of self-denial that leaves us and others stone cold.

We're the charitable ones who don't take, not because we fear being a burden, but because we don't want to be obligated. To receive is to be inferior, so we hide behind a charitable spirit instead. Instead of pride, we're falsely modest, pretending to possess a level of humility that is a churchy rouse. Instead of rage, we're indifferent, which gives the appearance of gentleness—the Gold Star of Sunday school behavior today. And instead of being slothful, we're hyper-concerned with other people's business, not because we care much about them, but because we fear what they're behavior might do to *us*.

The older brother, my fellow evangelicals, is too often the image looking back at us: joyless, trivial, bored, angry, and trapped by religiosity. God implores both brothers, the law-less and the hyper-lawful, to change.

So I fought the knee-jerk reaction to correct my son the way the older brother might and instead affirmed my son's inner heat.

If someone did mistreat or abuse Haggis, I *hope* Elliot would be angry—I hope he'd be indignant (which means "much to grieve"). If I can't feel grief, I'm either spiritually ill or spiritually emasculated. Grief is essential to a courageous, muscular faith and to a loving orientation toward others. You'd never know it from how we treat it today, but indignation actually is an indicator of a balanced and loving soul. (We'll look at grief in chapter 11.)

So instead I said, "He's probably okay, pal. Someone will take him in. They'll see our posters and call us."

That night, around three o'clock, which is maybe the hardest hour to keep one's courage screwed on, I stepped out onto the same porch and called for Haggis through the slight and dry summer wind. He didn't stir through the bushes or come running from down the street, haggard yet unharmed. No prayers were answered that night.

I was just a middle-aged man with a betraying hairline, standing half-naked on his front step with his heart torn open, unable to rest. My brindle-coated friend, brimming with tenacity and courage and eagerness and fervency and devotion, suddenly was gone. The void was so large that whole facets of me seemed to vanish within it.

After what felt like weeks, we got the "I have your dog" call the next afternoon. We jumped into our Suburban like Marines on a special op. Haggis was home within a half hour and received more hugs and kisses than he ever could have wanted.

Haggis continues to enliven and inspire us to go boldly forward throughout our days. We have grown to appreciate his courage even when it costs us rest, like when he hears a real or imagined bump in the night and fires off a series of semiautomatic warning barks. He is our sixteen-pound sentinel on the watchtower. He monitors our borders while we enjoy blessed REM sleep. He's our happy fighter, our dancing warrior of Celtic lore.

The martial spirit of Haggis affects us the way Vietnam veteran Tom Mitchell was affected by his unit's war dogs.

> When we were sick, they would comfort us, and when we were injured, they protected us. They didn't care how much money we had or what color our skin was. Heck, they didn't even care if we were good soldiers. They loved us unconditionally. And we loved them. Still do.[1]

Haggis's pugnacious nature takes its toll on him. When our children frolic in the pool, he's there, ever watching, his small, Canadian bacon pink-like tongue hanging out. "Uneasy lies the head that wears the crown," wrote Shakespeare,[2] and Haggis is plenty worried when our kids are exposed and vulnerable. Our cats have never guarded or worried about our children.

Recently I visited one of my best friends in his home as he was recovering from an accidental gunshot wound that almost took his life. His dog, Stella, made sure to keep her body between us. She didn't leave his side—no one trained her to be that way, but still there was visible strain on her dogged, worn face. What makes dogs do that?

Before Haggis there was Conrad Lewis, our German shepherd. When Elliot was just a toddler, Conrad put his body between him and two adult Chow Chows in our front yard.

Those were tough dogs—we later found out that the Chows had chewed the testicles off a Rottweiler weeks earlier. And Conrad was still a puppy. He literally put his life on the line for my son. What trait possessed him then?

Masculinity: Unwanted

I thoroughly enjoy Haggis's companionship while hiking, snowshoeing, and fishing, even though his fur only protects against so much—if we're in nature's raw winter elements long enough, he needs extra covering so he won't freeze to death. Have you tried lately to buy a jacket for a dog? It's a real education. Try it, and you'll see how we're even trying to drive the manliness right out of *canines.*

When we were going fly-fishing on the Klamath River for winter steelhead, I went to Petco and asked the clerk for directions to the dog jackets. She took me to an assortment that mostly were either fake leopard skin or (I kid you not) adorned with colored boas. "Do you have any jackets for dogs that are heterosexual?" I asked. Good night, I'd rather eat my own hair mixed with mayonnaise than put one of those things on Haggis.

And Haggis is a dog. We've gone mad, mad, mad at expecting little *boys* to behave like little *girls.* Boys are being gunned down by manliness gone bad and by those who do not accept or appreciate it. Our culture tells young boys that traditional masculinity is bad, that men are stupid and deserve to be the object of disdain, contempt, and ridicule. Then we expect them to grow up and exemplify honor, integrity, and valor.

Boys are vulnerable, and gutting a boy's manly courage is easy. Put him in the care of men or women who don't understand what creates a courageous soul, the kind of people who mistake manners for morals. Give him a Sunday school teacher or pastor who indoctrinates him into worshiping a false god, a gentle Jesus meek and mild.

Give him a mother who was beaten by her father. She'll do the best she can to attack burgeoning manhood in her boys. She'll look at powerful men with contempt and then use her verbal acumen to castrate young male souls. Thereby she condemns a boy's manhood: When she criticizes his father, the boy will struggle with the belief that he's the fruit of defective seed.

Or give him an overprotective parent who fights all his meaningful battles for him.

Give him coaches and teachers who refuse to push him further than he wants to go, or who don't get a kick out of irrepressible and sometimes irresponsible little-guy energy.

We strain our necks to get a glimpse of dogs that exhibit noble masculinity, whether in the Iditarod or in the backseat of a police car. Conversely, masculine-lite dogs lie on laps and shun uncomfortable weather. They cause no man to offer them his respect. Manly, courageous dogs are determined to pack multiple lifetimes into one, very much like manly men.

This same dogged attribute exists in you as well, and it will emerge and thrive if you will go against wrong-headed spiritual training to nurture and grow it.

Our Unnamed Spiritual Need

What is it about a dog that captures us so? Why, for example, is it usually guys in their twenties and early thirties—often an exceedingly fearful time in a man's life (underreported and under-ministered to)—who feel a deep inner need to get a big dog? Children yearn for them too. I read a few years ago that the number one topic kids look up in the encyclopedia is dogs.

I believe it, but why? What is it that captivates us? What quality, what trait, what x-factor are we trying to get from a creature whose bargain includes biting fleas, insidious ticks, smelly carpets, and outrageous vet bills? Is there an element we're trying to graft into our deficient, trivial, boring lives?

There's *something* that makes the words of animal rights activist Roger Caras ring true: "If you don't have a dog—at least one—there is not necessarily anything wrong with you, but there may be something wrong with your life."

Many of us, when we get a dog, think that our objective is somehow to make them semi-human. But have you noticed that there's a part of *you* that longs to be more like *them*? "The more I see of men," said Madame Jeanne-Marie Roland, "the more I admire dogs."[3] Me too. Some people think animals will be in heaven, and some don't. But I admit that if there are no dogs in heaven, then there's a part of me that wants to go wherever they're headed!

When Haggis ran away and got lost, he took with him a trait that I could sense I needed as much as I need air. I couldn't name it then. I can name it now.

This name, this container, answers a riddle that plagued me for a long time. Here's an example. A seminary professor's mind can ponder wisdom, order, and justice. His brain can help him to discern the weightier matters of theology and assist him with understanding sacred text in its original language. His heart can affirm what is valuable and beautiful and stir a desire within him to love God, his wife, his children, and his neighbor. It can inspire him to lift his hands toward heaven as he praises God in corporate worship.

But if he has no animating urge, no motivating courage or gumption compelling him to take the risks that are required to create and establish justice, he becomes a paper lion, a punch line, a cautionary tale. If he has no fire burning in his belly, no tenacity to inflate his chest and lungs, he won't be able to withstand, genuinely and authentically, the turmoil that accompanies the realities of loving people on earth or God in heaven.

What good is such a person who earnestly studies God with his mind, sincerely praises him from his heart, but fails to *actualize* either his thoughts or his emotions? Where is his fiery faith put into being—which, by the way, is something God expects from us? What if a man does not labor to put feet on the good desires born in his head and heart? Doesn't that make him the noisy gong that the apostle Paul denounces?[4] Isn't he what James would call a talker but not a doer?[5]

Maybe I just described your father. Or a sibling. Or a friend. Or you. I know this much: I just described the life *I* lived for far too long.

For years and years I was not connecting with or activating a special region within me, a dimension that my spiritual training didn't even address or, when it briefly touched on the matter, told me was off limits and sinful. It's a God-designed area, within me and within you, where courage and its fruits—unsentimental love and a martial spirit (to name just two)—are forged and stored.

This is a soul region that the ancient Greeks studied, praised, and placed warning signs around. It's a place that is a gift to those we love—if we'll do the soul-work required to grow it and unleash it. It's also a curse if it isn't seasoned and disciplined. At times it appears elusive. It's a lost piece in our spiritual puzzle. For many of us, it's our absent ingredient, the missing link in our spiritual journey.

The Greeks called it *thumos* (sometimes spelled *thymos*). This powerful word bulges with meaning, and it doesn't translate into English without some hitches. God created men and women with thumos, a "fight drive," a courageous and animating spirit, without which we don't grow in spiritual breadth and depth, are unable to deeply love, consistently fail to lead or surmount the sins of our flesh.

Think of thumos as a Thermos container of spiritual heat and spiritual juice. It's a pugnacious yet playful drive, an attribute that separates the men from the boys, the women from the girls.

Thumos, wrote the ancient Greeks, is one of three main parts of our soul, along with *logos* (head and logic) and *eros* (heart and emotions). It's found—or at least should be found—more in men than in women, making a man's spirituality and his earthly responsibilities similar but also different. It is largely due to this difference that men have become a cultural target of bigotry, resentment, even hatred. Thumos is a mighty gift and, like many giftings, can also be a burden.

Thumos is the reason two preachers will talk about God's requirement for social justice and mercy, yet only one will commit the deeds required to usher them in. It's why some men think that their men's ministry group at church should do more than flip pancakes every fourth Saturday morning. It's why one guy stands and denounces brutality while others pretend to have lost their vision and their speech.

Most Christians leave far more than their sin at the cross: We are admonished by the church and, in a different sense, by our culture to forsake our thumos and its fruit, courage—which is essential to deep and abiding love—as if they were a scarlet *T* covering our genitals. The church doesn't give us spiritual swords and other martial weapons for battle when we become Christ-followers. It gives us acoustic guitars and open-toed sandals, and then shows us how to become pacifist folk singers. "Jesus is our Savior," we're told in Sunday school. "Now let's make some rainbows!" No wonder leadership is so rare and elusive.

And this makes sense, given the hair-model Jesus many of us grew up with. He has a killer smile and is very popular with the gals . . . just not so popular with the guys. A neutered Jesus doesn't garner another man's allegiance and faith but rather his irritation and scorn.

It's Neither Heart Nor Mind

Your thumos is not a subset of your feelings or emotions. An awakened heart is invaluable for our spiritual life, but when overemphasized, it actually can lead us away from a rounded-out understanding of our God-created design. *Hearts alone do not lead us into worthy battle.* And hearts sometimes lead us astray. Rudolph Hess, swearing in the Nazi party in 1934, exhorted his hearers in a manner that should make all of us carefully evaluate our fickle home of emotion: "Do not seek Adolph Hitler with your brains; all of you will find him with the strength of your hearts."

Thumos is where our head and heart converge, quarrel, and then put feet underneath our courageous intentions. This is an integral part of our fulfilling the good works that God has prepared for us in advance[7]—if we have the guts (a blue-collar definition of thumos) to play our part by being obedient to transcendent causes larger than our own ego and appetites. It's the place where we talk to ourselves in the age-old effort to "screw on our courage." Men talk to themselves more than women, and again, this is not a coincidence.

Just as our heart alone isn't adequate to enliven our spiritual growth, reason (thoughts, mind) provides clarity but doesn't provide strength and impetus. Our lives are only strong, purposeful, and meaningful when we *do something* loving, beautiful, freedom-giving, redemptive, and worthy of respect. Or as J. D. Salinger's troubled Franny puts it,

> Everything everybody does is so—I don't know—not *wrong,* or even mean, or even stupid necessarily. But just so tiny and meaningless and—sad-making. And the worst of it is, if you go bohemian or something crazy like that, you're conforming just as much as everybody else, only in a different way.[8]

Go and *do,* the prophets and other malcontents tell us— don't just *think* and *feel.*

Those who have been shot at in the line of military duty will tell you that if they'd waited for courage to flow before they responded, it would have been far wiser just to have stayed in bed. Something else within them, from another region of their soul, kicks into action. Rarely does one feel courageous in the face of opposition, and so over-reliance on one's heart or mind can be a trap. Courage must be manufactured within another inner place.

Yet thumos-courage is not only part of the physical life, it also can have a moral dimension. When Boris Pasternak refused the Nobel Prize and with it the opportunity to deliver a speech to expose the lies of the former Soviet Union, Alexander Solzhenitsyn was mortified by Pasternak's lack of thumotic energy.

Solzhenitsyn's response, much like Martin Luther King Jr.'s "Letter from Birmingham Jail," shows us the elegant strength of thumos—the prophet-like justice it demands, the sacrifice it often requires from those who flex it, and the need for us, when necessary, to overrule our heart, because though love can flow from that region, so can life-stopping, love-freezing fear.

> All the more vividly did I see [the Nobel Prize], all the more eagerly did I brood on it, demand it from the future! I had to have that prize! As a position to be won, a vantage point on the battlefield! . . . I should resolutely accept the prize, resolutely go to Stockholm, make a very resolute speech. . . . [I would] touch off the explosive charge . . . [and] speak for all those who had been stifled, shot, starved or frozen to death! Drag it all to the platform of the Nobel Prize ceremony and hurl it like a thunderbolt.[9]

Those are passionate, heart-drenched words, but they are more than passion. They drip with courage as well, born from the thumos-place within the man that binds emotion and intellect together. The place where a man stands and says what he stands for is right, and that those who stand against him are wrong. It's the place from which Jesus was able to say, "He who is not with me is against me, and he who does not gather with me scatters."[10] Minus an appreciation for thumos, these are the ravings of a lunatic.

In *Unleashing Courageous Faith*, we'll explore the many facets of thumos: where we find it, what kills it, what fuels it, and so forth. For now, let me offer this hopeful insight up front: *It's already in you. The potential is there.*

We want men to have a heart so that they can more tenderly express love. Likewise, we need to help men, as the Wizard of Oz did for the Cowardly Lion, to have thumos so they can create a more muscular, manly form of love: that practical, unsentimental, no-strings-attached, kingly, prophetic, forceful love that lays down its life for another without fanfare or an arsenal of publicists—the kind that makes nations weep, faith grow, and God be glorified.

The Soul's Third Dimension

Gentler virtues, tougher virtues—we need them both—but they are found and forged in different places and through different practices and disciplines. The church, and some para-church organizations like Ransomed Heart, Promise Keepers, Iron Sharpens Iron, and Women of Faith currently are helping the Tin Men: those who need to find their hearts. This is a remarkable and noble accomplishment of immeasurable impact. But we also need to help the many, many Cowardly Lions find their courage as well. And note the three—not two—main characters who need to rediscover their essence: more than just brain (Scarecrow) and heart (Tin Man)! We're so familiar with this third facet of being that often we don't even notice or consider it.

These three soulish "parts" of us have been hiding for a long time. And, as the song by the band America goes, Oz never gave them nothing that they didn't already have. It's there, in you, simmering but elusive, like your last moment of déjà vu. We need each other to find it, grow it, and honor it, so that someday we can say, like the Cowardly Lion, "What makes a king out of a slave? Courage!"[11]

This force inside us is one that's shrouded in mystery like a mighty wind. Wind is an ancient symbol for thumos, and it's one of the ways the Holy Spirit is revealed in Scripture. This is where our heroic instinct is grown and where it's housed; this is where our innate longing to act nobly is found. We desperately need to tap it—this power that's missing in our culture and mostly missing in the church—but we don't know how. And, truthfully, we aren't even sure that we should. Our spiritual training has us believing it's a kind of Pandora's box, maybe best left untouched.

Listening to the well-meaning but naïve and spiritually negligent voices of mildness will lead to our demise. If you treat thumos as if it's just another flavor at the ice-cream counter of ministry, you will forgo love and the protection of what is good, right, and honorable. You will miss out on much growth and adventure, and the ability to subdue the cravings of your flesh. You will not have the skills you need to be the leader you want to be. You will remain fragmented and unstable in your nature.

All of us—and especially men—must lay claim to thumos so that God's grace in us can construct a new and dynamic person. Most of us will never fight a physical battle against an enemy; we will use our thumos, or not, for moral courage against both the evil spirit of the age that erodes human dignity and also against our own tendency to take the easy way through life, which halts spiritual growth. We must harness thumos to rise above the mediocre, trivial, social-club Christianity in which we too often find ourselves, shaking off the fearful and uninformed critics who worship comfort instead of truth. Because a shift is taking place: God is calling his people to fight for justice, and more and more of them are answering the call.

We have flexed compassion the world over to combat poverty and disease. But one of the most underreported reasons people's lives are so desperate isn't that they don't have the ability to feed and educate themselves—it's that others oppress them, rob them, maim them, and enslave them. Many don't need more bags of rice—not ultimately. They, like the estimated twenty-seven million people in actual slavery, like the 160,000 kids who stay home *daily* from American schools for fear of being bullied, need justice to rain down upon them from the hands of righteous people who will fight on their behalf. That's right, *fight*—one of evangelicalism's most feared words and even more feared actions. We need the men to move first—that's almost always how it works.

Thumos has a sinister side as well as a noble side, which should lead a man to embrace, not crucify, his martial spirit (that's the subject of the next chapter). Before we get into that, I need to give a disclaimer.

One of the hazards of being a writer, and there are many, is that you never quite live up to your words, especially if you write about spiritual matters. You always fall short. So just let me say straightaway that I do not hold myself up as some giant when it comes to thumos.

This will not shock those who know me. I've lacked thumos for much of my life. At the same time, I've undertaken a good amount of soul-work to grow it, season it, deploy it. I am guilty of cowardice, though I don't think this sin (yes, sin) defines me.

In this book I will share with you my victories and the victories of others. And if my thumos is strong enough, I will share with you my defeats, because it's not our strengths that make us relatable and lead to fellowship and even brotherhood or sisterhood. It's our weaknesses, through which we're perfected, that bond us.

And while we have sibling-hood on our minds, now's a good time to point out a distinction about this book that, like thumos, is bound to raise eyebrows. Both genders possess thumos, and it tends to express its animated spiritedness differently. Generally speaking, a woman's is expressed most strongly in intimate relationships, especially with children, and a man's tends to be deployed upon the world "out there," that is, outside the house. Of course there is overlap, and of course there are exceptions, and those exceptions should be honored instead of being used as material for jagged punch lines. We should applaud the good side of thumos wherever we can find it. (We'll talk about the other side in chapter 4.)

Here's an example. A friend of mine and his wife were having dinner with another couple and talking about gender roles. The other couple was more liberal, so they had a more general, less specific interpretation. In fact, the well-educated husband thought their understanding was so broad that if at nighttime they suspected someone was trying to break into their home, he said, it would be the responsibility of the person closest to the bedroom door to get up and investigate. His usually-just-as-liberal wife looked at him first with horror and then with contempt.

Liberal or conservative, theist or atheist—a man, muscular or weakling, is expected to confront the intruder. This has to do with more than innate physical strength. It's also because men possess a palpable thumotic energy that can either be valorous or sinister, depending on how it's used. God is thumotic, and as his image bearers, so are we.

Finally, a warning: Thumos is disruptive. Many people think disruption is sinful, and it's certainly unmannerly. In a church culture dominated by female sensibilities that make it wired more for safety than for battle, morality and manners are pervasively put forward as one and the same.

That Jesus was mighty unmannerly is just one indicator of our drift and diminishment.

Thumos bites into what's wrong with the status quo and will not let go, much like Haggis with a bone. There are people, lots of people, inside and outside the church, who love the status quo. They do not take kindly to anyone messing with *what is*—even when *what is* is killing them and others. So know that when your thumos urges you onto whatever battlefield has long been awaiting you, you're going to make some enemies. Jesus said to pray for your enemies,[12] and he wouldn't have said this if you weren't going to make some. And he never said you couldn't have any.

Notes

1. Quoted by Richard Ben Cramer in Matt Weinstein and Luke Barber, *Dogs Don't Bite When a Growl Will Do: What Your Dog Can Teach You About Living a Happy Life* (New York: Perigee Trade, 2003), 254.
2. In *King Henry the Fourth*, Part II.
3. Attributed
4. See 1 Corinthians 13.
5. See James 2.
6. In Eric Hoffer, *The True Believer: Thoughts on the Nature of Mass Movements* (New York: Harper Perennial Modern Classics, 1951), 81.
7. See Ephesians 2:10.
8. J. D. Salinger, *Franny and Zooey* (New York: Back Bay Books, 1961), 26.
9. Alexander Solzhenitsyn, quoted in Robert Inchausti, *Subversive Orthodoxy: Outlaws, Revolutionaries, and Other Christians in Disguise* (Grand Rapids: Brazos, 2005), 64.
10. Matthew 12:30
11. "King of the Forest," in L. Frank Baum, *The Wonderful Wizard of Oz: 100th Anniversary Edition*, illustrated by W. W. Denslow (New York: HarperCollins, 2006).
12. See Matthew 5; Luke 6.

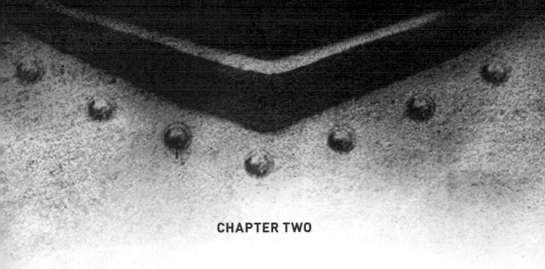

MIA—A MARTIAL SPIRIT

*Jerry Seinfeld: "What is this? What are we doing?
What in God's name are we doing?"*
George Costanza: "What?"
*Jerry: "Our lives! What kind of lives are these?
We're like children. We're not men."*
George: "No, we're not. We're not men."[1]

*From the days of John the Baptist until now,
the kingdom of heaven has been forcefully advancing,
and forceful men lay hold of it.*
(JESUS)[2]

What has been deemed the ideal man throughout history, what sociologists and others have called the male archetype, has been a combination of three potent forces: (1) what a given society deemed valuable; (2) what religion said a man should be and do; and (3) what the military said a man should be and do. This third facet is related to what we call a martial spirit, and it's also described as a part of the warrior ethos.

But the Sensitive Male, the new "man" that gradually was being forged in the smithy of the gender-confusing social upheaval of the '60s and '70s, culminated in the neutered archetype of the '80s and '90s that's still with us today. That process jettisoned the spiritual and military components of the ideal man. From a historical perspective, man left two-thirds of himself in the closet (next to his roach clip, argyle sweaters, Culture Club tapes, and pastel dress shirts).

Today's Sensitive Male ideal is a foreign and cruel creation: foreign because he's out of historical context, and cruel because society has compelled him to go against his created nature. One could say that he now is a male by anatomy but not by behavior and composition. The only attribute allowing him to cling to any semblance of a lineage is that he carries what society currently wants most: sensitivity.

In a way this is a beneficial development, because without sensitivity we can't really love. For love, though, more is required of a man than his often fickle, deceptive, and unreliable emotions. He *also* needs his soul to be vitalized, and he needs an internal fighting urge (martial spirit) to help him fulfill his roles of provider, protector, and guide. His thumos causes him to muster the inner heat—I describe this as "The Jalapeño Factor"—to undergo the criticism, suffering, and labor required to become a real leader, to fulfill his duty, and to reach the highest level of true masculinity: *love bolstered by courage.*

Why does a martial spirit matter? Because, wrote Thomas Hughes, in *The Manliness of Christ* (more than one hundred twenty-five years ago—it's harder to envision a book by that title today),

> [we are] born into a state of war; with falsehood and disease and wrong and misery, in a thousand forms, lying all around us . . . and the voice within us is calling on us to take our stand as men in the eternal battle against these.[3]

This voice is real, but presently it's crying out as one alone in the wilderness: repressed, stigmatized, and neglected. It seems that only oddballs hear it, and it's the oddballs who inspire others to heed it as well.

Why don't we honor this voice? Primarily, we church folk are not wave-making people. Mels Carbonell has given personality tests to thousands of churchgoers throughout the past twenty years. His findings show that while around 62 percent of Americans have developed passive personalities, a whopping 85 percent of Christians fall into the passive category.

David Murrow says of this finding:

> Any institution so heavily tilted toward passive personalities will itself become passive. It will tend to value tradition and stability over innovation and growth. . . . You might say that today's church is full of passivity activists whose greatest energies are devoted to fighting change.[4]

Passive people discard their strength and excommunicate their thumos as ungodly and wicked. Their spiritual growth is limited, and they flee from life's inevitable (and faith-building) hardships. The church has compelled overly passive people to become even more passive, and in doing so it has robbed them of the opportunity to forge life-blessing courage. This is like giving cough syrup to a diabetic: It's the wrong spiritual prescription.

Pastors' sons tend to be first in line at men's conferences after I'm done speaking. Their faces are an odd blend of mourning and the enthusiasm that comes from an insight that's real and useful but also frightening. Sometimes I can't tell whether they want to shake my hand or punch me.

"My father would let the congregation walk all over our family," one balding thirty-something man told me. He had a hard time keeping his hands still. "He would apologize for things that my siblings and I didn't even do. I hated him for it." His eyes were turning red; he drew deep breaths while shaking his head. "My dad lied, and I grew up just like him, a coward. I let people run roughshod over me too. I wasn't allowed to push back in life. I was bullied in school, and he kept telling me to 'Just ignore them' and to 'Turn the other cheek.' "

"You're divorced, aren't you," I said.

"How did you know?" he asked, amazed.

"I hear your story almost every time I speak. You let your wife walk all over you, and she didn't respect you. My guess is, she was testing you when she pushed you." (I said this with compassion, not judgment. This was once true for me as well.)

He nodded a resigned yes.

"A woman doesn't want a yes-man," I went on. "She wants a good man. Your spiritual training has betrayed you. Don't blame God. It's not his fault—blame the Official Script.[5] Today we have a false sense of what it means to be pastoral, and it needs to change."

Not like I usually need to spell this out to the sons of pastors. They know it deep in the marrow of their rage-filled thumos, even more so than most other men. In providing individual instruction to men across the nation who need help getting their thumos going, I work with pastors' sons more than any other group. Let that fact sink in. Consider the ramifications.

These men are taught to go with the flow so much that they end up going down the drain of most anyone else's will. This is what happens when people are taught from the pulpit to become doormats, to over-yes and under-no others. What's one of the heaviest insults you can drop on a guy? That he's a tool, a yes-man.

Think about it. We don't criticize people for their ability to say no. We actually are critical, even contemptuous, of people who are incapable of no. Something deep within us respects *no*. It shows backbone. When others throughout history wrongly said yes, or worse, said nothing, the greatest people of all time, when it mattered most, said *no*!

These pastors' sons are almost always separated, divorced, or on the verge of divorce. Their wives or ex-wives complain that they just don't possess the fire they want from a husband. They sometimes say that their husbands drain them of energy instead of invigorating them. These are hard words to hear from other men because I know the shame it creates in them, a shame they can rarely name and one they're hard-pressed to overcome.

These men often have no definable self, a fact their wives sometimes point out with disgust when walking out the door. We're encouraged to have self-control, but these men don't have a self to control in the first place because their self isn't yet defined—it's still runny in the middle. They don't know who they are, and this is what happens when churches don't allow them to be individuals. They're often anchorless, easily influenced by others.

Because they've been trained to be unfailingly pleasant, they usually say yes to everything. Many think it's simply wrong to say no. And when they do, they lose sleep at night. Being human, having boundaries, sequestering themselves (the way Jesus did), and not always providing an answer when questioned (the way Jesus refused to answer many inquiries posed to him) feels unnatural and sinful to them.

They're resentful of how people have treated them and their families, and because they don't think they should experience or own negative feelings, they don't know what to do with their frustration and bitterness. They tend to denounce the emotions as unchristian instead of being honest and working through them. As a result of being treated poorly, they don't trust others very much, including their wives.

They are known by many, but they're not knowable, in part because they possess personas, assumed identities, but not discernable personalities. They feel they've been forced to play roles, to wear masks. ("Mask" is one of the original meanings of *persona*. The word Jesus used for *hypocrite* while denouncing the Pharisees literally means "wearer of masks," as an actor would do.[6]) This has exhausted them and depleted their authenticity and confidence.

They know the right words to use in marriage—they know how to perform—but they don't know how to deeply love another person. This is what personas do: they're like holograms, which by nature are all surface, no substance. They know how to be really nice but not really good.

They think that always remaining gentle and pleasant, never showing indignation or other forms of healthy anger toward anything or anyone, is among the highest forms of spiritual maturity. More so, their upbringing has them believing that it's wrong *not* to be 24/7 gentle. (If this is true, then Jesus was wrong—Jesus sinned.)

Many ministers' sons had workaholic fathers who weren't there for them. Many also have slaved in never-ending, futile attempts to please a flock that in many ways cannot be pleased. A pastor friend told me that one of the most liberating moments in his career came when his church brought in a consultant; the man told him that if he did not guard himself against the mentally unstable people in his congregation, "they will chew you and your family up, then spit you all out."

There's also the weighty implication of appearances. If his son or daughter seems to be getting out of hand, the pastor fears losing his status, his home, his job. In most men, when money's involved, the flames of thumos shrink down to a nonthreatening pilot light. Most of them have learned to throw the martial spirit overboard so as to never rock the boat, even when a given boat would be better off at the bottom of the ocean.

What we often don't recognize or admit is that passive Christians tend to flee into the arms of Jesus not for strength to steer the ship but to avoid the waves of life—for *sanctuary*, which is what we call the room where we gather. But, not making any waves is the state that immediately precedes drowning.

First Turning

For those of us who grew up during the Sensitive Man era, Promise Keepers (God bless them) inserted the religious component back into the ideal-male construct. Promise Keepers deserves our heartfelt thank-you. I call their teaching "the First Turning." Now a Second Turning has begun.

Men across the globe hunger for a more earthy, raw, powerful, and pugnacious spiritual dimension that is—I'll say it—more manly than what they have now. I've talked with them face-to-face, at home and abroad. I receive their letters and e-mails from England, New Zealand, Malaysia, Japan, Germany, France, Uganda, Canada, and from countries I've had to Google to find on the map. They want a vitality of soul that their ancestors had but that now seems to have skipped at least a generation or two.

One man from Australia writes:

> The "nice" perversion [the misconception that being nice is the same as being good] is widespread across society, and as a parent of a five-year-old boy I am appalled at the prevalence of weak, non-masculine male role models in children's media as well as the church. Promo shots for leading male stars of the Christian Music industry look sweet, sickly sweet, to comply with the phony image of our Saviour.
>
> There has been a determination to recreate God in our own image and [to] give my son a complete "Queer Eye for the Straight Guy" makeover. That scruffy Hebrew carpenter

with questionable manners, too inclined to embarrass his betters, apparently became over time clearly unacceptable to the church he originally founded, much as he had been to the Pharisees and Sadducees of his time on earth.

No wonder there has been a crisis in church membership and a serious failure to bring seekers to the one true God.

Another from Kansas wants men to remain men when they come to Christ.

> What is it about church that turns us Christian men into such weenies? I've seen men come to our church, men who were known for being bold and decisive. And instead of blessing us with their boldness and ability to make tough decisions so we can take more hills for the kingdom, they become so pliable and innocuous. We already have plenty of those. It's the main reason why we don't do anything meaningful!

Perry Atkinson, a mentor of mine for nearly twenty years and general manager of The Dove radio station, often says that when his thumos gets rumbling, Christian men hide their cowardice behind a gentle spirit. But it's not fooling him.

> For some reason Christian men leave their guts [behind] when they enter the church boardroom. They forget about commonsense practices that make organizations healthier and better and instead make decisions that no one would make in their own homes. They don't want to make the hard decisions, so they make the easy ones, which ruin churches.

I think this is as good a definition of a martial spirit as any other: the ability to make the hard decision when the easy one looks so "Christian."

Have you tried to grow spiritually, love deeply, and lead reliably without a fighting animus? How'd that work for you? If you're like me—for decades I was told that all I really needed to do was pray hard, read my Bible regularly, and "sacrifice" everything for my wife and family—you'll conclude that this model is a colossal failure.

A non-martial approach toward male life doesn't work. It never has. The successful, handmade-suit-wearing ministers who have sold this recipe for disaster from expensive sanctuary stages don't live it themselves. I've met some of them, and I keep meeting them; they, like the Pharisees, are telling you to live one way while they live another (after the microphones and cameras are off).

One reason they do this is that they know a Christian man just can't be very honest about his thumotic nature. Most congregations don't want a tough minister (until they face hardship)—they want someone who's going to make them feel warm inside. So pastors think that if they reveal too much of their pugnacious spiritedness, the kind Jesus possessed, they'll be condemned as not being Christlike. So like Clark Kent, they keep their true identity hidden, especially from older congregants, the blue-haired mafia, which hold a lot of power in most churches.

One spiritually negligent pastor of mine, a man who punctured my martial spirit, was a stellar player of "the thumos shell game." His sermons were constant warnings against assertive and aggressive behavior. One of his favorite passages is where King David and his men were pelted with rocks by an angry man:

> [One of David's men, Abishai,] said to the king, "Why should this dead dog curse my lord the king? Let me go over and cut off his head."

But the king said . . . "If he is cursing because the Lord said to him, 'Curse David,' who can ask, 'Why do you do this?' "[7]

The pastor's clear message: If people attack you, it's the Lord's will. Give no place to your martial spirit—do not defend yourself or others.

Unfortunately, I and many other young men listened. Amazingly, hypocritically, this same man later hired bodyguards for personal protection. The only time he *publicly* expressed anger was when he attacked beliefs that threatened his fine-point theological stances. I never heard him get angry about injustice, or lack of mercy, or the other matters God says he wants us to take most seriously.

This spiritually naïve pastor told us that if we experience resistance in life, then God clearly is telling us no. Again, though, he had no interest in walking his own talk. For instance, when his church had a hard time getting building permits in order to expand—that is, it received resistance— he fought back (contrary to his constant harping about God's supposed will). And when the church still couldn't get the permits they wanted, they built anyway.

If resistance were God's way of telling us no, then no book worth reading would be written. There would be no *Pilgrim's Progress* (written in prison), and we wouldn't have most of Paul's epistles (written in prison). We can thank God that Martin Luther, Dorothy Sayers, Dietrich Bonhoeffer, Nelson Mandela, Mother Teresa, Martin Luther King Jr., Harriet Tubman, Tony Campolo, James Dobson, Chuck Colson, Mike Yaconelli, Gary Haugen, Desmond Tutu, and so many others who have changed the world for the better did not follow an insipid and simplistic belief that helps define invertebrate Christianity and that could have killed their godly martial spirit.

Most successful people, like the aforementioned pastor, regardless of the path they've taken or the path that has taken them, do have a martial spirit. Well, all people do. Let me clarify: *These* people tap into it while most other Christians don't. They feed it red meat. They train it, discipline it, argue with it, and employ it. But many of them compel *you* to scourge and crucify it because this is what the unbiblical, hypocritical, and spiritually destructive Official Script demands. The Official Script (see chapter 6) is what we come up with when we sift the Scriptures and only emphasize the mild ones so that we can sanctify mildness and eradicate discomfort from our lives.

Second Turning

Earlier I mentioned a "Second Turning," currently underway, of grafting the martial spirit back into men. This is one of my goals during conferences: to help men more accurately see their male essence, an essence that for decades has been portrayed as synonymous with their sin nature. The Second Turning retains sensitivity to women and children and God, but it shows itself in stronger, more emboldened, more courageous ways. It protects *and* cherishes the church as well as family, mercy, and justice.

This model provides wholeness, and with it, integrity. Men with integrity use force, but they use it justly. Remember Jesus' words at the beginning of this chapter—the words that, like so many other Jesus statements, appear so unchristian? "The kingdom of heaven has been forcefully advancing, and forceful men lay hold of it."[8]

We don't trust people who do not use force justly, or at least we don't trust them for very long. Women certainly don't trust men who lack the willingness to use force, and children are nervous around fathers incapable of using force. When these fathers fail their children, it feels to them like far more than a mere mistake. It is remembered as a betrayal. Children expect their father to flex his power when it's needed, and they are filled with disdain when he won't.

I was a paperboy in Reseda, California, when I was ten. And one day I came home from school to some very bad news: I broke someone's window with a newspaper—or so the owner said. So my dad drove me to the scene of the crime, an old two-story apartment complex. The window I supposedly broke belonged to an elderly couple who kept their apartment thermostat at around boiling. I could barely breathe when my father and I entered the low-watt-bulb apartment of this strangely quiet and very guilty-looking couple whose apartment smelled like an old shoe packed with Vick's VapoRub.

They showed us their broken window. I searched my troubled mind to remember if I had broken it and if so, how? I was a pretty good shot with a newspaper back then, so I actually never went up to the second story to deliver their paper. I would throw it from below, lobbing it over the guardrail, floating it onto their front doorstep. My father knew that there was no way such a small paper could pack that kind of wallop. But still, the window was broken, and these two old people were pinning it on me.

We were about to leave their sweltering apartment, guilty as charged, when my father stopped and, like Columbo, looked to his left at the window one last time. "Your window, it's broken from the inside," he said in his Irish accent. "It's sticking out, not in."

My father spoke as if you were fined for using too many words, which made him both intriguing and frustrating to me as a son. So instead of calling them rats, he just stared at them for their response. That sandcastle frail, ghost-like, and dishonest couple just stared back at us, more half-dead than alive, without a sign of remorse. We left silently as well.

This story may not sound like much to you, but on our ride home, next to my Old-Spice-smelling father in his mustard-colored short-sleeved permapress Penney's work shirt, my soul swelled, because I knew I had an advocate, protector, defender, a catcher in the rye—a father of quiet and judicious force that I could rely upon. I do the same for my three kids. I've done the same for other kids.

Unlike the contemporary synthetic male, men who complete the Second Turning are more organically connected to their God-created nature. They are more comfortable in their God-fashioned soul. As such, they're far better able to embrace and fulfill their destiny as a warrior of light.

The martial man will fight spiritually because not only will he have permission, he also will have a new set of spiritual weapons. Thumos, as the Christian monk and ascetic Evagrius Ponticus observed, is "an essential weapon in the spiritual arsenal which must be properly controlled and employed against the enemy."[9] Life without thumos is how men remain soulfully flat and self-absorbed. It's not because they don't have regular Bible studies or attend accountability groups, but because they fail to emulate biblical courage, and their gatherings usually lack thumotic earthiness, spiritedness, and playfulness. Take those qualities away, and you take away real male fellowship and brotherhood (see chapter 12).

The Prophetic Connection

I, like so many men, was told that biblical prophecy was primarily, if not exclusively, about figuring out future events, especially the return of Christ.

It wasn't until being part of the church for more than twenty years that I received a fuller view of prophetic writing: it inherently and vehemently critiques social evil and rallies a mighty call for justice. Thumos is indispensable to this redemptive work, not only because it musters the righteous indignation required to righteously render force but also because it links faith to real problems. Thumos drives a person to say no to a social ill and yes to the hard labor needed to combat it.

Have you noticed how angry the prophets got when it came to injustice? Have you ingested the fighting language they used in their denunciations? Look at these examples:

> How the faithful city [Judah] has played the whore,
> Once the home of justice where righteousness dwelt—
> But now murderers!
> Your silver has turned into base metal
> And your liquor is diluted with water.
> Your very rulers are rebels, confederate with thieves;
> Every man of them loves a bribe
> And itches for a gift;
> They do not give the orphan his rights,
> And the widow's cause never comes before them.[10]

> And now, you priests, this decree is for you: if you will not listen to me and pay heed to the honouring of my name, says the Lord of Hosts, then I will lay a curse upon you. . . . I will cut off your arm, throw offal [the organs of animals] in your faces, the offal of your pilgrim-feasts, and I will banish you from my presence.[11]

Most of us think the sin that brought God's wrath upon Sodom was homosexuality. According to Ezekiel, it included something much different. In his allegory of comparing unfaithful Jerusalem to Sodom, the prophet writes,

> This was the sin of your sister Sodom: She and her daughters were arrogant, overfed and unconcerned; they did not help

the poor and needy. They were haughty and did detestable things before me.[12]

It's safe to say that these blunt and spirited words from history's most captivating prophets will not be found on the wall of a Christian bookstore, framed and inset under a painting of an elk, sniffing the morning air, backlit by amber sunrays. Neither Isaiah, nor Malachi, nor Amos, nor many such others would be allowed into church leadership today. They'd be forced to take thumos-management classes instead.

Our thumotic inner heat fuels prophet-like indignation. Yet there are few directives as contrary to contemporary Christian belief as those of Paul: "Be angry, and yet do not sin."[13] Christians, especially men, aren't supposed to get angry about anything, are we? Give us a shot of sodium pentothal, and we'll tell you that anger itself *is* a sin. We are God's most denatured creatures.

Anger can be a *creative* force. It can crack inertia and drive us past persistent conundrums. Anger, properly handled, helps us fulfill our aspirations by causing blessed dissatisfaction with our lives and with the plight of others. Anger, seasoned to create courage, can be prophetic in the truest and best sense.

Righteous anger can compel a man to confront the world's deceptions and misrepresentations and rationalizations. It can shape his purpose and bring deeper meaning to his life. It takes thumos to confront suffering and misery, to rescue the persecuted, to stand against the crowd. This is what motivates a person to be like the *real* Jesus—not the sugar-coated Jesus we've been given.

Without this prophetic martial spirit, one not found in many believers today, a man can't serve God well because he doesn't possess enough urge to rise above the world's approval, attachments, and addictions. Without this spirit, men too often succumb to the "disease to please," the ailment Peter repeatedly suffered as he denied even knowing Jesus.[14] By contrast, through the prophetic voice born of thumos, a man can become free to serve in the way the prophet Micah told us the Lord desires: "To do justice, to love kindness, and to walk humbly with your God."[15]

Our spiritual training has us object and say, "A gentle answer turns away wrath, but a harsh word stirs up anger."[16] Generally this is true, and it's best—for instance, in marriage—to understand this sooner rather than later. But the Bible doesn't say gentleness is the only disposition that turns away wrath. A stern response can also do the job. Sometimes, depending on the circumstances, sternness does it even better.

Said Martin Luther,

> When my heart is cold and I cannot pray as I should, I scourge myself with the thought of the impiety and ingratitude of my enemies. . . . [Soon,] my heart swells with righteous indignation and hatred and I can say with warmth and vehemence, "Holy be Thy Name, Thy Kingdom come, Thy Will be done!" And the hotter I grow the more ardent do my prayers become.[17]

I call these moments "blessed dissatisfaction." Bill Hybels, a man with plenty of thumos (which has gotten him into trouble, especially with legalists), calls this attribute "holy discontent." It comes during instances where you don't ignore your God-given thumos. You grapple with it, learn from it, and let it propel you.

Hybels explains the power of this key to courageous living and muscular faith:

> This energy causes you to act on the dissatisfaction that's been brewing deep within your soul [thumos] and com-

pels you to say yes to joining forces with God so that the darkness and depravity around you gets pushed back.[18]

It was thumos that urged me to birth The Protectors,[19] so far the only faith-based solution of its kind to adolescent bullying. I was indignant that so many of the people to whom I minister were bullied as children, so I harnessed my discontent with the status quo and underwent the difficult work of creating a program that would provide a Christian response to this growing worldwide problem.[20]

The Protectors is one example of preventative medicine against future crimes and their crushing influence upon the living. Through our curriculum, Awanas, Boy Scouts, Girl Scouts, and other faith-friendly organizations around the world are learning how to push back against the scourge of bullying by taking seriously God's love for justice and his hatred for cruelty.[21]

Remarkably, interest in The Protectors is coming more from private Christian schools than Sunday schools. There's something about a martial spirit's penchant for forging courage and creating justice that doesn't go down well with many evangelical churches. Some churches feel it's off limits, but private schools know they can't succumb to such an illusion because they must grapple with the real world in real time. They can't afford the kind of Petri-dish thinking that survives in a cloistered environment but soon dies when exposed to reality.

Years ago a friend of mine, who's a kickboxing coach, tried to encourage his congregation to take their protection seriously by teaching them how to take down a potential bad guy at church. "Some of the elders and deacons loved it," he said, "but others were shocked and outraged that the church would even consider such training." As for the objectors, he had served with them for years and couldn't remember their ever expressing a strong opinion about anything—until it came to using force justly to protect the weak and the timid.[22]

Incredibly, we'll fight for our right to by-stand, but we won't fight for a righteous policing force that protects the innocent and the helpless. There *are* brave pacifists, such as Clarence Jordan (1912–1969), a powerful, visionary Christian who established an admirable interracial cooperative in the deep South during the 1950s—a courageous act that was met with prejudice, guns, and even dynamite. But there are also many cowards who hide behind pacifism and will contend only to maintain the status quo of their fearfulness. Anemic spirituality and a vacuum of courage have us believing that the most impact we can have is by dropping to our knees and praying really hard . . . even if a madman were to rip through our church, injuring and killing others.

Right Fighting

During conferences, I explain how Catholic priests in New York slums during the early 1800s weren't chosen only for their ability to comprehend God's Word; they also were selected for their ability to subdue an intoxicated man who was abusing his family. His wife would summon the church, which usually would dispatch two priests. They'd explain to the man that if he beat his family again, he'd receive a beating from them. This martial spirit kept many men in line during a time when police would not respond to such injustice. It reminds me of Shakespeare's wise observation: "Lions keep leopards tame."[23]

However, most guys don't know what to do with this information. Their gut and their lungs applaud it, but their spiritual training, so opposed to martial spirituality, has labeled it sinful. *Christian men can't act that way*, they think. Tell that to the wife and kids of an abusive man. Lots of church folk will call you a sinner if you behave like those priests. But vulnerable women and children will call you a hero. You'll have to choose whom to please and whom to offend.

And lest we forget, it's God—not the timid herd—we don't want to offend. When it comes to the truly weak, the outmanned and outgunned, we are to move *toward* them with power and boldness.[24]

Spending force virtuously, a hallmark of the martial spirit and of the most needed thumos fruits, is what happened September 11, 2001, on Flight 93, which was part of the worst terrorist attack on American soil. Jeremy Glick was a former NCAA judo champion, a water-skier, and a new father. Tom Burnett was former QB of his high school team and now a health-care company executive. Todd Beamer's Oracle co-workers called him the "go-to guy," a good name for a man of thumos.

When their flight from Newark to San Francisco was hijacked by four al-Qaeda terrorists, these men didn't believe there was a bomb on board. "I think they're bluffing," Burnett told his wife. "We're going to do something. I've got to go."

His wife, Deena, said, "Tom, sit down. Please! Be still. Be quiet. Don't draw attention to yourself. Wait for the authorities."

Burnett, a man of courage, realized they *were* the authorities. "If they're going to run this plane into the ground," he told her, "we're going to do something."

Glick told his wife that a plan was underway to wrest control of the plane away from the terrorists. When he asked, "What do you think we should do?" she said, "Go for it."

(As seen here, women are among the greatest thumos-builders in a man's life, in part because men are brought up to earn the approval of women, have an intrinsic need to impress women, and have an innate heroic desire to protect and provide for women. Inasmuch as feminine approval leads to what is right and just [it doesn't always—sometimes women use this tremendous power against men for selfish ends], it can be a profound impetus for positive change that fosters courageous faith.)[25]

Todd Beamer told phone operator Lisa Jefferson that he didn't think he would "make it through this" and asked, "Would you please call my family and let them know how much I love them? I don't think we're going to get out of this thing. I'm going to have to go out on faith." He said that passengers were talking about jumping the hijacker with the supposed bomb.

"Are you sure that's what you want to do, Todd?" Jefferson asked.

"It's what we have to do," he replied.

Those duty-bound words are not spoken from one's heart. They sure don't get spoken by our safety-geared brains.

Beamer then asked Jefferson to say the Lord's Prayer with him, after which he recited the Twenty-third Psalm, the one where hope fills a man though he travels through the valley of death's shadow.

Beamer sighed, then said to someone else, "Are you ready? Okay. Let's roll!"

CeeCee Ross-Lyles, an ex-cop flight attendant, shouted to her husband on her cell phone, "They're doing it! They're doing it!"

Much of the free world knows the rest. At approximately 10:03 AM, Flight 93 plowed into a field near Somerset County, Pennsylvania, not far from Pittsburgh. It fell short of the diabolical goal: the heart of American democracy, in Washington, D.C.

The flight's voice recorder reveals how those men willfully poured their strength into using a heavy service cart as a battering ram in order to crash the cockpit. Objects were thrown. Dishes were shattering. "Hold the cockpit door!" is shouted in Arabic. "Let's get them!" is shouted in English. There's more shouting, pounding, screaming, more screaming. The recording ends.[26]

> *"We're going to do something."*
> *"It's what we have to do."*
> *"They're doing it! They're doing it!"*
> *"Okay. Let's roll!"*

Let's never forget these earthy, authentic, rubber-meets-the-road expressions of thumos. Against incredible odds, the men of Flight 93 did not go quietly into the arms of hatred and evil. They fought by employing their martial spirit: this is the language of action, and, with it, hope, liberation, and rescue. It's the language of aspirations, believing in what's yet to happen. In this way, thumos is aligned with faith or, better put, *faith in action.* Accordingly, it is audacious to the faithless and folly to those more cowardly than courageous.[27]

Remember, too, that there were other planes on that fateful morning where the passengers and crew did not behave with bravery and valor. Their inability or unwillingness to use force justly shows how an existence void of sufficient courage is one of appeasement, not confrontation; of peacefaking, not peacemaking. Their passivity also reveals, horrifically, how we cannot *keep* peace when there *is* no peace.

Which plane are you on right now?

Becoming Whom We're Meant to Be

A Greek word for *manliness, andreia,* is the same word used for *courage.* Talk about setting the bar high. Can we say today, without blanching from embarrassment or growing queasy from remorse, that contemporary man, sweet lover of comfort, highly trained to be innocuous in and out of church, *is* courage?

Men: *Courage is what we were made to embody.* It's the very trait that must be manufactured in the neglected portion of our soul that is home to the martial spirit. It is from this deep, heated, rumbling place that our unique form of love flows—this is exemplified by police officers who risk their lives to safeguard citizens, by firefighters who rush toward (not away from) danger, by soldiers who fight for freedom and protect the weak. It's found in the teachers who denounce and defy bullying, thus defending human dignity. It's found in missionaries who sacrifice themselves for the lives of others.

Again, for many of us, this is the piece in our spiritual grid that when fitted into place electrifies and repairs the entire circuit. The military has shown us for centuries (if not for millennia) that it needs to be trained, not jettisoned. And the rediscovery of courage will prove to be providential right here, right now.

I have focused mostly on men in this chapter, and here's why: Men have more martial spirit in them than women. History confirms it, and our experience confirms it as well. Most women just don't have men's taste for fighting, physical or spiritual (though some do). My observation has been that most don't want it either—and again, that's *most* women, not all. As the expression goes, fighting is just not in their blood. By the way, *soul-blood* is another term the Greeks used to describe thumos.

I think back to my favorite Thanksgiving: My kids and I and another father and son got together to fire about six hundred rounds into an abandoned car. We took out taillights, headlights, windows, gauges, tires. My sons and I would do it again in a heartbeat. I hadn't felt such childlike glee and delight in a long time.

But not my daughter.

"Here you go, baby," I said, handing her my rifle. "Just aim and shoot."

Abby hesitated a very long while. Eventually she raised the barrel, sheepishly popped off one round, then asked, "Can I go inside now?" Her blood ran cold, not hot, from that visceral experience.

Shooting an abandoned car is not the same as fighting on a battlefield—I'm just trying to illustrate by example. Harnessing that sort of power, part of a martial spirit, just isn't in my wife or my daughter the way it is in me and my boys. And even if it were, this would be the exception, not the rule. That doesn't make either gender one bit better or worse than the other—it just makes us different. The company of the Thumos-Courageous includes both men and women, but this quality and its offshoots aren't brought out of us in the same ways, and this difference, like countless others, should be honored and respected.

I wrote a book a few years ago that's used by many counselors to help a certain kind of man—I call these men Christian Nice Guys. One counselor in particular has found the book helpful in her practice, and I had the opportunity to speak with her about it. She told me she'd noticed many of the same forces and factors that I argued have been ruining lives, but she was also very candid about her reluctance to be more forthright about her observations.

I saw the same problems you wrote about, but to be honest, I just didn't have the courage to come out and say it the way you did. We women like safety more than you guys—it's one of the reasons why we like going to church more than you—and I don't think I could have handled the criticism after writing such a provocative book.

That book,[28] like this one, was a battle cry, a declaration of war upon the status quo. This status quo, sometimes with the best of intentions, is injuring men, women, and children. My arguments were reformational in nature; reform will always draw fire, and reform is usually led by men who have—and use—a martial spirit.

Notes

1. *Seinfeld*, "The Engagement," 111th episode (7.1), originally aired 9/21/95. Written by Larry David. Directed by Andy Ackerman.
2. Matthew 11:12
3. Thomas (Q. C.) Hughes, *The Manliness of Christ* (Houghton Mifflin Publishing Co., orig. 1881), 29.
4. David Murrow, *Why Men Hate Going to Church* (Nashville: Thomas Nelson, 2005), 70–71.
5. I'll tackle this "Official Script" in chapter 6.
6. For example, see Matthew 23:13.
7. 2 Samuel 16:9–10
8. Matthew 11:12
9. Evagrius Ponticus, "Psalmody as Spiritual Remedy," cited in Luke Dysinger, OSB, *Psalmody and Prayer in the Writings of Evagrius Ponticus* (Oxford, New York: Oxford University Press, 2005), 130.
10. Isaiah 1:21–23 NEB
11. Malachi 2:1–3 NEB
12. Ezekiel 16:49–50
13. Ephesians 4:26, NASB
14. See Matthew 26:69–75.
15. Micah 6:8, NASB
16. Proverbs 15:1
17. Quoted in Eric Hoffer, *The True Believer: Thoughts on the Nature of Mass Movements* (New York: Harper Perennial Modern Classics, 1951), 99.
18. Bill Hybels, *Holy Discontent: Fueling the Fire That Ignites Personal Vision* (Grand Rapids: Zondervan, 2007), 26.
19. *www.theprotectors.org*
20. See *The Final Report and Findings of the Safe School Initiative: Implications for the Prevention of School Attacks in the United*

States. Created by the United States Secret Service and United States Department of Education, July 2004.

21. See Paul Coughlin, *No More Jellyfish, Chickens, or Wimps: Raising Secure, Assertive Kids in a Tough World* (Minneapolis: Bethany House, 2007).

22. For instance, see 1 Thessalonians 5:14.

23. In William Shakespeare, *Richard II*, Part One.

24. For just a few such admonishments, see Deuteronomy 10:18; Psalm 68:5; Isaiah 1:17, 23.

25. Men, especially churchmen, will do what women tolerate, and they will avoid what women will not abide. When women don't tolerate cowardice (during the Civil War they would hiss publicly at men who avoided military duty), men find themselves nudged out onto life's battlefields with few avenues of escape.

26. Alan Axelrod, *Profiles in Audacity: Great Decisions and How They Were Made* (New York: Sterling Publishing Company, 2006), 285–293.

27. For specific ways to foster greater spirited animation in men, see my book *Married ... But Not Engaged: Why Men Check Out and What You Can Do to Create the Intimacy You Desire* (Minneapolis: Bethany House, 2006).

28. *No More Christian Nice Guy: When Being Nice—Instead of Good—Hurts Men, Women, and Children* (Minneapolis: Bethany House, 2005).

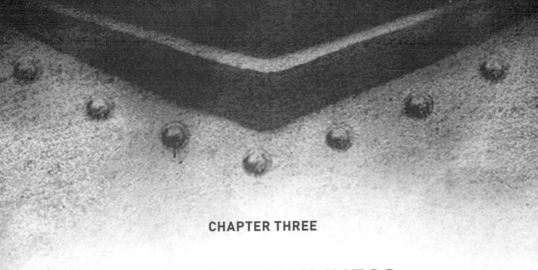

CHAPTER THREE

SOULFUL MANLINESS

Our task is to create a new vision
of manliness in a culture
that no longer believes in saints,
divinely revealed ideals, or absolute values.
(SAM KEEN)[1]

A true gentleman—a chivalrous man—
is just a bit more savage than most people imagine. . . .
A man who is not roused to combat evil
is no gentleman.
(BRAD MINER)[2]

In order for thumos to repair our emaciated souls by giving us staying power, combating the treason of cowardice and gluing us to transcendent causes, we need first to contend with what it really means to be a gentleman. Most people cannot say where the "gentleman" concept came from, or how it has evolved through the centuries. And most of us have no idea how offensive a historical gentleman would be today if we were unfortunate enough to be stuck in the same room with one for more than a half hour. He is our ideal in need of an overhaul.

The comprehensive evolution of what has been meant by *gentleman* is too extensive to cover here. And besides, much of that development is pretty boring. For our purposes, know this: the definition, which has changed throughout the centuries, has always been a construction of what society has deemed best in men, and what it has deemed best has undergone some drastic alterations. Those of us who respect liberty and equality would call a traditional gentleman, at best, a stuck-up weenie.

Though the Bible tells us a lot about the virtue of gentleness, it doesn't include the long-popular concept of a gentleman. In its original sense, the word *gentleman* described a male who came from an upper-class family—that is, he was of privileged birth. A gentleman didn't need to work, and if he did, blue-collar labor was far beneath him. That was reserved for "lesser" men, like us.

Through much of history, a gentleman would not be someone you'd want to sit next to at a ball game or in church. He represented the kind of rigid and punitive social order that revolutionaries saw and rebelled against. That worldview would make the average American's skin crawl.

Making matters worse, at times this privileged order was sanctioned by the church as being part of God's divine providence. For example, Charlotte Brontë was attacked by church people as godless and anti-Christian because in *Jane Eyre* she had undermined the God-given social order of her time. How? By the end of the novel she had allowed a mere governess to marry the lord of the manor.[3] For tradition lovers this was a scandal of biblical proportions—which is amusing, given Jesus' aforementioned unmannerly disregard for convention.

At the same time, though, there have been certain better concepts associated with being a gentleman. One is guardianship, or looking out for the well-being of those charged to your care. Also, the gentleman was thoughtful and courteous, and we need more of this today.

Looking to the East also helps us gain a more authentic understanding of this ideal archetype. For instance, Confucius called being a gentleman *chun-tzu*. Such a man is "distressed by his own lack of capacity," but he is never distressed at the failure of others to recognize his merits. He will be "slow in word but diligent in action," indeed he is "ashamed to let his words outrun his deeds." He remains "unperturbed when not appreciated by others."[4] Like you, I would be more than happy to spend time with this kind of man.

Conservative feminist Katherine Kersten has said well what an ideal man should be:

> True manhood means accepting responsibility for others, and making their welfare a primary focus of life. It means developing a capacity for judgment, courage, honesty, generosity, determination, public-spiritedness, and self-denial in pursuit of a larger good.[5]

Manliness, Kersten says, embraces both tough and gentle virtues.

All in all, it's important to understand that amid the shifting historical definitions, in large measure we men are expected to be more conformed to the image of Mr. Gentleman than to that of Jesus Christ. Nevertheless, we likewise must realize this: Mr. Gentleman doesn't have the last say regarding what it means to be a man among men.

Mr. Gentleman is a compilation of both helpful and hindering impulses and desires. He wasn't brought to us from Mount Sinai but from human fickleness, some of which is drenched in ugly tradition. And as scholar Brad Miner has pointed out in *The Compleat Gentleman*, "A true gentleman—a chivalrous man—is just a bit more savage than most people imagine. . . . A man who is not roused to combat evil is no gentleman."[6]

A gentleman once *was* expected to possess a martial spirit and, when necessary, to fight. That this aspect of his nature is largely lost today isn't accidental. It's a deliberate cultural jettison of valor in favor of a comfort-stupor. Now when we think of a gentleman, we think of a pleasant and amiable guy. He's swell, a sweetheart, everyone's buddy; he says "Golly," with a grin, when he's mad. As I've said before, we aren't very good at recognizing how cowardice and fear so smoothly masquerade as "pleasant and amiable."

One problem is that *gentle* is *such* a misunderstood word today. When Christian men hear or read about the virtue of gentleness, they often substitute "the vice of nice." This is especially true for younger men, and the results of confusing gentleness with niceness can be deadly when it comes to love, marriage, and fatherhood.

These guys get very nervous during conferences when I encourage them to embrace rugged virtues. Our male-disdaining culture already has geared them to think manliness is wrong, so they huddle after I talk, and they pull their pastor aside, and they express their "godly concern" for what I've said, and they have "a check in their spirit" (whatever that means). All the while their single Christian sisters pine for a man with some juice in him so they can respect him.

The force that a true gentleman brings into a situation or relationship is moderate and metered in its presentation—when being moderate and measured is an appropriate response. It's respectful—respectful enough to be both truthful and gracious. Sometimes we see this in a show or a movie, when a mature police officer is able to diffuse a volatile situation with diplomacy, eye contact, direct speech, a straight back, and—this is critical—the threat of further force if necessary. No need to use your Taser when its mere presence is working.

Chivalry is strongly connected to our current understanding of a gentleman, and that term comes from the French word for *knight*. Most generally, knighthood has codified a set of principles for men to follow in three major arenas of life: (1) man to man, with the virtues of courage, valor, and fairness; (2) man and his God, with faithfulness in promoting good and battling evil; and (3) man to woman, how he should serve and honor his wife, and then, after her, how he ought to treat other women. Chivalry had become established before the social invention of a "gentleman," who tended to be more concerned about self-preservation than with defending truth, justice, and beauty.

In thinking about a better understanding of masculinity, of what it means to be a good guy, let's go with chivalry, which is more receptive to our thumos than gentlemanliness. And when doing so, let's remember Edmund Burke's observation (paraphrased): Men who lack a sense of responsibility to a power above themselves are easily swayed by vanity or self-pity, and they come to prefer softer virtues. When men attach their strength to a power above themselves, they are better able to avoid the tendency to be sucked into the schemes of powerful and deceitful men who would employ another man's thumos for their own gain.

Gives Us Staying Power

Thumos brings wholeness to a man's fractured soul in many ways. Atop this list of healing is that it creates greater staying power, the absence of which is a source of great pain and shame for some men (especially Christian men). Another term for "staying power" is *fortitude,* the ability to stick to a task and not give up. Other words for this soul-repairing, meaning-producing attribute: *gumption, moxie, verve,* and the crowd-pleaser among young men, *balls.* From this seat of animation flow both strength and endurance to fulfill difficult responsibilities.

One of the unassailable facts of masculine life is that we have to fight to help foster our own spiritual growth and other attributes that help create a life well-lived. The version of "life in Christ" that's not about joining an army but rather a recreational co-op in which we watch our cholesterol and learn "Kumbaya" can sound appealing; it was to me for many years. But it's also incredibly boring after a while, and worse, it's misleading, for it leaves us turned away from the trials and struggles of others. This approach to life actually becomes a form of spiritual pot that causes us to languish.

In order for our thumos-courage to grow, and with this growth help to heal our own souls and to love others better, we need to sink our teeth into a juicier and grittier faith. We will have to break away from rec-center Christianity in order to find abiding maturity, guidance, and meaning. Especially during what I call Second-Half Spirituality—that time after a midlife crisis (which, in a healthy life, should really be a midlife celebration), where hopefully, if we've not yet done so, we discard our small lives for God's larger life for us.

On a daily basis, much of life's essence is about how much energy you give away and where you give it. Believe it or not, a passive and cowardly approach takes far more energy than an assertive and courageous approach. Cowardice puts us on the defensive, constantly covering up, being reactive, protecting ourselves from life's many blows—some of which are unjust, a fact that really steams cowardly and passive people, which derails and drains them even more. *We neither make progress nor replenish our resources while playing defense all the time.*

Defense destructs. Offense creates. Deconstructing, which is easier than constructing, has permeated evangelical spirituality. We judge our spiritual "progress" more in terms of what we don't do; this is intrinsically defensive. Think about it: Doing something good is more challenging than avoiding something bad. *Doing* good has an offensive orientation toward life.

We're more likely to be criticized for being offensive than defensive, so we usually settle for the less conspicuous position . . . and thereby avoid spiritual growth. Nevertheless, behaving flawlessly and having all your ducks in a row is no defense against criticism. Behave perfectly, or make a few mistakes—in the end, when it comes to being criticized, it doesn't matter. Have a more offensive orientation toward life, the kind thumos urges us to have, and you *will* be criticized.

There's no way around it. People love the status quo, and when you break from it, like a prisoner over a fence, all kinds of sirens and lights will be thrown on to get you back in the yard. Jesus warned us about this, saying that following him would tear families apart and cause hatred and even result in murder.[7]

At the same time, being on the offensive really scares passive men: it requires thumos, the employment of creativity and courage. However, it also creates much more progress, and with less energy. No matter that you have to fight and struggle to get there—you're already fighting, so you may as well be making more progress with less energy.

More than twenty-five times the Bible tells us to be strong and courageous. For Christian Nice Guys, a part of them knows that this is true, and it resonates within them, yet their spiritual background—what they understand to be "Christianity"—tells them it's sinful and wrong, dirty somehow. If this is you, then in order to light a spark and familiarize yourself with action, I recommend trying entry-level martial arts; or give archery or target-shooting a chance; or take up hunting or fishing. One or more of these endeavors may help you to experience the value of focused will and intention within a disciplined framework.

If you've been conditioned to listen only to music that's sweet and amiable, without a single rough edge, try listening to soul music; try some R&B; look for some good hip-hop; sample my favorite, jazz . . . at any rate, ingest some music that has fire in its belly, wind in its lungs, and dirt under its nails.

Too often when I make such suggestions, I'm met with a blank stare. "Um, I'll look into that," a man will say, with approximately zero conviction. For some, this concept of thumos-building is just too much, too far outside their domesticated, castration-producing background. At the same time, they wonder why they give up easily when the going gets tough. They can't figure out why they never really enter into life in the first place; the answer is: *They don't enter in because they aren't really alive.*

To show you what I mean, here's one of many such letters we get at Coughlin Ministries:

> I am a college student who has been struggling with being more courageous for years. Before and after becoming a Christian I was always picked on, abused, laughed at. I always thought that prosperity in my career was wrong and immoral. I thought as men we are supposed to be passive and not succeed in our work life and that doing something like that is "worldly."
>
> Sometimes I see myself as a dead dog that doesn't deserve anything better, while all of those secular people get to have all the fun. I'm not saying that we drink and party our way to heaven, but as Christian men, we should walk with integrity and stand up for the weak one and what is morally right.
>
> I don't want to be a wimp when it comes to being married either. Thank you for clearing up some misconceptions about my religion.

We can listen to this young man and say his real problem is that he doesn't have much self-esteem. While it's true that he's lacking self-worth, one of the reasons he undervalues himself is that he does not possess an inner sword, what I call a sword of willingness. Not will, in this case, but *willingness*, a spiritual eagerness (which is one way English Bibles translate the Greek word *prothumos*) to enter the fray, to confront, to clarify, to pronounce, and to protect himself and others so that he can deeply love.

This thumos-heated internal sword is recognized the world over and by different names, much the way thumos in general is recognized by different names. The Tibetans refer to it as the "Vajra sword." I wonder if it's from this attribute that someone created the word *Viagra*, an allusion to the tight connection between virility, sex, and thumos. Without this inner sword, they say, no spiritual life is possible, nor is manhood obtainable. Through spiritual atrophy, men without this sword are sitting ducks for spiritual abuse and sexual frustration.

Here's a taste of why such men drop the sword of their willingness, and what life looks like when they get it back:

> I recently read and am currently rereading *No More Christian Nice Guy* and *No More Jellyfish, Chickens, or Wimps*. They have been the most important books I've ever read. Nearly three years into a devastating divorce I now see how the recurring themes of fear and cowardice have wrought havoc in my life, starting as a young boy who was tormented relentlessly by a bully from 4th through 8th grades, and now have led me to my current shattered life—all due to spinelessness on my part as I bought into an over-domesticated and almost feminine interpretation of Christian life as a man. So much resentment and repression over the years have now begun to give way to mature wisdom that is quick to act when necessary and quick to react

appropriately when necessary as a strong and courageous Christian man should.

What a contrast to all the years I despised the aspects of church life that appealed to feminine sensibilities all the while believing that I just didn't like church life—and by extension that I didn't like God; I thought that being godly essentially meant being a woman. No thanks.

I still rage sometimes at the damage little 12-year-old Jimmy caused in my heart, using everything from vicious words to an excruciating torture, which ended more than 20 years ago when my family moved away. Of course, beginning days later and for the last three months of 8th grade I was tormented by a boy who was the spitting image of Jimmy only much larger.

I thought I was going to die from fear. The pain of those years of daily "mini-castrations" has never completely gone away despite building myself into 250 pounds of muscle over the years. But now, after reading your books and after two years of twice-weekly one-on-one Bible studies with two great mentors I've gained much-needed clarity about what God expects of me: what my purpose is, and how He expects me to go about accomplishing it. And it all begins by embracing my masculinity and understanding what it means to have real courage. I can't thank you enough for your role in helping me find my way, and I plan on helping others the same way through the Protectors.

The deepest matters are hard to put into words that go all the way down, which is one reason why Jesus told stories. He left us with images and characters that, like the prodigal son, may not be historical but nonetheless are vivid, engaging, and truthful. We give deeper truths a kind of "container," for instance, in the way we say emotions are found in our "heart," thoughts are in our "head," and courage is in our "chest."

And so it is with thumos. To better understand how it repairs us, we have to give it some shape and form. In Greek epics, thumos represents winds of change inside and outside of us: It's a life-wind that requires and facilitates action and boldness.

The fierce wind that blew through the upper room, igniting the early church with God's Spirit,[8] can be perceived in a larger and more metaphorical sense in terms of God's thumos visiting us. It is fierce and agitating, intent on change, and filling his people, like Peter, with boldness, and others with disturbing behavior, including tongues "as of fire," and speaking in foreign languages.[9] We can't miss this point, because if we do we miss what thumos does. *Thumos is disturbing, but at its best, it's good, necessary, and life-giving trouble.*

God's thumos troubles our air for our own good as part of his mysterious grace and his perfect will for us. Similarly, thumos is man's inner *wind* that disturbs, hopefully toward the deepest love, one that bears earthly energy, arising from a Latin word for *rush, run, flow*. At its best, it cultivates a desire to know and to alleviate the suffering of others, often (though not always) through our own suffering, when that suffering is unavoidable.

Suffering in and of itself is neither noble nor heroic. Viktor Frankl, concentration camp survivor and founder of Logotherapy, which is one of the most muscular attempts to make sense of life's inevitable suffering, wrote about the spiritual growth that can be the result of unavoidable hardship.

> Is this to say that suffering is indispensable to the discovery of meaning? In no way. I only insist that meaning is available in spite of—nay, even through—suffering, provided . . . that the suffering is unavoidable. If it is avoidable, the meaningful thing to do is remove its cause, for unnecessary suffering is masochistic rather than heroic.[10]

Thumos-courage helps us to do more than just endure suffering. It helps us thrive through the suffering, to learn from it, to grow into a better person on the other side of the trial. Otherwise, we're likely to remain impoverished and stuck.

But the view today that suffering born from sacrifice can somehow be exalted couldn't be more foreign. We think suffering is something of a mistake, a false accusation to our lives. Suffering and sacrifice are things to be eradicated and fixed. And with this mindset, we also jettison the framework of courage.

In addition to wind, thumos is also described as *breath*, which is airy and flexible, and which is not to be mistaken for mere life. Paul's eloquent dialogue in Athens[11] provides an important distinction that helps us get our minds around this somewhat mysterious, intrinsic-to-spiritual-staying-power attribute. He told those assembled that "[God] is not served by human hands, as if he needed anything, because he himself gives all men *life* and *breath* and everything else."[12]

Why does Paul use two words: *life* and *breath*? A foundational understanding of thumos may provide the answer. *There's a substantial difference between the state and gifting of being alive (life) and an animating quality that rests within this gift (breath).* All men possess life, but not all men possess breath—an animated spirit. You see it wherever you go—offices, churches, restaurants. Some men are simply and undeniably alive and vibrant and courageous. They, like Todd Beamer, are the go-to guys, men known for getting things done. Man is far more than a sophisticated organism capable of mere mechanical life. He has the potential to take life to a higher, more God-glorifying level to "make life [his] own" (Hebrews 10:39 NEB). Thumos men are too animated and vital to waste their lives.

Combats Cowardice

Despite our widespread contemporary disregard for it, courage, the reddest of the thumotic fruits, long was upheld as the virtue that underpins all others. Without courage, we are unable to create the deepest and most abiding form of love, *agapé*. Deep-abiding, soul-permeating love is risky, almost always making a man vulnerable to rejection and loss. People who have learned how to love deeply persevere through this very real possibility, yet if you're like me, the connection between courage and love has not been part of your spiritual training. This is one reason why, as the body of Christ, we aren't as influential and redemptive as we know we can and should be.

I believe cowardice is one of the most underreported reasons for depression in men. Cowardice builds up like gunk in a motor's fuel injection system. After a while, it shuts down the whole system, having robbed it of power and—here's that word again—*animation*. The self-loathing produced from cowardice injects a molasses-like pall throughout our entire being. Think about the times you've been a coward. Did you feel lethargic, lifeless, even poisoned somehow? It's like your body, designed to live off four D-sized batteries, only has one. You just want to crawl into a hole and shrivel.

Cowardice is one of the most shame-producing behaviors a man can commit, a malady that almost completely escapes the notice of most sermons that address negligent behavior. The fact is we feel guilty about our action or inaction, in part because we've been cowards; *when cowardice is not addressed spiritually, we are not given the opportunity to be healed spiritually.* We remain un-ministered to, and we remain in bondage to sin. Though most of us are instructed to confess our sins to one another, cowardice isn't even on our usual list. This is very bad news for us, especially men.

It's exceedingly difficult to forget the times we were cowards. Writes street evangelist and former Marine Truxton Meadows,

> I'm forty years old. And I've lived a lot of life and made many mistakes. I have regrets but have reconciled them.

The only nagging regrets I still have are the times that I could have stood up for a kid who was getting bullied. I was small and got picked on myself so I didn't want to draw the bully's attention and sometimes joined in to fit in. I regret that I never stood up for myself and others.[13]

If you want to get into the soul of a man, ask him about the times when he was a coward. It usually happens when we're kids, when we behaved *pusillanimously.* Among the meanings of that word are "small-souled" and "small-minded," that is, being weak in spirit and courage. As kids, we were pusillanimous when we succumbed to a bully or when we saw other kids being bullied and did nothing when we knew we should have acted.

Most men can tell you the first, middle, and last name of the bully who stole their dignity. They can sometimes even tell you what their bully was wearing. Cowardice is often indelible—and we need something very powerful, like grace, to help us remove it.

Cowardice makes us want to die, and I think it can speed up the dying process as well as lead to decisions for suicide. While women feel cowardice as well, it doesn't seem to steal their identity as much—it wounds them, but not so mortally. That's because courage is intrinsic to a man's purpose, to the very core of him. Cowardice steals our dignity and identity, our being-ness—our existence—as men.

Thankfully, God does not leave us defenseless or alone in this state. He gives us the potential to combat this soul malady through our thumos. For this, too, we are eternally grateful, because God himself said that "the cowardly, the unbelieving, the vile, the murderers, the sexually immoral, those who practice magic arts, the idolaters and all liars— their place will be in the fiery lake of burning sulfur."[14]

Wait a minute. God puts cowards in the same sinking boat as felons, sorcerers, and atheists, yet the topic is hardly broached by the church? God has been telling us a lot about courage and cowardice for a very long time. We just haven't been listening.

Courage—the ability to confront fear, pain, danger, uncertainty, or intimidation, whether for ourselves or for others—always includes some form of *sacrifice*, though today we use that word glibly, employing it to describe most any discomfort. Recently, when I heard a talk-show host say to a celebrity that it must have taken a lot of courage to get a boob job, I had to go for a walk. Just give me some real courage—like the Spartans had.

Picture this: In the fifth century BC, the Greco-Persian wars were fought. Persia ruled Asia, and it wanted Europe. Figures vary, but it is generally believed that at the pivotal Battle of Thermopylae, *three hundred* Spartans held off at least *two hundred thousand* Persian invaders for three days at a narrow land gap between the Trachinian Cliffs and the Malian Gulf. Then the Spartans were ambushed, most likely the work of the Greek traitor Ephialte (whose name means "nightmare"). They still fought for another four days, besieged on multiple fronts, fighting until their weapons were dulled and smashed, and according to the historian Herodotus, then having to fight "with their bare hands and teeth."

The highly skilled Spartans—free men defending native soil, wives, children, and honor—fought to the death against a force hell-bent on enslaving them, pillaging their cities, and raping and killing their wives and daughters. G. K. Chesterton captured the soul-power of such warriors when he wrote, "The true soldier fights not because he hates what is in front of him, but because he loves what is behind him."[15]

The Persian army was largely comprised of slaves, the king's property. They possessed little more value than goats or pigs, and in this fight they were whipped from behind to push into a death mill of superior weaponry and thumos training. Spartans were trained to spot *phobologic*—the loop of terror and fear that can consume a soldier and cause him to run away. Militarily, they were taught to ignore their hearts and follow their thumos.

The courage and valor of the three hundred Spartans, expressed that fateful week, is an astonishing symbol of bravery against overwhelming odds. Their valor inspired the Greeks to rally and to defeat the Persians in subsequent battles. It is not an exaggeration to say that the thumos of three hundred men preserved the beginnings of Western democracy and freedom "from perishing in the cradle."[16] In giving their lives, they provided Athens the crucial time necessary to prepare for a decisive naval battle that would determine the outcome of the war.

Why did the Spartans fight so well? How were they able to shun cowardice? Atop the list is that they were trained in how to handle fear, a training most Christian men do not receive. At times, in order to knock fear down, to mute its thunder, it's necessary to even mock it.

Paul did this when he wrote about our gift of immortality: "Where, O death, is your victory? Where, O death, is your sting?"[17] Death is our greatest fear; robbing that terror of its potency, Paul pokes fun at it. It's as if he puts his thumb on his nose and waves his fingers the way we did as kids, saying to death and fear, "Na-na-na-na-na-na—you can't touch me." Brash? Cheeky? It wouldn't be the only time that man of godly thumos behaved so.

You have sensed your redemptive thumos bristle in the presence of wickedness and evil even though you felt fear and were tempted toward cowardice instead. Next time, don't pretend this conflict isn't happening. Don't fool yourself into thinking that you aren't irritated, that you aren't indignant, or that there isn't a battlefield right in front of your very nose. Honor those moments. And don't avoid them like the herd does. That avoidance, wrote Martin Luther, is a form of spiritual treason against God.

Reason and emotion alone cannot deliver decisive action. It is through thumos that we marshal ourselves to join the battle, take charge of our family, and change the world.

Connects to Transcendent Causes

The third prominent way that noble thumos heals a man's soul is by reminding him that life is not about him. It drives a man to stubbornly connect his life to transcendent causes, to go out into the real world and redeem real-world problems, filling his life with the peace that only comes from consistently living out deep meaning and abiding purpose.

Thumos fosters enterprise and aspiration—two qualities many Christian men leave at the cross instead of having them redeemed to God's glory. These attributes compel a man to create acts of goodness and valor, to fight for truth, justice, and beauty, and to defend himself and those in his care. Without such men, malevolent forces take over.

As seen in and through the prophets, thumos brings clarity and cleansing. It helps us cut through the malarkey and roll up our sleeves to clean house, to clear the temple of the money changers (which today might mean knocking over the heavy cameras of televangelists who manipulate viewers to support their extravagant and sometimes criminal lifestyles). Thumos animates a man to be a doer, not a talker, creating vitality, light, and goodness.

Thumos gives us boldness and courage to follow God through all the heartache and pain that will come on account of following him. Remember how even when we stay on the defensive and reject courage, we're still fighting? We might as well do what's right: We must fight to do our part for the kingdom of heaven, alleviating suffering, protecting the weak, and creating justice and freedom.

This work is not done by mere sweetness or niceties. It is done through noble force. According to Jesus, the kingdom of heaven is not ushered in by timid and compliant men who are afraid or unable to employ thumos.[18]

Take William Wilberforce, whom we applaud today because history has allowed this once-controversial figure's thumos to cool and become less offensive, disruptive, and trouble-making. The church applauds him now—portions of the church did not, in his time. He was viewed as an enigma by many contemporaries: a popular but diminutive and sickly man whose single-handed energy and determination helped to eventually overcome the powerful pro-slavery lobby in England's parliament and put an end to the empire's trade.

Biographer James Boswell witnessed Wilberforce's eloquence in the House of Commons and noted: "I saw what seemed a mere shrimp mounted upon the table; but as I listened, he grew, and grew, until the shrimp became a whale."[19] Thumos makes small men huge.

Wilberforce fought for nearly twenty years to end the brutal trafficking of human flesh. He was initially optimistic, naïvely so, when he began his campaign, borne of Christian conviction, to fight for another's liberation and dignity. He expressed no doubt about his chances of quick success. As early as 1789, he and another elected official managed to have twelve resolutions against the slave trade introduced—only to be legally outmaneuvered on fine points. Other bills he introduced were defeated eight times.

When it became clear that Wilberforce was not going to let the issue die, pro-slavery forces targeted him, just as all men of thumos are targets because they are the right kind of dangerous. He was vilified; opponents spoke of "the damnable doctrine of Wilberforce and his hypocritical allies."[20] The opposition became so fierce, one friend feared that one day he would read about Wilberforce's being broiled by Indian planters, "barbecued by African merchants, and eaten by Guinea captains."[21]

Hearts can grow cold with time and age, especially from nearly two decades of struggle, ridicule, and scorn. Wilberforce's mind must have betrayed him as well: With time a man concludes, mentally, that the fight is not worth it, that it's unreasonable to continue. Wilberforce's health deteriorated, and his dreams were plagued by hellish nightmares.

But something else moored, buoyed, and compelled Wilberforce through these times, against the path of reason that's almost always set upon self-preservation, and beyond unpredictable and short-lived emotions, which often betray us in the middle of the night. *An awakened heart feeds the fire, but it is not the fire.* Wilberforce expressed his love for his fellow-man from a heated place within himself that was bolstered by a faith that would not let him forget: Human dignity is a gift, one that no man has the right to tear asunder.

I hope by now I've been making it plain that the form of thumos I'm promoting is not mere animalistic aggression—feral, raw, postal. Rather, it is assertiveness and aggression insisting that something is true and willing to battle for that truth—like Wilberforce, who knew that people are imbued with God-given value and that God is angry when our worth is stripped from us.

This truth-orientation is "fighting words" to others. It makes their teeth gnash. Every time this conviction is put forward, it becomes an assertion of truth and rightness. This is what spiritual assertions do: they fight and, in doing so, they help us transcend what is wrong with the world in our efforts to be part of redeeming it.

There is a force that helps us complete this fight, this good work. It's a gift from God to humankind, more powerful than fear, more noble than self-preservation. It is love, the great healer of our souls. And for men, the most distinctive expression of it is made through their thumos. It shows contempt for all forces of falsehood and darkness, recognizing them as foreign and ugly.

Without thumos, a man cannot truly love; extinguish this fiery core, taint it, or dumb it down, and you undo the man and the good he might have done. Thumos at its best helps men love, in a way—the way—they were designed to love: unsentimental, confrontational, sacrificial, practical, playful, powerful, prophetic, kinetic, unpredictable, and noble. It is a superior love, which, as Frederick Buechner described, "is not an excuse for the mushy and innocuous, but love as a summons to battle against all that is unlovely and unloving in the world."[22]

"To sentimentalize something is to savor rather than to suffer the sadness of it, is to sigh over the prettiness of it rather than to tremble at the beauty of it, which may make fearsome demands of us or pose fearsome threats. Not just as preachers but as Christians in general we are particularly given to sentimentalizing our faith, as much of Christian art and Christian preaching bear witness—the sermon as tearjerker, the gospel as urn of long-stemmed roses and baby's breath to brighten up the front of the church, Jesus as GregoryPeck."[23]

A man may have loving feelings. Even loving thoughts. But without thumos, he doesn't have loving *actions*. These and more are a man's gift to his world—if with God's grace he surmounts inner struggles and outer stereotypes. Through courage and action, a husband of goodwill learns to love his wife when he doesn't feel like loving her. Thumos-forged courage provides tenacity, fidelity, and fortitude, and these are essential; neither thoughts nor feelings alone create or keep commitment.

Something else inside a man has to kick in for him to love in a more mature way. That something is thumos, the place where his mind reminds him of his duties and his heart alerts him to what he feels (or doesn't feel). God's matchless love for us, fully revealed through the sacrifice of Jesus, shows us how thumos is required to carry out deep and abiding love, even when our feelings or thoughts are treasonous.

Our homes, our churches, and our nation need men with more than active hearts and keen minds. We need men with active thumos courage, and we need our culture to respect it and discipline it—not kill it. We face a battle to awaken it. The health of our souls depends upon this conflict being resolved effectively instead of conveniently.

Notes

1. Sam Keen, *Fire in the Belly: On Being a Man* (New York: Bantam Books, 1991), 83.
2. In Brad Miner, *The Compleat Gentleman: The Modern Man's Guide to Chivalry* (Dallas: Spence Publishing Co., 2004).
3. Dick Keyes, *Seeing Through Cynicism: A Reconsideration of the Power of Suspicion* (Downer's Grove, IL: InterVarsity Press, 2006), 158.
4. *The Compleat Gentleman*, 234.
5. Ibid., 150–151.
6. Miner, *The Compleat Gentleman*.
7. See, for instance, Matthew 10:21.
8. See Acts 1–2.
9. See Acts 2.
10. Viktor Frankl, *Man's Search for Meaning* (Boston: Beacon Press, 1959), 148.
11. See Acts 17.
12. Acts 17:25, emphasis mine.
13. Letter to author.
14. Revelation 21:8
15. G. K. Chesterton, *The New Jerusalem* (1921).
16. Steven Pressfield, *Gates of Fire* (New York: Bantam, 1998), historical note page.
17. 1 Corinthians 15:55, quoting (in part) Hosea 13:14.
18. Matthew 11:12

19. George Coulehan Heseltine, *Great Yorkshiremen* (Manchester: Ayer, 1932), 83.

20. Roger Steer, *Good News for the World* (British and Foreign Bible Society, 2004), 77.

21. Robert Isaac Wilberforce and Samuel Wilberforce, *The Life of William Wilberforce* (London: John Murray, 1838), 218.

22. In Thomas G. Long and Cornelius Plantinga, eds., *A Chorus of Witnesses: Model Sermons for Today's Preacher* (Grand Rapids, MI: William B. Eerdmans, 1994), 232.

23. Frederick Buechner, *Telling the Truth: The Gospel as Tragedy, Comedy, and Fairy Tale* (HarperSanFrancisco, 1977), 36–37.

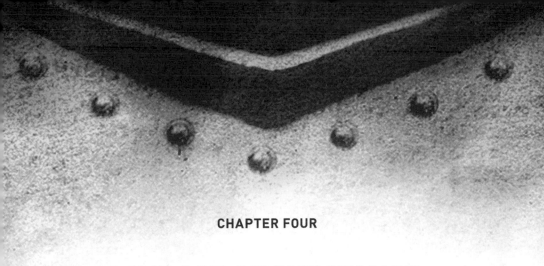

CHAPTER FOUR

COURAGE OF SUBSTANCE, AND OF SHADOW

Life is too short to be little.
Man is never so manly
as when he feels deeply, acts boldly,
and expresses himself with frankness and fervor.
(BENJAMIN DISRAELI)

A strong will is, I believe, the best asset
that a human being can possess,
not because it guarantees success or goodness,
but because a weak will pretty much guarantees failure.
It is strong-willed people who do well in psychotherapy,
who have that mysterious will to grow.
(M. SCOTT PECK)[1]

I've been explaining the vast upside to thumos, emphasizing how it's essential to spiritual growth and to a life well lived for all, and especially men. But as you've probably sensed by now, this animating and spirited quality that's tightly connected to our will and our willingness also has the potential to misfire and go bad. In fact, this is one of the most strenuous concerns on which I receive feedback during conferences.

"Aren't you worried that guys will get out of hand if they tap into this thumos you talk about?"

Yes, I am concerned about thumos getting out of hand, and I take steps to curtail this possibility. But—and here's where things get interesting—I'm equally worried that men won't tap into it at all. That likewise causes destruction, but because the damage isn't as obvious or apparent we tend not to think much about that side of the equation. This is one of the blind spots of Defensive Spirituality; we develop it when we adhere to the mindset that avoiding risk and remaining inconspicuous is somehow more "Christian" than actually risking a mistake.

Thumos is like gasoline. It can help get an innocent victim to a hospital in order to save her life. It can also take that same woman's life if someone hits her with a Molotov cocktail filled with gasoline. Its benefit and detriment depend in large part on how it's refined, handled, and applied.

Let's take a look at the positive aspect, what I call noble thumos. And then we'll look at the negative, what I call shadow thumos.

Noble Thumos

Noble thumos is redemptive, heroic, sacrificial, and tethered to the extension of love, and once again, to transcendent causes larger than our own ego and appetites. It's service-based, the superior but paradoxical form of leadership that Christ calls us to embrace. We're used to hearing how Jesus wants us to be *servants*, but our contemporary understanding of servanthood gives us the wrong impression.

When most of us think of servants, we envision hired hands, people without a will of their own, standing silently in the background, eyes slightly glazed, worried about slipping up, wearing a uniform and waiting to be told what to do. People who always say yes and never no; people wondering uncertainly about what their employer must be thinking. We think of people who are fearful of losing their jobs; people who will be punished if they don't do exactly as they're ordered.

However, I don't see this approach with the early church leaders. That's not Jesus, Peter, or John, and in no way does it describe Paul. Rather, they are *service-oriented:* they are involved and anticipating. They aren't waiting for commands. They sometimes give them. They are proactive, not reactive. They do say no, sometimes with thumotic fervor.

Interestingly, Jesus rejects the title of *servants* for his disciples.

> I call you servants no longer; a servant does not know what his master is about. I have called you friends, because I have disclosed to you everything that I heard from my Father.[2]

That really should make us rethink our exalted use of this term.

Another important distinction: This kind of servanthood is not motivated by fear. "There is no fear in love. But perfect love drives out fear, because fear has to do with punishment."[3] Our service, ideally, is to be love-based. Noble thumos says, *"I choose to serve."*

The following are some terms, flavors, expressions, and moods that describe noble thumos for us to consider, ponder, and pray about:

> Indignation, disruption, resolve, pugnacity, shrewdness, penetration, spiritedness, daring, solitude, demanding, opinionated, earthy, teasing, irreverent, impatient, sacrificial, firmness, philosophical, simple, playfulness, suffering, prayerful, activist, will to meaning, communal, determination, pro-social, subversive, weeping, freedom loving, exodus producing, conspicuous, cultivated warrior,

spiritual eagerness and readiness, enlivens, encourages, trustworthy, alchemy, fortitude, vitality, character, spontaneous, virile, enemy making, creative, protective, fathering, fidelity, natural, poetic, tickles, grief feeling, chivalry, dances, ecstatic, alertness, awareness, sympathy, Bushido, honor, willingness.

With this spirit in mind, fill in a few words of your own.

I've seen many examples of noble thumos throughout my years of men's ministry. One in particular grabs me because it helps show how a low-thumos man can rise up when he listens and responds to that place within him where reason and emotion duke it out, where passion and logic grapple and roll through the brambles of his third seat of being, pushing past self-preservation and fear of disapproval.

In this way a man's thumos-will interacts with his conscience; while conscience may tell him what to do, it does not provide the persistent vital force he needs to act. Conscience clarifies, but it does not create action. However, *conscience connected to thumos* tells a man that he should stop, set his feet like concrete, and stand for, or against, what he witnesses. This is how he forges character. This is how he comes to say, *and act on,* "Let's roll!"

I'm thinking about a professor at a large Christian university who attended our first GodMen conference in Nashville. (What a wild ride that was. The first time this small group of attendees saw the conference was also the first time I saw it.) Anyway, this professor was driving through town a few days later, when he saw a homeless man. Unlike the many previous times he'd seen homeless people, this time he was moved to action.

"The man was young, so young," he said. "I circled the block and this fight took place within me." He was outraged by what he saw: a young guy, with so much life ahead of him, had nowhere to go. He was probably filled with despair, maybe even consumed with hopelessness.

The professor circled the block. Again. His mind lobbed the first shot for self-preservation and against love. *Don't get involved in other people's business—it just leads to trouble.* And then his heart betrayed him, playing upon his fears. *Your roommates will be mad at you!*

Then his thumos spoke up: *Whatever. Be irresponsible for God. You're already helping your roommates out, so who are they to complain?*

Then, and this is important, he acted sooner rather than later. We do our souls no good by deliberating too long about such matters. God opens the door to these moments, and the openings don't last long. One gift of a noble-thumos moment is that it is a test of our commitment to love God and to love our neighbor as ourself.

Love is serious business, so it's best not to pretend that this inner debate isn't happening. Furthermore, don't pretend that more deliberation will help you make the right decision, because the longer you wait, the more being a coward looks right. Thumos rises. And then it falls. It doesn't point the way toward courage and toward a more muscular faith for long.

The professor stopped and naturally fumbled his way toward rightness and goodness, even though he didn't have all the answers. (Who would?) It's this factor alone that stops so many from doing the right thing: We're petrified of making a public mistake, and we've fortified this fear by beating only one drum, that of personal purity. This causes us to slump quietly to life's sideline and disqualify ourselves because we don't think we're pure enough to minister, to love and to be loved by God.

A recent experience in men's ministry illustrates this point. A guy I'll call Brian really hates himself. He's constantly comparing himself to the "towering religious figures" in his life: his wife's two brothers, both ministers. "I can't even begin to be like them," he told me, resigned to everlasting spiritual loserhood.

I know one of those brothers. He's not the got-it-all-together guy on Monday that he pretends to be on Sunday.

"Well, Brian," I said, "I sure hope not." I told him how his brother-in-law has learned to put on a show but actually struggles mightily with fear in real life—though frankly I don't think he even notices what fear has done to him.

A weight lifted from Brian. Hope—and with it some green courage—began to flow through him as he came to realize that those who usually are the heroes of their own stories are not coming clean. He began to talk as if God could accept him, could really love him.

Back to the professor: Thank God *this* man pushed past a common spiritual misconception and didn't disqualify himself. He let heated, protective, rescuing love flow through him. He took the young man home and fed him. He gave him clean clothes to wear and a bed to sleep in. His roommates weren't crazy about the situation. (Welcome to the real, messy, *disruptive* world of thumos love!)

Professor Thumos also noticed that the young man's teeth were bad. He got on the phone and called a dentist friend in another state to ask if he'd help. The friend paid for the young man to come and receive extensive dental care (free of charge).

I think the dentist heard in the professor's usually mild voice something more than compassion. I think he felt the low but distinguishing rumble of noble thumos: warm and penetrating, like the bark of a large dog hitting your chest. You can't help but respect that kind of power; if you allow it, your own embrace of goodness will move you to action.

His story highlights a problem and danger associated with compassion that often goes overlooked: The impulse itself can be shifty and even fickle. Compassion must be translated into thumotic action or else it disappears. And worse, we lose a portion of our integrity when we don't act. When we fail to act upon our compassionate impulse, we sear a portion of our conscience. We feel sick inside because we were created to act and do.

Our capacity for compassion is a summons to action, not just feeling, and we denigrate a part of ourselves when we don't act because unredeemed compassion actually shrivels sympathy. Much hopelessness, apathy, and cynicism toward our own lives and the lives of others can be traced to compassionate emotions that did not become actualized, real, and tangible through our willingness to act.

Thumos made a mild-mannered man larger than life. It gave him charisma, which others noticed and responded to. He told me that if he hadn't come to GodMen, if he hadn't heard about a man's unique expression of non-sentimental love, and how deep love is almost always risky some way, somehow, he never would have helped that young man. "But I was angry at what I saw," he said, "and you helped me honor my indignation. I just couldn't take it. I had to do something about it."

Does his story thump well with your thumos? It makes my chest swell, and it makes me want to act the same way. When it's deployed and actualized, noble thumos is contagious; I think this is what happened with his dentist friend. I don't know for sure, but I doubt the man thought about his decision for long. That's usually how matters like this go down. Too much brain time leads to increased emphasis on self-preservation, which extinguishes thumos.

This helps to explain how some of the most "reasonable" people you know are also the most cowardly. I see this in men who possess what I call "Head Religion"—the kind of "faith" that described my life for way too long and was a hiding place for my fear of life in general. These guys are mostly about theological minutiae and not much about love-extension. They do not see, or they refuse to see, that *nuanced ideology means nothing to the average person's life unless it's connected to matters of his or her soul.*

Such "head people" over-reside in the spiritual but spend dangerously little time in the soulful; this is part of what Francis Schaeffer described as "the great evangelical disaster."[4] Too often, what matters to those who live in their minds just doesn't apply to how real people really live. One accurate and embarrassing example is escapist end-times theology. How will obsessing over jots and tittles of eschatology possibly help a single woman with two kids whose cowardly man of the house has abandoned them?

When Head Religion is on the throne, you can be prideful, have a sham of a marriage, possess cowardice that's mistaken for gentleness, do nothing truly virtuous, be unrelatable to the average person, lifeless, obese, coldhearted, but if you possess the right doctrine—you're in. A Head Religion minister looks at people and says with his eyes, "Do you have the dogma? We need to know."

That minister often has a wife who's pining. She puts on a good front for an hour or so, but when you see her away from the public eye, when show time is over, she appears unfed and starving for a man's affection. This soul-frail woman is drawn toward more animated men, then looks away and beats down her heart with a disciplined resignation.

Alongside Head Religion is Heart Religion, which is primarily obsessed with expression and experience.

It's far more "showy glow" than transformational heat, but people are happy to shell out serious money for a spiritual tan. This color can last for a few hours or days, like what happens at many retreats and conferences. People get jacked up on God for a while, but it doesn't really go anywhere.

Heart Religion love is sweet and sentimental but foolish and naïve. It gives little or no wisdom, and it doesn't prepare anyone for how to serve and love people in the real world. Being told about anything that sounds like an admonition or a warning is a bummer, because it takes the glow away, and we're all about the glow. Doctrine is mistaken for an irritating roadblock instead of a life-preserving guardrail.

Anything that sounds like conflict or difficulty or challenge is a huge Heart Religion no-no. Keep the blood and guts of life away, please—that's just not entertaining or sunny. It's hard to focus on self when that stuff is in view. And hearing about people's needs is no fun. It makes it seem like Scripture is supposed to speak to more than our personal, heartfelt wishes.

You don't see Religion of Head *or* Heart, on their own, leading to deeper faith and muscular love actions. Both are wacky in their own self-justified way.

Shadow Thumos

Dark, sinister, wicked thumos—*shadow* thumos—is undisciplined, reckless, and selfish. Instead of being willing, shadow thumos is *willful*. It's consumptive and thievish; its prowling, arrogant nature is hell-bent on satiating one's inflated ego and sordid appetites. Shadow thumos puts a man, or more accurately a man-boy, at the exclusive center of a universe in which all others are to serve and soothe and please and change his diapers. Shadow thumos ultimately is childish by nature, but it's extremely developed and proficient in its ability to harm and destroy.

Visually, for instance, shadow thumos is a guy ostentatiously grabbing his crotch and thrusting his hips; this is where such a man pours his thumos, into the messenger of his distorted obsession with self-gratifying pleasure. This is a zone of trickery for women who are attracted to thumos but unaware of or unwilling to recognize its dark side. (Much, though not all, of rap music is the unofficial soundtrack to shadow thumos; its "artists" give ample and ongoing illustrations of its imagery.)

Men with low or no thumos often complain of this. Whether out loud or to themselves, they ask, "Why do the jerks always get the women?" The answer: Even dark thumos usually is more attractive than low or no thumos. (That's the subject of the next chapter).

Men commit more than 90 percent of sexually predatory crimes. It's sinful thumos that makes men willing to commit acts of profound and vicious evil, stripping others of their God-given dignity and marring their essence for a cheap and abusive thrill; this malevolence crushes weaker people in its winepress of wrath. When propagandist Joseph Goebbels said that Nazi fascism was "in its nature a masculine movement,"[5] he was describing one of thumos's blackest expressions.

The following are terms, flavors, expressions, and moods that describe shadow thumos for us to consider, ponder, and pray about:

Rage, wanderlust, isolation, remote, domineering, selfish, bravado, machismo, simplistic, wife beating, child abuse, gang rape, gang violence, domination, road rage, incest, violent fundamentalism, anti-social, dry-eyed, draining, insulting, immature, blaming, shaming, overbearing, untrustworthy, reckless, rigid, will to pleasure, will to power, abandons, non-fathers, superfluous, hubris, cynical, over-tickles, arrogant, disruption, enemy making, honor, dissed, blasphemous, revenge, malice, strife, outbursts of wrath, defensive, willfulness, prejudice, rash, Islamic radicalism, Crusades, narcissism.

With this spirit in mind, fill in a few words or phrases of your own.

Unfortunately, our minds tend to remember more examples of shadow thumos than noble thumos. The reasons are many, and I don't claim to understand them all. Psychological theory tells us, for instance, that in our lives we retain the memory of roughly nine negative events to every one positive. It seems that in the present conditions of our reality, here and now, pain embeds itself in our souls more easily than pleasure.

Shadow thumos is a once-good attribute—often a strong will—that has gone in the wrong direction, and because it's not tethered to a higher power, it isn't kept in check or harnessed. As Scott Peck pointed out, a strong will is among the greatest faculties we can possess, but it also carries with it the potential to curse ourselves and others. "The worst side effect of a strong will," he warned, "is a strong temper—anger."[6]

Shadow thumos widely reduces itself to bullying. Courage-gone-wrong delights in unfair power—as long as it's one's own. Older brothers often give in to shadow thumos against their younger brothers, which reminds me of an Old Norse proverb: "Brothers will fight together and become each other's bane." Sad but true for many. With their extra bit of muscle, brainpower, and street smarts, the older ones often lord it over the younger with subtle and not-so-subtle acts of abuse that cause humiliation.

Why? "Because they can," I've said to my second-oldest son while remembering my own childhood. Notice, however, when someone treats older brothers with similar disdain or contempt, they come unglued. They often weep bitter tears and rail like Old Testament prophets against injustice, demanding that all wrongs cease at once. And so it goes.

Once, long ago, I was camping with two high school buddies, Ed and Kelly. Ed and I had ridden our bikes to the end of a road that brought us to the beach in Astoria, Oregon. This was the '80s; we were wearing 401 Levis and had long-johns under our T-shirts. Suddenly, out of nowhere, a lean-faced, dark-haired, twenty-something man-boy pulled up in a muscle car with two women.

Why does the bad guy always seem to have not just one but two girls? Again, thumos of any stripe is tremendously attractive. Even so, what amazes me is that such a woman grows accustomed to seeing her man let loose his shadow thumos upon others—and then, nonetheless, is shocked when he unleashes it upon her.

He told us to stop, which was an easy order to fill; we were at the end of the road. Then he ambushed us. He pulled out a fixed-blade knife, held it up, and commanded us to ride our bikes into the ocean. We refused.

In a moment that seemed to last forever, he walked behind me. I was straddling my ten-speed, awkwardly. As he lurked, I could hear the blood in my head course by my ears—it sounded like someone sanding old cedar with a scrub brush. For some reason I didn't run. He was very close to me, so I don't think I imagined I could get away. Something told me he was bluffing, but I wasn't sure.

I breathed deeply, tried to relax, and closed my eyes. I prepared myself to be stabbed in the back through my rain-soaked jacket. I heard the sound of cutting—through the bag that dangled under my seat. He appeared over my left shoulder, threw my bag on the ground, and said something about how that could've been me. Then he went to torment Ed.

Neither of us road our bikes into the surf. Neither of us ran. And, mercifully, neither of us got stabbed.

Many times, shadow thumos dominates not for survival but for kicks. And practitioners almost always get their kicks off weaker people. In this way they are cowards, because they rarely, if ever, pick on peers. People of shadow thumos devour and don't consider; they consume and don't replenish.

One summer I was unfortunate enough to work with a delinquent named Larry. Larry usually wore blue jeans that could stand on their own and a white wife-beater T-shirt that was too short to be tucked in. What covered his uncovered skin were many, many scars from bar fights and prison rumbles.

We actually were a three-man crew, and I was the odd man out: Larry the ex-con, Marty the high school dropout, and me—College Boy—making some pre-senior-year money by building fences, moving large rocks, and doing whatever else people wanted done outdoors. Our job was digging post-holes. A posthole digger is a large drill with a motor on top; this one had four metal rods coming out from the middle like bike spokes. At the end of the rods were handles.

We bore holes in the soft earth by going from a standing position to a kneeling position while revolving in unison— not easy. It was while being on our knees that things got dicey. We had to be close enough to the handles to maintain leverage, but far enough away so if the bit grabbed a root or a rock we could get out of the way. The incentive was strong: If the bit caught in the ground, the four handles would whirl counterclockwise like helicopter blades toward exposed ribs.

Making matters worse was that there was only one kill switch; this cut the motor off right away by touching a piece of metal to the spark plug. If we didn't reach it in time, the digger would send one or all of us tumbling across the ground—it was like getting thrown off a bull and then contending with thistles and blackberry bushes. We had to get to the switch at the first sign of the drill snagging, otherwise it would catch and the top would spin out of control.

When I didn't get to it in time, I would send Larry tumbling. And he already didn't like me. He had started putting me down the very first day we worked together.

Larry was proud of his scars—mostly on his arms, with some around his neck and a few on his face. To him, they weren't disfigurations, they were ribbons. He fingered them during lunch breaks and sometimes, between his broken teeth, he'd tell us how he got them. Most were from knives, though some, he said, were from broken bottles, which he worried about more because "instead of one blade, you gotta worry about all those other ones."

Larry made it sound as though he could never tell why he was always in the wrong place at the wrong time. He was just Joe Six-Pack, minding his own business, when some random guy would try to land a sucker punch from behind, and then of course he'd have no choice but to reach for his blade and defend himself. Women were always involved somehow, and it was this part of his story that rang true for me.

The day Larry threatened to kill me was the same day that the daughter of the ranch owner came on to me. I was nineteen; she was in her mid-twenties. She was blonde, medium height, well-maintained. She used to sunbathe in a two-piece suit while we worked in her father's field, behind their house, and was much nicer to look at than Hairy Larry.

She gave me her phone number and wanted me to call her. Larry and Marty must have seen her hand it to me. Marty was cool about it, but now Larry hated me even more. The green monster of envy was kicking him up good. His look went from "You're a jerk" to *pure evil.* A primitive fuse was lit, and he became a man looking for an excuse to maul "Paul, the school puke."

Speaking of education, I was well-schooled in being a doormat; I hadn't responded when he'd started taunting me the first day we drove to work, the three of us in the front of Marty's small truck. I pretended his put-downs didn't bother me, when undeniably they did. He called me more rotten things than I can remember, but I was going to love him into the kingdom of God, so I didn't defend myself. I'd been told I shouldn't; it was my gentleness that would reform him.

Anyway, on that afternoon, I didn't get to the kill switch in time. Larry and I both tumbled across the ground. Between rolls he managed to scream profane invectives, all of them directed at me. Each of us came up ready to kill the other.

And I did want to kill him. Despite the games I played with myself, his insults had cut me deep. I'd fantasized about beating him senseless for giving me so much hell. I was ready to rumble.

I was a top athlete back then—quick, light on my feet, pretty strong for my size. But Larry had me by about forty pounds, and while most of that was belly jelly, beer fat counts for something in a fight, especially if it gets on top of you. Weight itself provides leverage when you're on the ground wrestling for control, and most fights end up on the ground.

I wanted to attack him with my fists and elbows, feet and knees. I wanted to smear his mug into Oregon's loamy soil. I wanted to break his nose with my forehead.

I wanted to grab him and jam his face into a cow pie. I wanted that pie to be warm, runny, and gritty. I wanted to force that grit so deep into his mouth that he'd have to floss it out. I wanted to rub excrement into the nucleus of every atom of his being. I wanted to humiliate him as he had humiliated me.

I believe I could have choked the life out of a man that summer day. My shadow thumos possessed me.

Most people who preach Bunny Rabbit Christianity never worked with a Lumbering Larry (or met one in seminary). They most likely will never get to know anyone like him; they would avoid such a sinner-man at any cost once they were in his company. Larry was a primitive beast in many ways, a man who carried a knife (almost certainly a parole violation) while making fence-post holes, not to cut away brush but to cut away the flesh of another man.

To such men, a gentle word doesn't always turn away wrath. It may well invite exploitation. To such a man, gentle = sucker. Gentle = easy mark. That was me, Sucker-Mark Boy. Larry wanted to kill me *before* he took a spin on the dirt, *before* the most beautiful woman of that summer approached me. That day was the perfect storm for envy, fury, and those other twisted motives that make one man want to end the life of another through dark courage, through an animated will going hard in the wrong direction.

I had to get to Larry before he got to his knife in his back pocket.

That's when Marty stood between us and gradually, blessedly, helped cool the inferno of our repelling and repellant shadow thumos.

Practitioners of shadow thumos have not indignation but hate, disdain, pride, terror, and supremacy heating their courage. They are sinners, but remember: so are men who extinguish their courage. The shortcomings of cowards are just less noticeable than those of criminals.

And it's so easy to respond in kind, as I did. Larry wounded my dignity, and unless a man adheres to a faith that exalts love above *all* else—even honor and dignity—he will seek to steal another man's honor and dignity in return . . . maybe even his life. Shadow thumos met by shadow thumos creates cyclical hatred and retribution.

But when I say "a faith that exalts love," I don't mean the weak-wristed kind of sentimental feel-goodish stuff we mistake for love today, especially in church and especially through popular worship music. It's not an either/or: *either* retaliation *or* reticence, *either* monster *or* mouse. We can preserve and protect without being vicious or vengeful; noble courage doesn't say we cannot defend ourselves from shadow thumos. But it does tell us that our motives shouldn't include revenge: eye for an eye or tooth for a tooth.

You probably noticed that some words and concepts in the lists describing noble and shadow thumos (above) appeared in both. Three, actually: they are *honor, disruption,* and *enemy making.* Once again, this is because, like gasoline, combustible thumos can go both ways, depending on motives and depending on the outcome. Assault is disruptive . . . and so are the wounds of a friend that can be trusted.[8] Each might well create an enemy. Protecting the honor of another person can be an act of noble thumos, yet the belt buckles of Himmler's Nazi SS troops read, "My Honor Is Loyalty." We'll put that one on the shadow side.

Notes

1. M. Scott Peck, *Further Along the Road Less Traveled* (New York: Simon & Schuster, 1993), 36.
2. John 15:15 NEB
3. 1 John 4:18
4. Francis Schaeffer, *The Great Evangelical Disaster* (Wheaton, IL: Crossway, 1984).
5. Quoted in Martin Durham, *Women and Fascism* (Milton Park, UK: Routledge, 1998), 168.
6. Ibid., 36–37.
7. See Proverbs 27:6.

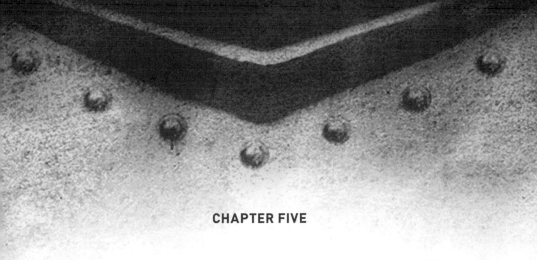

CHAPTER FIVE

LOW ON LIVING, LOW ON LIFE

Be on the alert, stand firm in the faith,
act like men, be strong.
(Paul the apostle)[1]

It's not the men in your life that matter.
It's the life in your men.
(Mae West)[2]

We men, at our best through noble thumos, are life-supporting and life-donating. Though we don't give birth, we were designed to sustain, grow, and protect life; we're wired to charge it with energy and verve, going ahead of and providing for those we love.

Though the results of shadow thumos are real and treacherous, there's still another condition that's at least as perilous: possessing little or no thumos at all.

Low-thumos living is one of the biggest challenges of ministering to men who go to church. They can't seem to get animated about anything. They're unable to stoke an inner fire that gets them moving to improve the quality of their life and enhance or safeguard the well-being of others. They feel stuck in the gear of "apathetic neutral," and they're living off the vitalizing will of others. Usually this will belongs to their wife, and that dynamic does *not* go down well in families.

"My husband will not take the initiative about anything!" one woman vented at a writer's conference. "It's like he's dead, but he's not. Can you help him?" The answer depends in part on how deep Neutered Christianity has gone into such a man; it depends even more on his willingness to exorcise it.

The event that usually stimulates men to take an honest look at thumos is their realization of the sorry state of their marriage. Often, by this point, they're about to be separated, they are separated, or they're about to be divorced. At long last, their wife's finally not being able to take it anymore has given them the gift of desperation.

They really want to keep their marriage together; up to now, though, they've utterly failed to muster the fighting spirit necessary to contend for it. And here is where, once again, their background betrays them. Their Bunny Rabbit faith has them believing that all fighting is striving, or as a pastor of mine used to put it, that they're supposed to "stop trying to make things happen and let God take over."

One younger man facing divorce told me, "I know this sounds crazy, but all I need to do is lay this situation at the Lord's feet, and then get out of the way and let him take care of it." Jesus as Super Sherpa, waiting to carry us up life's jagged slopes without any human willingness, cooperation, or synergy—sound familiar? This is the language of a man who is too "spiritual," and who is insufficiently soulful, to be of any real good. What do you think would happen if he behaved this way at work when his quarterly report came due or when his assignment had been left undone?

Another definition of *thumos* the Greeks gave us is "soul-blood," which represents a vital capacity for life: a living, an expression, a movement, and an action that's ever right here and right now. Women leave weak men who do not care for their soul-blood and who hide their soul-neglect behind a façade of spirituality. They can tell at an intuitive level that such a man is unreliable, unsoulful, inauthentic and untrustworthy. They desire a man who has soul-juice.

I worked with one juiceless man for months, helping him battle his fears and become a more proactive husband and father. He did want to make the adjustment, but he hadn't yet actualized it; his wife, who'd long waited for him to step up to life's plate, also had complained bitterly, even saying, through disdainful lips, "You suck the life out of me."

It hurts to so often hear such contempt from wives of low-thumos men; I know how shame-producing it is. As a young Christian Nice Guy who for years followed the CNG script to the letter, I once heard it from a girlfriend I really loved, and being sliced open by the jagged blade of that comment remains one of the most painful experiences I've ever had.

If you've experienced this, you know what I'm talking about. It feels like such a sucker punch. The voice of your emasculated spirituality says that if you're a swell guy, the road to relational happiness will be cleared for you. It doesn't happen this way. Many Christian men come to feel like a mushroom: kept in the dark about how the real world operates and fed a lot of manure. Eventually they tend to turn around and reject the worldview that gave them this worthless outlook.

It's the life-draining, soul-sucking aspect of low thumos that drives a wife to express disgust toward her husband. And for most men it is their wife—not God—who drives them to their knees; by the time they've hit the floor they feel shattered into a million little shards. A woman's rejection is the pinnacle of shame for most men.

Here are some words and phrases that help to describe low-thumos life:

Numb, passive, whining, feckless, anxious, yes-man, acedia, sexually bland, pleasant, agreeable, nice, hands in pockets jingling change, innocuous, beautiful loser, let's just be friends, wimp, passed by, divorced, naïve, can't knuckle down, dainty, disease to please, procrastinator, doormat, picked on, held down, no boundaries, always a groomsman never a groom, irrelevant, lukewarm, rootless, failure to launch.

With this spirit in mind, fill in a few words and phrases of your own.

Low-Fire, Lonely Lives

Single Christian men who do not have the gift of celibacy, who want to be married, and who are unanimated by courageous vitality have it especially hard. Their letters are among the most heartbreaking that we receive at Coughlin Ministries. Most of them struggle with pornography, and their dating life is a veritable sea of disappointment.

Their low-thumos ways pretty much ensure they won't kindle any kind of spark with the women they date. Many of these women say things along the lines of, "I wish I liked you more." They really do want to like such men; in many ways they already are so likeable. Yet in a foundational, crucial, inevitable way they are not *want-able* to women. Most women, most of the time, are attracted to men with thumos heat.

I remember the conversation I had with a single man who works for Compassion International. He caught only a few minutes of a presentation I gave, but he said he felt as if I'd been reading his mind. He said I'd mentioned things I don't remember saying, statements that weren't even in my notes. He told me he wanted to be married more than anything and that he *knew* something significant was missing in him.

I said that if he's like many other men today, his Achilles' heel is his backbone. I encouraged him to disagree with his next date, when appropriate, without being dismissive and to stick to his guns without being obnoxious. I also suggested that he gently tease his date, to show he wouldn't be rigidly fixed upon her complete approval (something most healthy women will appreciate).

But, like many Christian men, he was an approval junkie, so my advice sounded almost sacrilegious to him. He was shocked, even scandalized. I wish he'd have been willing to give something else a try; it was obvious his blueprint wasn't getting the house built.

The Bible tells us it's not good for the man to be alone,[3] and upon this biblical truth I rest my case against Nice Guy theology and all the damage that goes with it. Men are alone because of an orthodoxy and an orthopraxy—a belief, and that belief lived out—that's constantly been draining and disposing of their God-given thumos. Their boldness, their courage, their will needs to be animated and seasoned by the Holy Spirit; it's *not* to be suppressed, it's *not* to be destroyed, and it's *not* to be crucified!

Among the countless examples of what inanimate living is like, *The Weather Man*, a film starring Nicholas Cage as meteorologist David Spritz, sharply illustrates a man who through bottomed-out thumos suffers across-the-board collateral damage. And, unlike some other examples, you can view this one over and over.

Spritz is financially successful, but he's a lousy husband and father. He's separated from his wife; his kids flounder aimlessly through life, because he just can't bring himself to become more of a man. A part of him knows it, too—his muted, unfulfilled desire drives him crazy, and his failure to develop as a person drives others crazy.

People who recognize him on the street sling fast food at him. "Always fast food," he ruminates to himself. ("*I'm* fast food," he realizes later, in a moment of epiphany.) In fact, the movie's promo poster shows his left shoulder splattered with a Wendy's chocolate Frosty.

Like what's thrown, Spritz has no substantial character or substance. He feels humiliated and angry, but people take aim at him because they know they can get away with it; they can tell by how he carries himself that he possesses no backbone, no thumos. He's pretty much a shell, an empty hull.

Spritz does not possess fortitude, or, as he himself puts it, the ability to "hunker down." (That's another way of saying "to man-up.") To some extent, the obscene amount of money he makes shelters him from the full consequences of his courage-void; all the same, his ailing thumos leaves him out of sync with the regular rhythms of life, much like what a drug addiction does to others.

One of his sons is so alone, so without guidance, that he is seduced by an older homosexual man. David senses that something isn't right, but like so many men of low thumos he does not have the courage or the ability to heed his chest and lungs as they scream for him to lovingly protect his son. To his father, Robert—a loving man and a Pulitzer Prize–winning author played by Sir Michael Caine—David laments, "I just can't knuckle down!" (That's a street-level definition of low-thumos living.)

Over dinner, after he hears about David's separation, Robert speaks of how life *really* is lived among real men and real issues. Here are just a few of his gems:

> "To get anything of value, you have to sacrifice."
> "Did you know that the harder thing to do and the right
> thing to do are usually the same thing?"
> "Nothing that has meaning is easy."
> "Easy doesn't enter into grown-up life."

These trenchant proverbs, spoken in love by a father, are found throughout the tougher portions of Scripture, spoken in love by our Father. David says he knows everything his dad is telling him; Robert looks at him knowing he does not. Or rather, he knows that knowing is not the same as doing. Knowledge isn't enough to make us doers; information alone is an insufficient cause for action.

Eventually David Spritz embraces a new hobby, one that reaches deeper into his soul than even he realizes. He takes up archery with a long bow, even though he "doesn't know why." This lethal and graceful pursuit helps him get in touch with his martial spirit; it helps him focus his scattered will, and with this acquired capacity he benefits from the sense of well-being that comes from completing a task, from hitting a target.

One definition of sin (from the Greek word *hamartia*) is to "miss the mark." This is an archery term, and that connection pretty much escaped the notice of the critics who reviewed *The Weather Man*. David was missing the mark in his life because of his inability to knuckle down and do what's right, or as Jesus states it, "to be rich in good deeds."[4] His capacity to do the right thing improves as he grafts thumos back into his life. (Remember the "Second Turning"? He was becoming a participant.)

Growing through his martial pursuit, Spritz soon walks with more confidence—not arrogance—and people no longer throw food at him. He feels, and acts, more like a man. His developing focus helps him to see the value of directed force and the power of distilled intensity. Aiming an arrow at a target over grass and snow has helped enable him to become newly alive.

David Spritz didn't just take up a hobby. He took up a discipline, a practice that his soul desperately needed in order to help him create the kind of love he wants to give his children and, hopefully, to assist him in winning back his wife. His practice has been breaking up and dissolving the life-threatening blockage of his soul's arteries; though like you and me he remains a very flawed person, he's increasingly better able to "knuckle down."[5]

Helping the low-thumos David Spritzes of the world can be hard slogging. While the vast majority of them know they're missing something they absolutely must obtain, many of them have not yet identified their specific need. As men fight through the bleariness or vagueness to gain clarity and vitality, most of them can find huge benefit in taking up archery, target shooting, hunting, or a martial art—*something* requiring focused will that carries with it some level of risk (not to be mistaken for rashness or foolhardiness, which are born from risk that is unjustified and not tethered to a noble purpose). Except for southerners, though, many guys feel that these practices are unbecoming of—even an embarrassment to—Christian men. There is a pudding-middle soul-pudginess in them that we the church, incredibly and indefensibly, somehow have sanctified and ordained.

Criminal Cowardice

Lack of thumos disgusts more than wives—it disgusts us as a culture as well. You might remember seeing footage of or hearing about an elderly man being assaulted by a young man trying to steal his car. That elderly man was ninety-one-year-old war veteran Leonard Sims of Detroit, who was punched in the face and neck more than twenty times during a brutal carjacking in 2007. The attack was caught on video and broadcast throughout the world. But what most of us didn't see was the wide-angle footage that showed four bystanders watching the attack—and doing *absolutely nothing* to help the man being pummeled like a punching bag. They stood there like ravens on a power line, like the proverbial monkeys who saw, heard, and spoke no evil.

Mr. Sims was unable to lift his hands—he used them to brace himself against the gale-force attack until he was knocked to the ground and was almost run over as the shadow-thumos thug pulled away. The punk stood only five-foot-nine and was slim; the crowd could have taken him easily. Instead they just watched. They didn't even call 9-1-1. A nearby convenience store clerk did.

We witness low-thumos life and feel gut-piercing remorse, righteous anger, and stomach-turning disgust. We're *designed* this way. This is a natural, God-given response to one of the most despicable behaviors in humans (especially men). God *made* us to disdain cowardice, not so that we'd be consumed by guilt and shame, but so that when we face trials we'll be compelled within to forge greater character: fortitude, strength, boldness, courage, and love.[6]

British preacher Paul Scanlon talks about a baby who was dying in a nursery ward in England. The child's chart showed how doctors conducted every possible test to find out why this child was dying. Then, at the bottom of the chart, in the sobering diagnosis field, was written, "Failure to thrive." This child had no fighting spirit, no lust for life. Unlike other children in that nursery, he was missing an animating quality or soul-blood that would compel him toward the activity necessary to survive. He seemed to have been born without the essence that no machine could install or induce; he needed an animus to help move him past adversity and into a life of vitality and growth.

Many of us adults have the same actual but mysterious ailment that's killing us spiritually. Gichin Funakoshi, known as the creator and founder of modern karate, gave us something essential to chew on regarding this lack: "That in daily life, one's mind and body be trained and developed in a spirit of humility; and that in critical times, one be devoted utterly to the cause of justice."[7] He meant real humility, not the false form of humility that tells us that we are nothing but worms—that's just another form of lying.

Worse, our false humility undercuts our God-given gifts and power, and I don't think this is a coincidence. When we reject our strengths or our talents it's often because, like thumos, they make us conspicuous. We show up on people's radar. In other words, if we woke up to their *realities*, then we would wake up to their *responsibilities*. Fearful and selfish, instead we slink away with a pious smile, a pledge to pray, and a wish for blessings.

Thumos helps us to play our part in the kingdom of heaven, a kingdom of love, light, and truth. It also helps us to avoid what Francis Schaeffer noticed with chagrin:

> One of the greatest injustices we do to our young people is ask them to be conservative. Christianity is not conservative, but revolutionary. To be conservative today is to miss the whole point, for conservatism means standing in the flow of the status quo, and the status quo no longer belongs to us. If we want to be fair, we must teach the young to be revolutionaries, revolutionaries against the status quo.[8]

Schaeffer wasn't using the word *conservative* in its popular and narrow political dimension. He meant it in the broader sense of how young Christians are inculcated into maintaining what currently is. What currently is includes a vast indifference to the well-being of others and catering to our own comfort. Cain's comeback to God—"Am I my brother's keeper?"—is often our unsaid snotty remark, except that we usually lack the audacity to be so direct.[9] Nonetheless, our actions too often are the same.

We know that thumos deficiency is a spiritual ailment. But is it a psychological disorder as well? Counselors complain that sometimes their best insights go unheeded by clients. They often scratch their heads as to why one finds his way to healing and spiritual growth while another barely moves in a better direction. I think thumos has a lot to do with this quandary. If one has no internal urge to push past a misconception or neurosis, does he really have a chance? If he has no inner urge to grasp the better life above him, and if he's too cowardly to face his fears, he simply isn't going to make much progress.

Thumos is part of what philosopher William James described as "reserve energies," a capacity that every person possesses and that should be depleted by the end of life. The energy in this reservoir lifts people to higher and better places; as a man who was horrified by the waste of human energy in armed conflict, James believed this energy should be used to "drain marshes, irrigate the deserts, and dig the canals, and democratically do the physical and social engineering which builds up so slowly and painfully what war so quickly destroys."[10] This energy recognizes that while there will be defeats, there also are victories yet to be won.

As a lay minister, I know that people who are unable to carry on through life's inevitable suffering and pain are eventually somehow stuck, very much like people addicted to drugs. If they are skilled at manipulating others, they usually will prey upon the weak and the earnest to meet their cravings. They will line others up like bowling pins and mow them down. Cowardice is an orientation toward life that leads to apathy in all who possess it; in some it likewise leads to manipulation. These sound like psychological ailments.

Making matters worse, we don't live in a world that rewards courage, except the selfish kind where we'll applaud others who have enough thumos to keep our borders safe.

But what about the kind of courage that rushes toward Twin Towers ablaze? "What happened to the respect for that kind of manliness?" a friend asked me during a recent fishing trip. "For a time we really appreciated people like that. Now we've just slipped back into a flat existence where we don't even acknowledge heroes, much less honor them. We're not even sure they exist anymore. I mean, everywhere you turn, including church, it's as if everyone is trying to rip courage out of you."

This is a man with a prophetic nature, a man who believes that some things are right and others wrong. He recently had to clean up after a head pastor made a shambles of his congregation and was eventually fired. The wreckage took place right under the noses of deacons and elders who did virtually nothing to contain (let alone stop) it.

This angered him profoundly. "You guys are a bunch of cowards," he told them. "One of the reasons he [the pastor] made such a mess is because you watched it happen and did nothing." He said there's still more cleanup to do, and he's afraid there isn't nearly enough will to create the necessary healthy changes.

"Can you create a coalition of the willing?" I asked.

"I really don't think it's there," he said, sounding tired. "What do you think I should do?"

This is among the hardest questions to answer since I know what it often leads to. In an average group of ten people, one, two at the most, have a functioning thumos. That's plainly a minority. You can comfort yourself by saying that one person plus God is a majority—and it may be. But I speak from experience in affirming that it doesn't always work that way. People of noble thumos often get their head handed to them on a platter, actually or figuratively.

So I replied, "It may not be a battle that's worthy of your blood." After thinking about it more, though, I said, "But then again, your integrity and your loyalty to Christ will take a beating if you *don't* speak up. If you do speak up, make sure it's done lovingly and with wisdom, but then expect to be slandered and ostracized later. Planning on this can take out some of the sting and disappointment. And, if you're right, time eventually will vindicate you."

I'll say it again: Thumos is a burden made lighter by Christ, who is life itself, who is disruptive courage, and who honors those who tell the truth the way he did, does, and will.

Notes

1. 1 Corinthians 16:13 NASB
2. Attributed
3. See Genesis 2:18.
4. 1 Timothy 6:18
5. *The Weather Man*. Gore Verbinski, director. David Alper and William S. Beasley, producers. Paramount: 2005.
6. See James 1.
7. Gichin Funakoshi, *Karate-Do Kyohan* (Toyko: Kodansha International, 1973), 3.
8. Quoted in *Ministry Today* (July/August 2007), 12.
9. See Genesis 4:9.
10. Will Durant, *The Story of Philosophy: The Lives and Opinions of the World's Greatest Philosophers* (New York: Simon & Schuster [Pocket], 1961), 387.

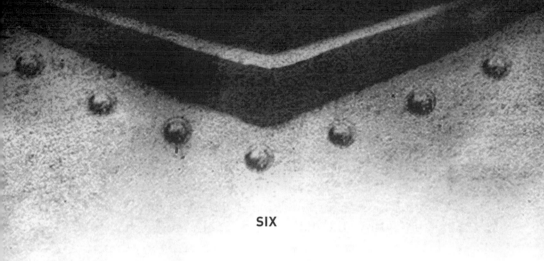

SIX

TRAINING THAT DRAINS—A SCRIPT THAT NEEDS REWRITING

No man is strong unless he bears within his character antitheses strongly marked.
(Martin Luther King Jr.)[1]

While there have been many, I particularly remember one sermon illustration that drained my thumos and yet at the same time unfairly, even cruelly, was designed to compel me to lead with boldness and strength. I call it the Parable of the Good Chauffeur, and it was pivotal to my early spiritual development.

As the story goes, there was a wealthy man who needed a new chauffeur. He tested three.

The first took him up a windy and dangerous road, and in order to showcase the fine points of his skill, he drove near the edge of the pavement—so close that the wealthy man could see to the bottom of the canyon below.

The second drove quickly and efficiently; he preferred the left lane on the freeway.

The third drove slowly and safely down the middle, taking no chances. You can guess by now which chauffeur my pastor lavishly praised and the one he said was most pleasing to God.

Through this and similar anecdotes that promote the Official Script, the message is clear: The Lord favors caution-oriented men who play life safe, who refrain from taking risks. Don't climb any spiritual trees—you might get hurt! (This same pastor also was wont to say that women are more sensitive to the Holy Spirit than men.)

Divine blessing, then, is said to rest upon placid men who stay within the bull's-eye of God's breezy, status-quo will. Like many men, I was taught to be overly cautious, continually concerned about what others thought of me, never to offend and always to please. Such fear-encrusted, smotherly-motherly advice leads to a life that's very much unlike the life of Christ.

Here's the ugly irony: While this pastor heaped shame onto people of thumos, behind the scenes he was a man of tremendous thumos. Because he so carefully kept it concealed— he hoarded power to lord it over those he weakened—he was viewed as a spiritual traitor, a grim reaper of masculinity. A number of men have told me they can trace the destruction of their marriages back to the deception and naïveté of the man's teachings.

Exhausting people of their courage, or preventing them from developing it and then exhorting them to be strong, is an equivalent to the pharisaical sin of heaping onerous burdens upon others while refusing to offer help. Ministry should lift burdens, not make them heavier. Without thumos, life is depressing.

We're often told to stay away from any behavior that could be deemed irresponsible. You know, like what Simon and Andrew did after Jesus invited them to be "fishers of men": They immediately "left their nets and followed him."[2] Notice, though, that *he* didn't scorn their seemingly careless action.

They didn't drop to their knees and pray really hard about their decision. (Oops.) They didn't consult their wives. (Those cads!) And they didn't go to their elders for counsel. (Yikes—weren't they worried they'd lose their "spiritual covering"?) If they were anyone else, we would denounce their gutsiness as rash, foolish, and of course, anti-family. We'd regard them as heathen—not fervent men following God himself in the flesh.

The common belief that everything in life is predetermined doesn't help either. Dallas Willard writes about the troubling connection many Christians have between fatalism/determinism on the one hand and apathy/cowardice on the other:

> If you were to get to the bottom of my theology you would find me pretty Calvinistic, but my sense of ministry is to judge the lay of the land for your times and shoot where the enemy is. The enemy of our time is not human capacity, or over-activism, but the enemy is passivity—the idea that God has done everything and you are essentially left to be a consumer of the grace of God, and that the only thing you have to do is find out how to do that and do it regularly. I think this is a terrible mistake and accounts for the withdrawal of active Christians from so many areas of life where they should be present.[3]

In order to help thumos create spiritual growth and strengthen our soul, we will need to amend, while not destroying, some very pivotal and popular teachings that comprise much of the Official Script.

Fruit of the Spirit: Nine—*Plus*

At the top of this "reassessment list" is a better understanding of what we've been told are the fruits or manifestations of the Spirit. Jesus told us that after he returned to heaven God would send us a Comforter that would help direct our lives. He called him "the Holy Spirit," and Paul apprised us of the qualities a life has when the Spirit is in the driver's seat.

> The fruit of the Spirit is love, joy, peace, patience, kindness, goodness, faithfulness, gentleness and self-control. Against *such things* there is no law.[4]

These nine traits have been taken by many to be exhaustive. But it's erroneous to believe that there are no other attributes of the Holy Spirit's living in a person's life to strengthen, comfort, and direct us. It's also untrue that God does not expect us to graft other qualities into our lives. A more comprehensive understanding of his Spirit likewise can give us a better comprehension of this mysterious power.

Note Paul's qualifying statement that "against *such things* there is no law." He didn't write this because he was trying to add more words to his letter or fill up his parchment. He wanted us to realize and understand that there are additional manifestations. He didn't intend for his letter to the Galatians to put forward a complete list.

Paul refers his readers back to their initial experience with the Spirit, which included, for example, illumination[5] and moral transformation,[6] neither of which are in the Galatians list of attributes. In Acts, the most regularly mentioned spiritual manifestation is inspired speech—speaking in tongues, prophecy and praise, and bold utterances of the Word of God.[7] These also are not listed in the "original nine." The Spirit is invisible, but for those willing to take a broader and deeper look, the manifestations of the Spirit's presence were readily detectable.[8]

For the sake of your thumos, consider a few things. First, notice the words "bold utterances of the word of God" as a manifestation of his Spirit. As our spiritual training has many of us compliantly and pleasantly behaving like Pavlov's dog, you'll likely notice that boldness appears to clash with the Galatians list that today holds court over all others, the list that contains the word *gentleness*. We don't think legitimate boldness and actual gentleness should come out of the same person, but looking at the life of Christ and the lives of the godliest people we know reveals that boldness and gentleness aren't at all incompatible.

Those in whom the Spirit reigns are gentle when gentleness is required, and they are bold with the life-giving Word of God, sharper in truth and wisdom than any two-edged sword,[9] when that's required. Here there is no contradiction but rather completion. Martin Luther King Jr. put it this way: "No man is strong unless he bears within his character antitheses strongly marked."[10] King used *antitheses* to mean that men should possess tender hearts, tough minds, and a heated thumos in order to play our part in God's plan for our lives.

The spiritual fruit of love is not always gentle or pleasant. Surgeons and dentists and physical therapists and psychiatrists bring pain into (or reveal pain already in) our lives in order to help us heal, to escape disease, and to experience freedom. Their love for others brings creative tension, significant discomfort, and healthy disruption to the object of their care.

The same is true for God, who disciplines those he loves.[11] And friends sometimes wound each other because they care— they don't want the ones they love to screw up their lives. Wounds from a friend have love as their motive, so they can be trusted,[12] but they sure don't feel gentle at the time, do they? If this experience is foreign to you, then chances are you've not yet experienced the tremendous blessing of brotherhood.

The Relationship Between Power and Peace

When I want to burrow deeper into a word or concept, I sometimes turn to sign language. Recently, during a break in a Michael McDonald concert, I noticed a woman, to the right of the stage, signing to a small group of people. I was mesmerized by her unvarnished and unblinking use of signs to describe everyday life.

There was no posturing or pretense as this gifted communicator reflected the mood and nature of the songs. When I asked her for the sign for courage, she clenched her fists, knuckles away from her body, elbows bent—the position your arms would be when finishing a pull-up, where your fists rest just below your chin.

"Courage means 'strength, power,'" she told me. And that sign is the visual equivalent of the Hebrew word for courage (*hazaq*), which means "to show oneself strong." Thankfully, there are expressions of Christianity that put forth courage as a gift of God's Holy Spirit.

Anglicans, Catholics, and Lutherans believe there are seven primary gifts of the Holy Spirit, as found in Isaiah 11. Here we're told that the Spirit of God rests upon Messiah, helping him and those who know him to do their part in the messianic kingdom. Isaiah gives very specific information:

> The Spirit of the Lord will rest on him—
> the Spirit of wisdom and of understanding,
> the Spirit of counsel and of power,
> the Spirit of knowledge and of the fear of the Lord.[13]

This word *power* is also translated as *strength* and *might*, derivatives of courage. Thomas Aquinas unfolded this spiritual gift when he wrote that the gift of fortitude (courage) allows people "firmness of mind [that] is required both in doing good and in enduring evil, especially with regard to goods or evils that are difficult."[14] According to Aquinas, the gift of courage compels a Christian's will toward doing God's will *here and now.*

Another view of the intriguing Isaiah passage says that the gifts listed are threefold: (1) wisdom and understanding for government, (2) counsel and power (courage) for war, and (3) knowledge and fear of the Lord for spiritual leadership.[15]

We must also pay attention to what Isaiah writes next because it's intrinsic to our comprehension of what the Holy Spirit will compel us to do with our thumotic courage.

> With righteousness he will judge the needy,
>> with justice he will give decisions for the poor of the earth.
>
> He will strike the earth with the rod of his mouth;
> with the breath of his lips he will slay the wicked.
> Righteousness will be his belt
> and faithfulness the sash around his waist.[16]

Biblically, again and again and again, we see that courage is intrinsic to justice, faithfulness, righteousness, and peace. Through the Prince of Peace,[17] we learn that peace itself is hard-won. Here we learn, specifically, that peace follows judgment and springs from righteousness—not from perpetual pleasantness and never-ending niceties.

Please don't miss how this remarkable passage so vividly reveals God's heart and will for the needy and the poor. We are to do more than merely provide food and shelter—we are to judge on their behalf, to move their direction, to plead their case for them when necessary. We should be more than their dietitian or landlord: We need to be their *advocate.*[18]

Unfortunately, our current notion of peace itself is poorly conceived, even self-serving. We usually think of it in the framework of inner peace, an inner sense of well-being. We also frequently regard *peace* as being "about me, my feelings, my thoughts, my experience, my needs." There is an inner peace that comes from the Holy Spirit, yes, but why wouldn't we think this would include the likelihood that God would gift us with the ability to help bring about peace on earth as well?

Furthermore, regarding inner peace, we need to admit that this also comes from a life well-lived through the discharge of one's duties. Simply *doing what one ought to do* is a strong vaccine against the malaise of existential anguish and depression that haunts many people. We fulfill our responsibilities and continue moving toward our aspirations in part when we possess and employ our fighting spirit.

The fruit of peace likewise should lead toward the proliferation of peace; it shouldn't result in appeasement. Unfortunately, we're not very good at distinguishing peacemaking from peace-faking. Rick Warren reminds us:

> Peacemaking is not avoiding conflict. Running from a problem, pretending it doesn't exist, or being afraid to talk about it is actually cowardice. Jesus, the Prince of Peace, was never afraid of conflict. . . . Peacemaking is also not appeasement. Always giving in, acting like a doormat, and allowing others to always run over you is not what Jesus had in mind.[19]

The falsehoods in our worldview have us believing we're the world's doormats. In his oft-overlooked bluntness, though, Jesus sets us straight: "If your brother wrongs you, reprove him; and if he repents, forgive him."[20] That's pretty straightforward and assertive. He likewise once told his disciples that if they had no sword they should sell their cloak to buy one.[21]

The Bible gives us many examples of the rugged virtues we're called to embrace, so why do we focus only on the sweet and sugary ones that, when overemphasized, give us spiritual cavities and further deep-freeze our already frosty thumos? The answer is that we don't want toughness in our spirituality, even when it's unavoidable, and even when it can save lives. We don't want creative tension and unsettling disruption—we're afraid these might be offensive to others and, from a leadership angle, thereby lower the body count on a given Sunday. We like numbers. Numbers keep our budgets growing.

I understand budget problems. I've gone months unable to pay my bills due to ministry expensees, and I've hated how that feels. But service to others is a priority we make, for right now seekers coming into our churches aren't seeing fervent love and action but rather the ordination of mildness and conformity. On the most segregated day in America, they are seeing people "more cautious than courageous, [people who] have remained silent behind the anesthetizing security of the stained-glass windows" regarding matters of justice and cruelty.[22]

So we only quote the things that make our faith feel safe and comfortable; we hide from stuff that's revolutionary, adventurous . . . truly transforming. We'll do most anything to escape or ignore what seems threatening to our status quo.

Remember, though: The Bible commands us to be strong and courageous more than two dozen times! (Interestingly, it also lists about the same number of examples of cowardice, *each* a cautionary tale. It's as if God is instructing us to embrace courage each time there's an opportunity to flee it). We're told that the righteous are as bold as lions;[23] how on earth have we come to think we should be as sugary as cotton candy or as saccharine as diet soda ("sweetness"—both real and fake)?

The health of our thumos, the state of our spiritual maturity, and thus our ability to live well depend upon our accepting this revelation of what it means to follow God and reflect his true nature, which brings *both* disruption and comfort. Once more, here there is no contradiction, but rather completion.

Thumos in the Bible

Thumos is found eighteen times in the New Testament; seven of those occurrences refer to God's wrath. In Galatians, we see an example of shadow thumos in the word *jealousy*, which when smoldering breaks out in wrath.[24] Thumos and another word for "wrath" (*orgé*) are coupled in two places in Revelation: "the fierceness (*thumos*) of His wrath [*orgé*]" and "the fierceness and wrath of Almighty God."[25]

For most of us, that's as far as our one-dimensional understanding of this beneficial-slash-harmful attribute goes. The following is a good example: One popular New Testament commentary shows how narrow is our comprehension of this vibrant attribute. The author states that *thumos* means "wrath" and "hot." "Wrath is like a volcano. . . . Stuff a cork in it."[26]

This perspective leads to the emaciation and wilting of many souls, largely because it ignores the creative seed in properly handled anger and because it overlooks anger as an intrinsic component to righteous indignation, which should lead to deep and abiding love for those who are weak and oppressed. The Bible shows a more noble side to this attribute in the way Jesus demonstrated muscular indignation—the kind that battles for transcendent truths, protects others who are being stripped of their worth, and loves those in need in practical ways—as opposed to anger that stems from not getting what we want. In Jesus we see a thumos that guards and provides for those whom leaders have exploited and abused.

Noble thumos burns for the good of others, for God's will to be done on earth as in heaven, and thus it causes people to act; wrathful anger is usually personal, born of envy, self-absorbed, and vengeful. Stuffing a cork in thumos will diminish your spiritual growth and weaken your faith-in-action!

Anything that says otherwise is a misguided recipe for being unable to wrestle with and tackle real issues in real life.

Today's Official Script, though, favors lower-thumos and contemplative folks over bolder and more active ones; people who prefer reading to doing; theological polemicists and parsers to mission-minded burden lifters. Today we applaud the kind of strength that suffers but not the kind that says no, lives courageously, and rescues others the way Christ did. *Why not honor both?*

And why do we applaud heroic strength in films (for instance) if there's something wrong with having it at church? This is a sign that we don't honor what our souls tell us is right and good because somehow it doesn't appear "spiritual" enough.

Machiavelli observed:

> This way of living, then, seems to have rendered the world weak and handed it over as prey to wicked men, who can safely manage it when they see that most men think more of going to Heaven by enduring their injuries than by avenging them.[27]

The world, he concluded, "has become effeminate and Heaven disarmed"[28] by this kind of faith—the version of Christianity I call "the Official Script."

So far I've been giving Official-Script illustrations without providing a real definition of what it is or where it came from. The Script is a cut-and-paste version of a biblical outlook; while it's an essential part of a life well-lived, it masquerades as the entire thing. In that sense it's similar to Thomas Jefferson's homemade New Testament, which he called *The Life and Morals of Jesus Christ of Nazareth.*[29] Jefferson jettisoned everything supernatural—angels, prophecies, miracles, divinity, and of course, the resurrection. He considered belief in the metaphysical an embarrassment to a learned man.

Our Official Script today retains the supernatural, but it does something similar. It's scandalized by the *mysterious* rather than the miraculous. In an attempt to make the gospel appealing to contemporary bias and prejudice, the Script endeavors to explain and reason through everything.

Its grasp overextends its reach and thereby renders God's Word increasingly flaccid and lifeless. Again: *Reason alone has never created or brought about virtue.* The French Revolution is one of many historical examples showing that the idolization of reason often leads instead to destruction and misery.[30]

News flash from God to us: *It's okay not to know everything! In fact, it's good—this leads to deepened faith, spirited animation, and established righteousness in you. My mysteries keep you hooked, curious, aware, motivated . . . and I designed it that way.*

Yes, righteousness. In Paul's first epistle to Timothy, a letter full of warnings, probes, admonishments, and direct judgment upon those who work against the addressee, Paul concludes with a description of righteousness that sometimes snares today's evangelical eye.

> Pursue a righteous life—a life of wonder, faith, love, steadiness, courtesy.[31]

Wonder is integral to what it means to pursue righteousness, just as it's inseparable from the creation of courage. Today's evangelicals often read this verse, miss Paul's point about wonder, and say or think something like, "Hey, wait—what about keeping the main thing the main thing? What about piety?"

The Official Script, ultimately, is what we want to hear as opposed to what we need to hear, and I'm no different than most people when it comes to this convenient game. I'd rather avoid the things I don't want to hear. And sometimes I do.

There's no better explanation for the Official Script's predominant trait than what we discover in Paul's other letter to his beloved protégé. With patches of Paul's loving thumos threaded throughout, 2 Timothy deals primarily with the character of a Christian minister. And here he exposes the underlying motives of those who cling to the Official Script:

> The time will come when men will not put up with sound doctrine. Instead, to suit their own desires, they will gather around them a great number of teachers to say what their itching ears want to hear. They will turn their ears away from the truth and turn aside to myths.[32]

I don't know when that time began, which is irrelevant anyway. What I do know is that when I compare the Bible's overall content, tone, and flavor to what I hear when I flip through the "Christian" programs I find on TV, I can hardly locate similarities. The only exception I've found recently is on a Catholic cable channel.

What we want to hear is pretty much that which makes us comfortable and preserves that comfort. For example, Scripture doesn't show the luminaries of our faith turning to Christ so they can climb corporate ladders. But as Americans, we love our money, our bulbous cars and our bulbous homes, so we turn many portions of God's Word into business training classes. Many of the biblical passages used to promise wealth and advancement are tortured beyond recognition. The deception continues and at a blistering pace.

The Official Script is part myth, part lullaby, and part nursery rhyme. It's unable to alleviate real suffering and in the process emulate the real Christ. Also, no one denomination or person defines it or owns it. It's one large act of group-think (as opposed to God-think).

The truth about life—primarily, that it's hard—is less appealing than the illusions currently swirling around. Like one of the real biggies: that you can have a really peaceful life right here, right now. (Yeah, you *can*, if you duck and flee all the battles that rage.)

Intriguingly, but also frighteningly, this is one of today's main evangelical credos *and* a basic premise of Eckhart Tolle's *A New Earth: Awakening to Your Life's Purpose*. Neither evangelicalism nor the New Age is accepting (much less embracing) the fact that deep and abiding love, like deep and abiding courage, is risky and sacrificial. There's no legitimate or truthful way around it: You live, you get hurt. "Take your share of hardship, like a good soldier of Christ Jesus."[33]

> "You are a king, then!" said Pilate.
> Jesus answered, "You are right in saying I am a king. In fact, for this reason I was born, and for this I came into the world, to testify to the *truth*. Everyone on the side of truth listens to me."[34]

Truth is demanding and uncompromising, but it's infinitely better than illusion. Still, most of us prefer illusion—it's less taxing and less disruptive. This brings us to the Script attribute that's perhaps the most damaging.

The Official Script pretends that the narrow path of spiritual growth and maturity is wide. The fact remains, as it's always been, that those who love God, exercise genuine faith, and love truth, are in the minority. Love, faith, and truth are simply too much hassle for most people to care about.

The Official Script makes people feel good as opposed to helping them become good. It's what our fears and our ego want to be true—we want self-preservation and self-glorification to be true and right, to be essential to reality, as opposed to what the Holy Spirit reveals to us as being unassailably and everlastingly true and right. Things like losing oneself so that one will live, and bringing glory to God instead of to ourselves.

The Official Script is hell-bent on removing challenge and difficulty, which are two of the most effective raw materials in forging growth and faith; they're God-given materials that lead to the kind of life that people remember when you're gone. The Script, instead, erases legacy, deconstructs potential heroism, and wipes away adventure. It continually reminds us about our sinfulness, hardly telling us anything about our God-given glory. It mistakes feeling horrible about ourselves for being humble.

Finally, *the Official Script has one ironclad law: It will always bunker around and suckle the status quo in crowning* mildness *king over and above all other temperaments.* Some of the status quo is good, and some of it is not. But because the Script-holders have been blinded in pursuit of comfort and mildness, they rarely are capable of distinguishing between them.

You Can't Script THIS!

Scripturally and soulfully, noble thumos is called *prothumos,* which means "predisposed, willing," and is akin to *prothumia,* which denotes spiritual readiness and spiritual eagerness: "That is why I [Paul] am so eager [*prothumia*] to preach the gospel also to you who are at Rome."[35] The apostle had seasoned courage coursing through him that spurred him ever onward to good and loving deeds.

Prothumos also is found in Jesus' own words to his slumbering disciples in Gethsemane:

Stay awake, all of you; and pray that you may be spared the test. The spirit is willing [*prothumos*], but the flesh is weak.[36]

This forward-moving, proactive spirit is found again in 2 Corinthians:

> I [Paul] know your readiness [*prothumia*], of which I boast about you to the people of Macedonia, saying that Achaia has been ready since last year; and your zeal has stirred up most of them.[37]

Paul *boasts* about their good thumos! He *doesn't* "put a cork in it."

Seasoned boldness is intrinsic to spiritual willingness, readiness, and eagerness. And get this: it even plays a role in being cheerful and merry. *Euthumos*, "to put in good spirits, to make cheerful," is found in Acts 24:

> When the governor had nodded for him to speak, Paul responded: "Knowing that for many years you have been a judge to this nation, I cheerfully [*euthumos*] make my defense."[38]

Even more intriguing is how *thymia* (a variation of the word *thumos*) is intrinsic to a biblical understanding of equality. Remember: Thumos is a product of our will that drives us to be recognized by others as *human*, which includes being made gloriously by our Creator and thus deserving of respect and dignity. Such a desire is not sinful—thumos is enflamed when human glory and honor as coming from God's image are not valued.

We fight for the respect and dignity of others in part because we sense these qualities in ourselves. Because we possess them we grow heated when others are *dispossessed* of them. Oppression bothers us, and God, because it removes what should never be taken away: intrinsic dignity. Thumos is dignity's guard dog.

We saw in chapter 4 that, like all good things, this bristling quality can "go bad." And so to differentiate, we need to be aware of two crucial thumos "qualifiers": *Megalothymia* and *isothymia*. Megalothymia is the sinful need to be recognized as superior to others (shadow thumos), while isothymia is the healthy need to be recognized as equal to others (noble thumos).

It's from this distinction that we get our support for liberal democracy, equality, and freedom. When megalothymia is in the driver's seat, we have inequality and chaos. When isothymia reigns, when people are recognized as intrinsically valuable and inherently equal, there is harmony, the kind of harmony we find in the book of Acts:

> They devoted themselves to the apostles' teaching and to the fellowship, to the breaking of bread and to prayer. Everyone was filled with awe, and many wonders and miraculous signs were done by the apostles. All the believers were together and had everything in common. Selling their possessions and goods, they gave to anyone as he had need. Every day they continued to meet together in the temple courts. They broke bread in their homes and ate together with glad and sincere hearts, praising God and enjoying the favor of all the people. And the Lord added to their number daily those who were being saved.[39]

In his story about the vineyard workers,[40] Jesus says that the kingdom of heaven has isothymia at the core of its nature. All laborers are treated equally—even those who work less than others—no matter that such generosity may lead to resentment. We see this noble boldness in Paul's first letter to the church in Corinth.

> [God's purpose and desire, he wrote, are that there should] be no division in the body, but that its parts should have equal concern for each other.[41]

And in his second letter to them, he says, "Our desire is not that others might be relieved while you are hard pressed, but that there might be equality."[42]

Low Thumos Has a High Cost

Oh but how very hard our unbiblical spiritual heritage dies. I hail from a long line of Corn-Syrup Christianity, and the "faith" I grew fat on just won't disappear. Many times when I open my Bible and see plainly how it's not a "nice" book of pleasantries and platitudes, bickering voices in my head conflict, and one of them tells me not to challenge Jesus' manner of presenting the truth. *That boldness and indignation and intensity—all that "thumos" can be explained away.*

It doesn't help that I've been program director of a Christian radio station, where I endured more denominational squabbling than I will ever allow myself to hear again. I saw a lot of Scripture verses strapped to arrows and theological javelins hurled across rooms. Most of this had much more to do with sectarian pride and factional distinctions than with wanting to get to the root of what God's Word really says.

"You're stealing my joy" and "You're stealing my peace in the Lord" are two responses I commonly get when someone becomes uncomfortable around these insights. This is a big, big deal for those people who come to church not to join God's army but to take part in a kind of recreational group-bonding ritual with religious overtones. I smoked this spiritual weed for years, and sometimes I can still smell it.

However, I hope you realize there's something that actually *will* "steal your joy." If the enemy of your soul is permitted to tie you up in knots of deception and hollow you out with the vacuum of apathy, you can kiss joy good-bye. You *need* a fighting spirit to break free and to stay free; that's how we become, and remain, truly joyful.

"Aren't we supposed to be content in all things?" I'm asked. Well, yes and no. Jesus did tell us to be content with regard to material matters and not to spend our lives striving for more. But we are never told to be content when it comes to others who need us: like prisoners and those who need clothing and shelter, food and water, the sick and dying; we're told to visit and assist those who need our compassion and help in seeing justice done. *Being content concerning the suffering of others is sinful.*

As for losing your peace and contentment, there's something that really is worth fearing: getting to the end of your days and realizing you've been in a "Sweet'N Low" daze for most of your life: All those Bible studies, books, and sermons didn't amount to squat because you smothered and buried the internal urge God gave you to live them out. You can't remember doing much that's been truly meaningful and redemptive, and neither can those who know you. You've turned your vitality into a waste of oxygen. You've celebrated birthdays not because you invested and served from year to year, but because you managed to keep breathing. (The heathen do that every day.)

Maybe inside your chest this potential realization has never really settled with you. Maybe you've managed to push thoughts of those regrets down; perhaps you've anesthetized them with television, sentimentality, getaways, drinks, or even as-needed helpings of porn (usually visual for a man, emotional for a woman). Have you, with the help of cozy routines, been able to hide the discontent that may have bloomed into the blues, or even depression? Is your life low on meaning, purpose, and integrity? If any of this describes you, consider this: God has laid out good works for you to do, and he has promised to provide what you need in order to fulfill them, and yet you have managed to turn them down, all in the name of maintaining your "peace" and your "joy."

I'll make this personal. I used to "live" in a stupor too. I spent many years in apathy's bottomless canyon. I wasn't serving or helping anyone.

Fear used to consume me. I'd get stuck in suspended animation—and my spiritual training just made things worse. I had both loving thoughts and loving feelings toward others. But I was low on loving actions. I wasn't sufficiently animated to truly care about and impact the world around me. My will was too weak (not too strong). I had dropped the sword of my willingness; it's what I'd been told to do.

If I hadn't been rescued; if I hadn't gradually climbed out; if I hadn't learned how to honor my grief and indignation; if I hadn't stoked my noble thumos; if I hadn't turned my back on false church teaching (however well-intentioned), I'd still be going that way.

I wouldn't have become part of a ministerial work where people who were contemplating suicide did *not* take their own lives. I wouldn't have people stopping me to say that my writing and our conferences have saved their marriages, bolstered their faith, strengthened their families, and compelled them back, regularly, into the Bible. By God's grace, I have been privileged to be part of a remarkable ministry where people's histories have been changed within a larger history.

I had a pastor, keeper of the Official Script, say that if I met resistance doing something, it was "God's way of telling me *no*. Don't try to make anything happen. Just pray and get out of God's way." Sound familiar?

Remember how I said if we stopped every time we met resistance, we'd get nowhere? Just one illustration is that there never would have been a *Pilgrim's Progress*, which John Bunyan wrote from prison, from where he said, "I will stay in jail to the end of my days before I make a butchery of my conscience." We would have been without Martin Luther's Reformation: "Here I stand; I can do no other, so help me,

God." There wouldn't have been Abraham Lincoln's call to an end of slavery in America: "This nation cannot survive half slave and half free." There would have been no Declaration of Independence: Thomas Jefferson began, "We hold these truths to be self-evident, that all men are created equal...." And there would have been no victory at Calvary: "My God, My God, why have you forsaken me?"[43]

At times I feel as if I've been part of a grand and optimistic but disastrous experiment with popular Christianity during this time in history. Every day something like this happens:

"Is the new congregant asleep, Brother Smith?"

"He is, Pastor Tollman."

"Okay then. Time to remove his thumos. Bible?"

Smith hands Tollman his tattered black Bible along with his favorite seminary texts and notebooks.

From these Pastor Tollman pulls out sermon after sermon and subliminally hammers the new congregant with just how *bad* he really is.

He tells him how every fiber of his being is dyed in sin, how his very existence is an affront to God, and how he doesn't possess one good impulse within him.

He piles on hundreds of nitpicky rules to be followed to the letter—which, according to Paul, actually "chips away at the faith."[44]

He already has extracted two-thirds of the new congregant's thumos—the steamy and easier portions to reach—which has cooled the unsuspecting man to a mild shade of yellow, the color of a nursery wall.

And the guy is only twenty-five. *The process of sanctification,* Tollman thinks, *is nearly complete.* Now for his final stab: the will.

"Wait!" the man's young wife suddenly interjects as she gets to her feet in the pastor's office. "Don't you want his will redeemed? If you extract it he'll be lost in this world—he'll just become the fodder of other people's agendas. He'll have no aspiration, no drive. He will be a boat without a tiller, a horrible husband and father!" She cradles her obviously pregnant belly in her hands.

"Whooo . . . What? But his will is sinful!"

"But so are his heart and mind. Are you removing those too? You spend sermon after sermon trying to feed his mind, as if that's the only path to his soul and spirit. Why do you ignore his will—that's his seat of action! Please put his thumos back, or he'll be the kind of man you constantly complain about: a hearer but not a doer. You're mistaking his capacity for willfulness as a sin. Which is amazing, since Jesus, Paul, Mary, Priscilla, and others were people of tremendous will, especially in comparison to those around them."

The distraught wife's argument is lost on Pastor Tollman, whose Official Script contains none of this philosophical stuff. And since it's not in the Script, it's wrong. *She must be in the Peace Corps, or a Democrat or something,* he thinks.

Now he starts burning with indignation—having been challenged (and corrected) by a woman, no less—so he summons his own thumos, doubling the ferocity of his sermons, using the might of his will to extract that of another.

Well, What Do We Expect?

The primary reason this surgery keeps getting performed is that we've been expected to conform to a ridiculous caricature of Jesus; as a result, believers have been sent into the world armed with the innocence of doves but without the wisdom of serpents, the way Jesus wants us to be.[45] He didn't tell us he would send us out like his disciples—like sheep among wolves—because he wanted to impress us with his ability to formulate metaphors. He said this because it's true and because he loves us.

But wisdom is not our strong point; in fact, it's currently one of our weakest. In one Barna study, laypeople rated church leaders on thirteen major characteristics, including love and compassion; wisdom came in dead last.[46] And I don't think this is a fluke. When we obtain wisdom, we obtain discernment, and discernment can lead pretty quickly to conflict. Most Christians fear and avoid nothing so much as conflict.

The lack of wisdom in our teaching has filled Jesus' words with even more pathos and irony. His warning that we were going into perilous territory was meant to be heeded so we would be prepared and armed—it wasn't a command to go get slaughtered. But because we've been stripped of thumos and its related attributes, isn't this what has happened? We've been massacred in the workplace, in our homes, and in civic life, ceding the Culture War by refusing to acknowledge that thumos is required to fight and to win.

It's not coincidental that we haven't been allowed to emulate the tender-to-tough Jesus and that we've been outgunned in most every theater of life. As Teddy Roosevelt lamented, why should wicked people have all the virile qualities? Roosevelt was, in essence, affirming Jesus' teaching in the parable of the shrewd manager.[47] We have skipped onto the battlefield without a martial spirit and without a functioning thumos. Essentially, we've been untrained, unmotivated, and unarmed.

What's so frustrating about how poorly thumos is handled, corporately, is that even though it's been hidden like an illegitimate child, *many* successful Christian movements have thumos in their blood and in their mission statements. There would be no Focus on the Family, no Prison Fellowship, no trailblazers like Wilberforce, Luther, or John Paul II without the motivational blessing and empowerment of thumos.

Leaders: I implore you to let your congregations and your other audiences see your bold courage, your empowered willfulness. Let the men in particular see how you season it, contend with it, subdue it, fire it up, prod it, poke it. Show us how you handle it, and we will be inspired to do the same.

Unscripted: Thumos in Action

Parade magazine has called Baltimore minister, former pro-football player, and high school football coach Joe Ehrmann "America's Coach." It's crucial to him that boys adopt a more noble understanding of masculinity than what our sex- and fame- and power- and money-obsessed culture tricks them with. He confronts the sins of our nation with strength and courage.

Ehrmann's form of masculinity is far from machismo. It's both tender and tough, like the real Jesus of the Gospels.

"What is our job as coaches?" he asks his players.

"To love us!" they yell back in unison.

"What is your job?" he shoots back.

"To love each other!" the boys respond.[48]

But Ehrmann's love is not sentimental. He sweats to help boys comprehend and embrace masculinity, without which, he says, we won't be able to address other issues like divorce, poverty, abuse, crime, and racism. He and his coaches provide boys with a threefold code of manhood: accepting responsibility, leading courageously, and enacting justice on behalf of others.[49]

Ehrmann expects his players not to allow any high school boy to eat lunch alone. His guys are expected to tackle the largest of all high school oppressors—peer pressure—and sit next to the lonely and the despised, spreading love and growing courage. Has your child heard *that* in Sunday school? Has his or her spiritual lineage provided the courage they will need, the kind God tells us they should exercise?

I have never heard the prophets of old speak. I've never actually heard the pitch and timbre of their voices. But I'm confident I heard their tone when Joe Ehrmann was a guest on my show.

Unlike most of my guests, he gave my audience an uncensored view of his thumos, which was seasoned by the

Holy Spirit. His voice grew louder, lower, and more distinct when he talked about poverty and racism and about the false understanding of masculinity that molests the boys he loves. He was indignant, but it was not the kind of anger that turns your ears to wax or makes your eyes glaze over. It wasn't feral; it was harnessed and redemptive. It animated me and my listeners to be stronger and more courageous. It was true to the original meaning of the word *encouragement*: to grow courage in others.

Injustice angers Ehrmann without making him hysterical. It gets him off his spiritual duff and makes him a *doer*. What did this Hall of Famer talk about? Remarkably, he focused on empathy, without which we cannot be courageous.

Ehrmann told us about the importance of letting the world's pain get under our skin. Like Bill Hybels and Chuck Swindoll and Rick Warren, Ehrmann exhorted us to be *discontented* with what we see around us and to muster all that is within us to fight it, hand in hand with God. "I think the alleviation of pain is a fundamental root for understanding some kind of cause," he said. With the kind of growl my chest recognized as righteousness, he continued: "Wherever there is injustice, we ought to show up, stand up, and speak up."

Injustice angered Bob Pierce, who in 1950 watched with disbelief, horror, and indignation as orphaned children dropped dead in food lines in third-world Asia during the Korean War. There wasn't enough food to feed them, so his thumos burst into movement. He returned to America, gathered his most affluent business partners, and birthed World Vision, one of the largest Christian relief and development organizations in existence today. He said, "We're going to get food at the front of the food lines. If it kills me, we're going to do it."[50]

In 2005 alone, World Vision helped more than a hundred million people in ninety-six countries receive physical, social, and spiritual support. Pierce's anger at what he witnessed was noble because it transcended himself. Like all people of thumos-courage, he saw the world as it was and decided that it wasn't what it can and should be.

You know what might be the best-kept secret in the Bible? The thumos of the real Jesus, who prayed and wept, who was betrayed and was abused, who was battered and murdered, and who harnessed his astonishing courage to accomplish the will of his Father in the ultimate spiritual war. If Jesus had listened only to his heart, what he would have heard was fear, anguish, and sorrow "to the point of death."[51] If Jesus had listened solely to his reason, he would have heard a less noble calling, safe but not redemptive. Jesus heeded another inner dimension. The human heart alone isn't strong enough to overcome such obstacles.

Jesus loves us with more than his heart and his mind. He loves us also through that third region, that God-breathed part of us where thumos is found, the part of our soul that when seasoned, comprises part of what Abraham Lincoln called our "better angels."[52] It's a place from which love can emanate as well and as powerfully—and certainly *more steadily*—than our heart.

The greatest commandment, Jesus said, is to "Love the Lord your God with all your heart and with all your soul [the seat of thumotic will] and with all your mind."[53] We've read it so many times that we don't even notice that three "parts" of us are capable of and called to love.

What are further practical ways we can reverse the trends of anti-thumos and non-thumos? Straightaway, we must endeavor to provide a more biblically balanced understanding and application of the attribute and its spiritual benefits. For one thing, I think the application process to all seminaries should incorporate a Courage Assessment Test (CAT). Questions like this should be asked:

- Can you tell us about a time when you showed courage?
- Why did you do what you did?
- Can you tell us about a time when you showed cowardice?
- Why did you do what you did?
- What happened after each occasion?

Today thumos-powered courage is in startlingly rare supply, so we must prioritize and emphasize grace when we discover this treasonous state of our soul that has rendered us cowardly and innocuous. Calling forth an absent attribute doesn't get it onto the front burner of our spiritual lives right away, but at least it will be moved onto the stove top.

These same questions should be revisited upon graduation. Perhaps they should be requirements to the point that candidates do not receive their degrees until (for example) they have a witness to at least one courageous deed. Deacons and elders should be asked these seminal questions as well. So should Sunday school workers.

Perhaps questions about cowardice will be the most important. You learn a lot about a person by his cowardice, not so we can condemn but rather help. This isn't information that should be shared with just anyone; perhaps before the questions are asked of a potential student or leader, members of the review board should profess an act of their own cowardice in order to warm up the room. In this way—whether the setting is academic or familial—we can pray for one another and bind up each other's spiritual wounds, since cowardice brings up a degree of shame most of us don't want to remember.

We need to talk sense to one another. We ought to reassure and re-empower each other. We must allow love and mercy to patch up the cowardice-wrought hole that still smolders in our chest. And we should emphasize the importance of telling each other stories of courage, thereby encouraging boldness in the lives of fellow believers. This is especially significant when it comes to asking others for forgiveness, since we rarely talk about how essential courage is to this godly action.

I know a man who was a bully in high school and who is now part of The Protectors. He became a Christian in his thirties, and part of his soul-work was to contact the men he had tormented and apologize. He found three. Two told him to "go to hell." (No surprise there.) But one, who also had become a believer, responded well to this courageous act of contrition. They talked and helped bind each other's wounds. He told me he wouldn't have done this if he hadn't stoked his courage first. It takes a lot of thumos to repent and to fulfill the greatest of all commandments.

One of my best friends is a pastor, and he sometimes gets called to be with people during their darkest hours. He told me about the time he visited a family whose son had just committed suicide. As he walked through the front door, he saw a distraught father standing at the fireplace mantel. He was running his trembling fingers over the pictures of all his children. They stopped upon the face of his dead eighteen-year-old son. And he said, "He was such a *nice* boy. He just didn't have what it takes to make it in this world."

The young man had not shown the usual signs of depression. He attended the same emasculating, anti-thumos church I'd once attended. When life got hard, when his girlfriend broke up with him, he had no inner fighting spirit from which to draw comfort and hope. His spiritual training did not honor the boldness and courage he needed, and like so many young men, he was a sitting duck when buried under unexpected, bitter disappointment.

Let's write courage back into the Official Script.

Notes

1. Quoted in Stephen Oates, *Let the Trumpet Sound: A Life of Martin Luther King Jr.* (New York: Harper Perennial, 1982), 41.
2. See Matthew 4:19-20.

3. From an interview with Andy Peck, "Kingdom Living," in *Christianity + Renewal* (May 2002). See text at *www.dwillard. org/articles/artview.asp?artID=92*

4. Galatians 5:22–23, emphasis mine.

5. See 2 Corinthians 3:14–17.

6. See 1 Corinthians 6:9–11.

7. For example, see Acts 2:4; 4:8, 31; 10:46; 13:9–11; 19:6.

8. Cross-reference John 3:8.

9. See Hebrews 4:12.

10. In Oates, *Let the Trumpet Sound*, 41.

11. See Hebrews 12:6.

12. See Proverbs 27:6.

13. Isaiah 11:2

14. Thomas Aquinas, *Summa Theologica*, II.II.8.

15. D. A. Carson, R. T. France, and J. A. Motyer, *New Bible Commentary: 21st century edition*, ed., Gordon J. Wenham (Downer's Grove, IL: IVP, 2003), 641.

16. Isaiah 11:4–5

17. See Isaiah 9.

18. This currently is uneasy ground within evangelicalism, where courage training has been almost nonexistent, but we are seeing ground broken for these endeavors in the writings of certain leaders—for instance, Joel Hunter's *A New Kind of Conservative* (Ventura, CA: Regal, 2008).

19. Rick Warren, *The Purpose-Driven Life: What on Earth Am I Here For?* (Grand Rapids: Zondervan, 2002), 153.

20. Luke 17:3 NEB

21. Luke 22:36

22. Martin Luther King Jr., in his "Letter From Birmingham Jail."

23. See Proverbs 28:1.

24. See Galatians 5:20

25. Revelation 16:19; 19:15 KJV

26. Jon Courson, *Jon Courson's Application Commentary: New Testament* (Nashville: Thomas Nelson, 2003), 1318.

27. Quoted by James Bowman in *Honor: A History* (New York: Encounter Books, 2006), 58.

28. Ibid.

29. Thomas Jefferson, *The Life and Morals of Jesus Christ of Nazareth, Extracted Textually from the Gospels* (Philadelphia:

David McKay Co.).

30. For more, read Gertrude Himmelfarb, *The Roads to Modernity: The British, French, and American Enlightenments* (New York: Vintage, 2005).

31. 1 Timothy 6:11 THE MESSAGE

32. 2 Timothy 4:3–4

33. 2 Timothy 2:3 NEB

34. John 18:37, emphasis mine.

35. Romans 1:15

36. Mark 14:38; cf. Matthew 26:41

37. 2 Corinthians 9:2 NASB

38. Acts 24:10 NASB

39. Acts 2:42–47

40. See Matthew 20:1–16

41. 1 Corinthians 12:25

42. 2 Corinthians 8:13

43. Matthew 27:46 NASB

44. 2 Timothy 2:14 THE MESSAGE

45. See Matthew 10:16 KJV.

46. For instance, see *www.barna.org/FlexPage.aspx?Page=Barna Update&BarnaUpdateID=81*

47. See Luke 16.

48. Jeffrey Marx, *Season of Life: A Football Star, a Boy, a Journey to Manhood* (New York: Simon & Schuster, 2004), 3.

49. Ibid., 36.

50. Bill Hybels, *Holy Discontent: Fueling the Fire That Ignites Personal Vision* (Grand Rapids: Zondervan, 2007), 46.

51. Matthew 26:38

52. *www.smithsonianmag.com/history-archaeology/man-of-his-words. html*

53. Matthew 22:37

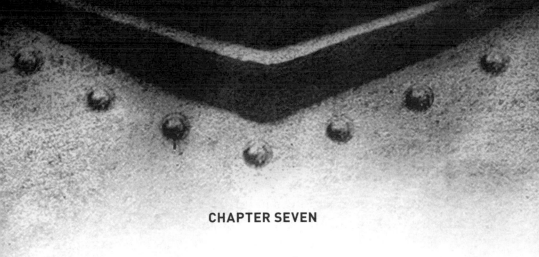

CHAPTER SEVEN

SPIRITUAL ABUSE: THUMOS-SPILLING

Gradually, I began to resent Christian school
and doubt everything I was told. . . .
Fools aren't born.
They are watered and grown like weeds
by institutions such as Christianity.
(MARILYN MANSON)[1]

A person who cannot feel anger at evil
is a person who lacks enthusiasm for good.
If you cannot hate the wrong,
it is very questionable whether
you really love righteousness.
(DAVID SEAMANDS)[2]

I grew up with plenty of false guilt, shame, and self-recrimination. As is often the case, I was unable to show myself anywhere near the same level of grace I showed others—even to strangers and people I didn't like. My worst enemy, in many ways, was me, and because I was often attacking myself within the confines of my troubled mind, I was unable to forge the thumos that would help me excel in life. I exhibited particular gifts as a child, but I tried to kill them because, I see now, I didn't have enough fire to be true to my nature. Gifts make you different, and "different" can get you criticized.

Around age fifteen, I started attending churches that were well-intentioned but spiritually abusive, which also handed me a bag of false guilt, shame, and self-recrimination—talk about going from the frying pan into the fire! My tour of duty through these institutions, which varied in their abusiveness by degree, did not end until my thumos was large enough to lay claim to spiritual freedom and to have the necessary courage to disagree with ideas that would never live long outside the walls of these kinds of churches.

Sadly, that wasn't until I was in my thirties. I had visited non-abusive churches during that time, but they just didn't feel right. Back then, if I didn't leave church feeling beat up, something was wrong; I would conclude that the congregation or the message was not "Spirit-filled." So for many years I languished in the confusing, rigid, soul-killing, thumos-deflating, fear-producing, resentment-growing realm of lifeless legalism, the armpit of human spirituality.

Legalism is a collection of beliefs predicated on the notion that if we follow a certain variety of very specific disciplines, we will receive God's approval and secure his blessings and their related rewards. Legalism includes lists of do's and don'ts that change from one legalistic church or denomination to another. It puts people on a treadmill; leadership usually increases the speed or raises the incline so that people perpetually must strive harder and harder to obtain acceptable piety.

For example, one pastor would yell, "If you're reading your Bible for a half hour a day, then read it for an hour!" "If you're tithing 10 percent, then you need to tithe 20 percent!" On and on he went, raising the bar, applying the whip, month after month. This eventually leaves a person exhausted, and exhaustion is one of the main causes of cowardice. It also leaves a person very angry, and that's the wrong kind of anger when it comes to thumos growth. Rather than going through the kind of mournful grief that leads to redemptive animation and the outward radiation of thumos, we're implanting the seeds of spiritual discontent that sprout into the crabgrass of cynicism (see chapter 9).

To be fair, there can be benefits of sorts to a young man or woman within such a system. It can designate a straight-forward path for navigating through our confused and permissive society. One problem with this is that such young people end up fighting for things that aren't true, spilling much energy and credibility on useless issues and silly battles. When eventually they realize they've been trained to major in minors and to defend what turns out to be one person's or one group's subjective opinion or preference, they will have to face and surmount the inevitable negative fallout that's sure to follow.

One potentially silver lining around this dark cloud is that at least they've been receiving opportunities to practice spiritual activity. They've been learning how to hold some spiritual weapons (even though they often move in the wrong direction with them); while they've likely been fighting poltergeists rather than the real enemy, they *are* becoming spiritually active. They haven't achieved any lift yet, but they are strengthening their spiritual wings and may grow up to fight significant battles in a significant war.

These poltergeists take many forms in legalistic churches. Whatever they turn out to be, the spiritual carnage from such manmade standards and beliefs is real and lethal. God *can* use such spiritual foolishness for good in the lives of young people, if they're willing and able to embrace a spiritual life that's more than do's and don'ts, isn't fear-based, and opens spiritual eyes to wonder, mystery, even the original meaning of *weirdness*, which meant "supernatural" or "uncanny" and carried with it connotations of God's amazing ways.

One person who was jammed through the meat grinder of legalism and hasn't been able to surmount the rage and bitterness of being hoodwinked spiritually is Brian Warner, who uses the name Marilyn Manson. In his fuming autobiography, *The Long Hard Road Out of Hell*, the shock musician reveals how years of misguided fundamentalist teaching about the return of Christ—and the always-attached apocalyptic conspiracy theories—left him feeling abused and cheated and eventually motivated him to reject Christianity. Year after year he endured pounding lecture upon pounding lecture about future events involving things like the mark of the beast.

"Those who don't receive the mark, the number of his name—666" warned his Friday-night teacher at Heritage Christian School, "will be decapitated before their families and neighbors."[3] The kids were told that the mark was concealed as the Universal Product Code (UPC) that appears on things like grocery store items. All of this was presented as fact—not opinion, and never speculation—that was straight from God himself. And it couldn't be challenged, because it was drawn from words that are in the Bible.

Nightmares soon tormented Warner's preteen mind.

> I was thoroughly terrified by the idea of the end of the world and the Antichrist. So I became obsessed with it, watching movies like . . . *Thief in the Night*, which described very graphically people getting their heads cut off because they hadn't received 666 tattoos on their forehead.[4]

After a year passed, then another, then another, and the terrifying eschatological predictions panned out to be false, Manson, who says he still has end-times nightmares, felt deceived and defrauded.

Gradually, I began to resent Christian school and doubt everything I was told. . . . Fools aren't born. They are watered and grown like weeds by institutions such as Christianity.[5]

Warner and countless others in their formative years throughout the last four decades have been "God-shocked" by leaders who thought that was the best way to guarantee their obedience and secure their salvation. Their innate fear of the future has been exploited by (mostly) earnest elders in an attempt to drive them into the arms of a loving Savior. But *perfect fear often casts out love.* Worse, troubled adolescents come to deeply resent the terror when they recognize the manipulation, and many of them curse the little god they were told is behind it all. As preacher David Hawking said it:

Some of the prophecy preachers got a little out of hand . . . and we were even told that . . . when Israel became a nation in 1948, it would be forty years and then the Lord would come. So we back it up seven. So the rapture is coming in 1981. I've met people all over this country who believed that, followed that, anticipated that. It did not come and as a result many of them bombed out, dropped out, copped out; they're not around anymore.[6]

That deserves the Understatement of the Year Award. People who once looked to the church for help and healing no longer do—yeah, that's "a little out of hand." As does most of fundamentalism, Hawking ignores the career-building political utility of conspiracy theories, one that's been exploited throughout history (both inside and outside the church).

It's fitting but distressing that Marilyn Manson, who adopted the names of two pop culture icons as his own—the first, Marilyn Monroe, a casualty of pop-culture fame and power; the second, Charles Manson, a sinister predator hell-bent on fame and power at any price—has himself become an example of pop culture's corrosive and abusive nature.

Legalism, which implies that we should pay, pay, and pay again for our sins, promotes myriad forms of self-scourging. Some forms are overt and obvious, such as when people in Latin America beat themselves or have someone else beat them; some carry an actual cross on their back, and some have large fish hooks barbed into their flesh. Most are less explicit and culturally startling—we in the U.S. consider ourselves "more civilized" than that. But our legalistic systems and their unattainable challenges do no less violence to human souls and spirits.

When we do wrong, we need to feel guilty about our sin so that we can distance ourselves from its corrosive nature. Legalism, though, makes guilt almost the entire focus of spirituality. To show us our vile fallenness without also revealing and highlighting our value and honor is to sentence us to spiritual claustrophobia and hopelessness, and both of these drain us of thumos.

As Francis Schaeffer explained, we are "glorious ruins,"[7] and when we fail to realize both of these realities—that we're wondrous *and* flawed—we're unable to find harmony with God, ourselves, and our neighbor. We're far less likely to extend love for another's dignity when we don't believe in God-given dignity in the first place.

Attributes of the Spiritually Abusive

Still, spiritual abuse can be hard to clearly recognize and decipher. We need reliable guidance, and we need to get a good read on this problem if we want to take our thumos seriously. The following are some of the characteristics of an abusive leader and an abusive belief system. This list isn't exhaustive; it's designed to help us see common expressions of spiritual abuse as they relate to depleting us of courageous boldness and courageous love.

- The leader is usually the hero of his own stories.
- The leader assumes power and authority that the New Testament does not give.
- The leader cares more for polemics than people. Specifically, he will spend much more time and energy on sermons that espouse a particular theological nuance than in seeking to nourish and nurture those in his care. Perhaps he also will take denominational distinctions to the extreme.
- The leader places heavy burdens on others that he himself does not lift. For example, he will reprimand his flock for not volunteering more time at church, yet he himself volunteers nowhere.
- The leader is big on making a solid religious impression on others, specifically in terms of personal piety. As Jesus said of the Pharisees, the spiritual abusers of his day, "Everything they do is done for men to see."[8]
- The leader goes to great lengths to ensure that people call him or refer to him by his religious title: Senior Pastor, Bishop, Reverend, etc.
- The leader's thumos rarely goes toward or is applied to life's weightier matters. Also, some spiritually abusive leaders believe that all thumos heat, which they mistake for raw anger, is sinful, so they're careful never to express it—in public. (One abusive pastor of mine praised his father from the pulpit numerous times for never, *ever* expressing anger. I thought, *This man grew up during World War II. He was alive during the atrocities of Hitler, Stalin, Jim Crow, Pol Pot, and apartheid. None of this unthinkable destruction made him angry? Not even* once?)
- The leader believes he is above correction by an "average," non-religiously titled person.

- The leader probably will adhere to the belief that he is part of your "spiritual covering."
- The leader expects others to clean up their act when in his presence.
- The leader carries and displays a worn-out Bible (usually black) to imply his spiritual maturity and also as a weapon that warns, "Don't question me."
- The leader sometimes will abuse prophetic portions of Scripture, ultimately to the benefit of his own popularity and to compel the growth of his church.
- The leader is arrogant, and the rules don't apply to him the way they apply to other people. (A roommate of mine once saw our legalistic pastor leaving a Denny's restaurant. Turns out he was short on cash; to help pay his bill, he pulled quarters out of a donation display by the register, one that was designed to raise money for kids in need of life-saving surgeries.)
- The leader might have a "dark curmudgeon" side to his personality, but more often than not he's very smiley. He's almost always "up," never unhappy like you and me. And he doesn't acknowledge having the same weaknesses others have—he may admit to getting grumpy with his kids or doing 30 mph in a 25, but that's about it.
- The leader frequently surrounds himself with earnest but low-thumos people. This way he can ram his agendas through with very little resistance. The rare person with thumos, the one who objects, soon finds himself on the outs.
- The leader has lost perspective on what really matters in life. He makes moral and theological mountains out of molehills.
- The leader's attitudes and actions make him, and Christianity, look mighty irrelevant to the real lives of other people—he truly doesn't seem to care that much. Some

prefer "church" to be this way because it effectively keeps them in power. Their big molehills form a sort of mountain range around them.

- The leader extols the feminine at the expense of (instead of the completion of) the masculine. That is, he crushes thumos. I've talked with numerous men who have been commanded, from the pulpit, during a service to "go home and apologize to your wife for being such a poor husband."

- The leader creates and delivers fine-tuned messages about not questioning authority.

- The leader has an unhealthy preoccupation with purity, which makes him an odd duck around others; he knows this and takes it as a positive demarcation of his spiritual growth and superiority. He actually thinks his lack of engagement with and investment in others will eventually convert them to his way of thinking.

- The leader (usually unintentionally) assassinates spiritual wonder, mystery, and "weirdness"—essential sources of spiritual growth and thumos health.

The most spiritually abusive people in turn-of-the-era Israel were the Pharisees. By looking at how Jesus dealt with them, we get to see not only what God thinks of such people but how he lived and acted among them. Seeing and embracing that reality is a huge factor in rescuing and salvaging our thumos.

And that's especially important, because people with wounded low thumos are drawn toward abusive institutions. They usually came from homes where approval was rare, so they're prone to attend churches that emphasize religious performance and where pleasing the pastor is paramount. *They have yet to discern the difference between real guilt and false guilt.* If such people are young, bright, and idealistic, they're often drawn to charismatic leaders who express grand-scale and heroic plans for God but who spiritually abuse people along the way.

What did Jesus do when he witnessed such abuse? He said nothing about playing nice or putting a cork in it or "Can't we all just get along?" Rather, he confronted the abusers powerfully, aggressively, and courageously. In fact, I think Matthew 23 should be renamed The Great Diatribe. Writes minister Ken Blue:

> Jesus was so focused on the problem of spiritual abuse that it was the only social evil against which he ever developed a platform. It was the only cultural problem that he repeatedly exposed and opposed. This is amazing when we recall that his culture was plagued by a host of serious social ills. Jesus took no public stand against slavery, racism, class warfare, state-sponsored terrorism, military occupation or corruption in government.[9]

Christ's thumotic anger toward spiritual abusers was unleashed without apology and in public, which gave those who were being spiritually abused permission to get out from under a crushing grip. It gave them permission to affirm what they must have been pondering for a long time: *These guys aren't as good as they say they are, and somehow they're damaging me; I don't know how to describe it, and I don't really understand it, but it's messing me up and it's got me down.* Even after the cells have been opened and the razor wire has been cut down, those who've been imprisoned by spiritual abuse usually need someone to give them permission to leave; they require a rescuer. Can you name one rescuer who did not possess an inner heat and martial spirit?

Indignation toward spiritual abuse—or lack thereof—says a lot about whether or not someone is capable of true ministry. Writes David Seamands:

> A person who cannot feel anger at evil is a person who lacks enthusiasm for good. If you cannot hate the wrong, it is very questionable whether you really love righteousness.[10]

And it's obvious that person does not possess a functioning courageous spirit; furthermore, he's probably hiding this fact behind a counterfeit gentleness.

A truly gentle person doesn't just lie down and let life happen to him and to others. Gentleness means, even requires, that you use force—justly, yes, but you *use* it. A truly gentle person is a truly virtuous person, and it's worth repeating here that part of the definition of *virtue* is the word *force*.

But what we often describe as a "gentle spirit" can be a mere disguise for timidity, passivity, even indifference. This makes me think again of the smashed-down pastors' sons who've disguised their timidity as a gentle spirit; it's almost always their wife or ex-wife who points out the damage that's been done and is still being done, and by then it's often too late for their marriage.

Though we certainly need more of this virtue, our current gentleness-at-any-price policy is unbiblical. (If we're always required to be gentle, then Jesus sinned.) Here's what this fallacy often leads to in real life: One pastor's son who asked me to help him overcome passivity in marriage told me how his mother's "gentle spirit" made her the perfect Christian woman.

"She was always so gentle," he said warmly. "She never got angry about anything. She was perfect!" he gushed.

My inner Dr. Phil came to the forefront. "Perfect?!" I exclaimed. "In more than twenty-five years of ministry, she had to have seen wickedness and evil tearing people apart. She had to have seen divorce, adultery, child abuse, drug addiction, homicide, and even suicide. And she never became indignant, the way Jesus did, when she saw that kind of destruction?!"

As healers and rescuers, our proper expression of anger should be part of affirming to the abused that what happened to them was real and that it was wrong. Our anger, rightly deployed, can serve as a beacon, a lighthouse, a lamp unto their feet. Have you noticed that abusive people lie to their victims in some way or another? That's not a coincidence. Victims need thumos people to point this out for them and to shine light on the truth with thumotic power and conviction when appropriate.

There is much to grieve in this life, and responding to destructive forces without thumos power may well make us accomplices. For many, gentleness is a disguise for being dispassionate spectators.

Why Our Happiness Is So Sad

Becoming a dispassionate spectator of life often happens to us from one of the most unexpected sources.

Within the framework of Christianity, legalism is the belief that a Christian must always stay on the sunny side of the street, a requirement that hit me between the eyes two days after my mother died.

I was broken inside, as if I had fractured a soul bone or collapsed a lung. A lot of swelling had formed around the traumatic break in the inner me. I was numb to the core, and I thought church would be the right place to help bind up my burden. But given the kind of church I attended at that time, this decision was one of the biggest mistakes I've ever made.

After the service I was in a room with a young and energetic associate pastor. In a moment of what turned out to be both weakness and foolishness, I shared with him that my mother had just died and that I was in awful pain. He didn't even turn to look at me; his back was toward me while he rooted around for something—I think it was a patch cord for the worship band—and he said, "Consider it all joy, brother." He hadn't missed a beat, as if he were reading from a cue card.

This leader told me that when I thought about my mother's last hours, which brought a morbid rattle sound as she struggled to breathe, her lungs filling with fluid—that clogged-coffeemaker sound she made for hours through that dark night as she slowly drowned—I was to be consumed with joy?! To rejoice in the death of my troubled mother and her tormented ways, her unresolved soul, her fear-horrified and truncated adulthood, her unfulfilled little-girl desire to return to the land of her birth and beloved family, her strong but squandered mind, her wasted potential and complaining bitterness . . . I was to delight in the death of this courageous heroine who so egregiously lost her way, the woman so bitten by evil that she struck others with even more toxic venom. . . . I was glibly to consider all this wreckage a wonderful matter.

The Lord knows and I know that this peddler of quick-fix religious pabulum didn't know what he was doing. I hold no ill will toward him today. He was parroting what he'd heard from others in the discombobulated world of legalistic religion. He was playing his role, too eager to do his part, to do his thing, to show his faith, to glorify his God with his "biblical" approach toward life and ministry. He was following the Official Script, saying what he thought God wanted him to say; after all, those words are found in Holy Writ.

Of course he tortured them by taking them out of context. The same Bible tells us to weep with those who weep, but his cocksure mind was liquored up on a tight-fisted theology in which God is safe and manageable and tame. Weeping with those who weep probably wasn't crossing his mind—maybe it never had crossed his mind. (Fact is, too often it doesn't cross my mind either, at least when it should.)

Here is the one pathetic, regretful word I said in reply: "Yeah."

I may as well have said, "Penguin."

What does one say while in spiritual shock, while coming face-to-face with a mentality that does not allow a man to be human, that bars a man from coughing up that grief at *church*, in God's house with God's people? I was like a man seeing actual concentration camp photos or footage for the first time. I was stunned, and as the stunned are prone to do, I spoke nonsense.

You can see how devastating is today's Happiness Mentality. It claims to be for the good of others, and it's intended to buoy sinking emotions; in reality it makes people callous to suffering, which leads to anger and resentment, which erodes a loving orientation toward others. It keeps life on a superficial plane, leading to shallow living, which renders indignation impossible. And I don't think this is a coincidence, either, since we desire comfort rather than thumos-born, love-born disruption.

And as we'll examine in chapter 11, in order to grow thumos courage, we have to be able to feel emotions such as grief, sympathy, and compassion. They're raw material for your thumos mill, yet they're largely eradicated from our lives due to the spiritually abusive Happiness Mentality.

I used to attend a church whose leadership was trained *not* to enter into the suffering of others. They were to "point people to Jesus" and Jesus only. They were instructed to tell others to pour their heart out to God but to keep their distance from difficulty, as if the human-connection side of our lives didn't matter or even exist—another example of too much spirit, not enough soul.

Their denomination is extremely "anti-counseling," and I've noticed that the people who stay there begin to take on a plastic and homogenized nature. Deeper conversations and deeper expressions of faith just don't happen much. They're very pleasant (until you ask a weighty question) but certainly not ministerial when it comes to traversing life's weightier side.

And let's not pretend that today's prevalent mindset does not have a benefit for those who follow it. Much like the fake smile some people wear to hide overarching fear, the Happiness Mentality allows an effective hiding place for those who are terrified of brotherhood or sisterhood, which lends the appearance of spiritual maturity and wholeness. Woe to those unable to discern this kind of spiritual dissimulation; it can take decades, if ever, to unravel its corrupting influence in their life.

The Happiness Mentality has another related benefit: It helps ward off the disruptive nature of Christ. If everything we do serves the idol of happiness, and if we can pass off our "happiness" as peace and joy and spiritual growth, then we feel we're justified in not doing things that bring "non-happiness." We can avoid love-extension and keep life self-indulgent while retaining the appearance of purity and maturity.

Game over.

We hate thumos disruption so much we'll do most anything to avoid it. The courageous Russian novelist Fyodor Dostoevsky explained this tendency in his ingenious and haunting book, *The Brothers Karamazov*.[11] The story takes place in Spain, where many of the worst acts of the Inquisition took place. Dostoevsky brings Jesus back to life, walking the streets; remarkably, everyone recognizes him, including the Grand Inquisitor.

Jesus heals the sick and resurrects the dead. The Grand Inquisitor has him jailed, and then at night, visiting his cramped prison cell, he asks Jesus, "Why did you come to bother us?" (What is it about religious leaders visiting Jesus at night?)

Christ's love is both penetrating and troublemaking—love so amazing that it inspires us to lose our life so we can have a better one. Good thing his love is all-consuming, because the truth is we *will* be consumed by something—every one of us. We'll either be consumed by our will, or someone else's, or a combination of both.

God's love consumes us, owns us, and then—we often miss this part—he gives ownership of our life back to us, except now we're connected to his love, assistance, guidance, grace, light, truth, and correction. It's his unique owner-protection program, a kind of dual stewardship that's impossible to explain or grasp in complete detail. That he does not give ownership of us to someone else helps us to avoid many aspects of spiritual abuse and shields us from one of the worst stumbling blocks to carrying out good deeds.

Jesus, as Dostoevsky showed, is a disruptive bother to the yet-to-be redeemed soul *and* to the soul in the process of renewal. In order to ward off his disruption, we have come to emphasize pet Scriptures that, by avoiding the rest of the palette, paint reality almost exclusively in pastels, colors that are only part of the mosaic and that cannot illustrate or reflect the real weight or real image of real life for long.

Consider this: Whatever we may glibly say and sing about God and life in a pleasantly decorated church, from pulpits, risers, and stages, must also be true when said over a burning pile of babies. Pastel Christianity is not only incapable of properly explaining such a horrifying event but it's also insulting to legitimate human sensibilities. Pastel Christianity is repulsive to our God-designed souls.

I experienced a less dramatic example of this when I attended the funeral of a loved one.

The minister said we should not shed tears for the man who'd just died because he was with Jesus now. "This is not a day of mourning but of celebration!" he bellowed, with enthusiasm that appeared contrived.

Celebration? I thought. *I loved him. I will miss him so very much. Today I won't celebrate his death. I must and will grieve over this loss.*

True to the Happiness Mentality we slavishly idolize, that minister did not allow for the expression of the whole spectrum of human life, love, and longing; this spectrum is not considered "spiritual," which, in some circles, is code for "disruptive." He didn't allow for both mourning *and* celebration. True to his training, he axed the negative soul-stuff and gave us a plateful of over-sugared metaphysical dessert. And instead of leading everyone toward a loving and compassionate orientation toward life as it truly is, he encouraged a selfish approach. Why express your condolences to the twelve-year-old daughter who just lost her father when our spiritual leader just told us there's really nothing to cry about? So she remains untouched and unloved. "Happiness" in this model actually yields inconsideration, coldness, and even cruelty.

This plastic world of our own making, one that serves to make the Christian faith appear more and more irrelevant, erases the need for courage training; why would we need it if life is meant to be lived on the mountaintops of human experience? We're so ill-prepared for valley living, where thumos is required for ourselves and for love-extension toward others. One ordained minister (also the son of a pastor) said to me, when I asked for insights regarding how important courage is to our spiritual growth: "I don't understand the connection between courage and faith." Let that sink in for a few moments.

In legalism there is no room for the courageous prophets, the rebellious but godly philosophers, for the person who loves God but loves him differently. This religious orientation is hell-bent on homogenization and taming at any price. It makes its converts double sons of hell, because these then take the battle against mystery and against thumos-building creativity to new diabolical levels. These churches hardly lift a finger on behalf of social justice.

Here there's no room for the dogged soul who sees wonder and tries to explore it; he finds his hand (or his soul) slapped when he does. There's scarcely room for the courageous artist whose work contains fire that grabs the world by the neck and won't let go. There's no place for people who dance to another beat—never mind that it's still God's beat. This way of life says it's trying to conform us to the character of Christ, but mostly it pressures followers to be conformed to the charismatic nature of the one in the pulpit and the status-quo nature of the Official Script.

Spiritually abusive institutions drive out creativity, which sees options and avenues for love-extension that wouldn't be seen otherwise. Creativity is a pathway to hope, and hope opens gateways to courage. A ministry that does not fit within "traditional" confines gets viewed and portrayed with dark suspicion through legalistic eyes and lips; usually all that's accomplished therein is the diminishment of our ability to be light in a dark world.

The Happiness Mentality has a uniquely American distinction. As a first-generation citizen with European roots, I know how suspicious constant-grin Americans appear to others. Most other humans on this planet can tell that something just isn't genuine, and here's what I think it is: Christians in the U.S. are constantly pressured to be happy, and people aren't capable of happiness on command. Requiring happiness is as silly as mandating laughter. I don't trust people who smile all the time; I'm even more wary about people who smile all the time and yet don't have a sense of humor.

Spiritual abusers also bank on guilt and shame. Though they would deny it, these leaders believe deep down that being human is itself somehow sinful. They do not acknowledge our divinely endowed glory and dignity.[12]

Once again, real guilt is good. As with the woman Jesus met at the well,[13] real guilt helps us realize and deal with the wrong we do, so we can ask for forgiveness, make restitution, and return to or get on a better path. But false guilt isn't good at all. For example, some people feel guilty for disagreeing with another person, not because it's wrong but they've been conditioned since childhood to never question authority, upset others, "make a scene," or hurt someone's feelings, and so on.

The point is that feeling false guilt or shame—two hallmarks of damaging religion—leaves us confused and distracted, careening around in a soupy spiritual fog. It leads a person to depend too much on the opinions of others, which in turn leads to a life that is not one's own, which saps us of cheerfulness, decisiveness, animation, willingness, volition— all fruits of thumotic-born love.

When we become enslaved to the will of others, we begin to live lives that weren't meant for us. This depletes our ability to make vital and courageous decisions. Horrifically, we become lost in the very place we've been told we're found; the subsequent tension and anxiety strips us of our capacity to deeply love and cheerfully (euthumotically) give. We're so unsure about what to do that we become inert; eventually we just wearily sit down.

People who are low on thumos are better suited to play the spiritual shell games of legalism than those who have boldness and courage. One of the many significant attributes of thumos is that it impassions people to maintain their Christ-granted freedom and God-given dignity. Timid, inert people often find that it takes too much energy to be bothered by having their freedom and dignity stolen or crushed. Tragically, many such people find this a relief, because accompanying freedom and dignity are certain burdens and responsibilities.

It could be said that this is a benefit to being cowardly, since you usually don't get shot at if you never poke your head up. But the cost of this "safety" is incalculable. Caring so much about what other people think, out of fearing disapproval, makes such people putty in the hands of those who mete out spiritual mistreatment. And the longer low-thumos people stay under such degradation, the lower their thumos becomes and the harder it is to turn the wagon around.

One of the most damaging results of legalism is confusion and bewilderment toward God's Word. Frankly, many times I'll come across a Bible passage and suddenly, like the voices

of several dysfunctional siblings, I'll hear all the denominational bickering that is built up in my brain. I hear the party-
line polemics arguing and shoving for their position over and
against all others. I see red-faced zealots, rage-filled hard-liners,
tight-minded hair-splitters, heart-miserly gnat-strainers.

Honestly, if you get enough of that stuff in your head,
you're going to start opening your Bible and find it's like one
of those greeting cards that plays a song. Except it's not a
song—it's an all-out brawl of head-religion finger-pointing.
People that bicker and clamor this way do not lead to love;
if you listen to them you might begin to find that you don't
know what to think. And when we don't know what to think,
we don't know how to act.

I think theological discussions should end by making
the following statement: "We've heard a lot of talk about
God today," and asking, "What is one way the insight we've
gained will help us love him and our neighbor more?" We
will hear three types of answers: Nonsense, nonsense that
looks true but isn't, and truth. Asking and answering this
question, over time, could help us avoid a lot of misspent
energy and the kind of ineffective disorientation that hinders
our faith in action.

Protect Your Thumos

What should you do when caught in this type of a sticky
spiritual net? In a word, *leave.*

I'm this blunt for two reasons. First, because Jesus was
this blunt when he said of the first-century Jewish religious
leaders, "Leave them; they are blind guides. If a blind man
leads a blind man, both will fall into a pit."[14]

Second, because I must. The unfortunate reality is that
most people who recognize that their church is abusive either
will do nothing or will try to change it. The former is a disaster; the latter rarely works. Most spiritually abused people, in

their current state, have neither the power nor the ability to strategically and effectively use it. This evil often is highly entrenched; what really needs to happen is for that individual church to die its own death.

Spiritually abusive leaders usually come from spiritually abusive institutions, and those rarely change unless and until they face extreme desperation: financial collapse, catastrophic health problems, or unavoidable scandal. Chances are they'll already have heard anything you would say—it won't be news to them. And some are just too spiritually immature to understand what you're saying.

However, don't miss this: *Most spiritual abuse is not intentional.* We still don't have to like it, but we do need to forgive. This doesn't mean we pretend damage didn't take place when it did; rather, it acknowledges that if we don't forgive we're like the man drinking poison across the table from his enemy and waiting for the enemy to die.

Resentment mistakes the quarrel for the battle. I believe that one reason Jesus said to pray for our enemies is that if we don't pray for them, we'll curse them. Cursing others is loser-speak. It doesn't generate any light, *and* it leads to cynicism, which depletes thumos.

Conversely, forgiveness keeps us vitally alive, which is crucial to our thumos courage. Forgiveness cleanses our thumos of fear, which allows even more growth. It also gives us an odd power in the relationship. Forgiveness is an indicator of an inner strength; as I have noticed during a conversation with a formerly abusive boss, this can put the abuser on his heels, especially when you project a kind, non-threatening demeanor.

Bullies don't know how to deal with this. They see that the handles they used for past control are no longer present on you. They move on, and away from you, because your forgiveness makes you harder to manipulate.

One of the unexamined reasons we don't want to forgive is that doing so makes us feel like we no longer have a boundary up against that person. Forgiving someone makes us feel vulnerable. But lack of forgiveness actually isn't a boundary—it's unable to keep him from hurting us again, and, in fact, it pretty much ensures that he can. *Courage and wisdom are the best boundary materials.* Because of what it bears—bitterness and resentment, for instance—unforgiveness is fragile, and it's easily exploited by a crafty adversary.

If spiritual abuse has been part of your spiritual heritage, submerge yourself in God's mercy and grace—these are two of the greatest expressions of his love for us. We can't deeply love others when we're disconnected from God's lovingkindness toward us. Well, we can, for a short while, straining forward on our own power to temporarily light up a few lives. But we won't make it on that road for the long haul; legalism is a spiritual undertaker that separates us from God's love.

There's no substitute for experiencing God's inexpressibly profound love, the kind with no strings attached, the kind that makes us want to complete good works for him—not because we're trying to earn our salvation, or because we're afraid of what will happen if we don't, but because we find him so good for our souls that it's a natural expression of our love back to him. We become reflectors of his love through our heart, mind, and (thumos) strength.

One final piece of hard-earned advice: If you have false shepherds in your life, don't think too much about them. When you do, think like Stephen did[15] and ask God to be gracious to them and forgive them. Know that in most cases, most of the time, they didn't mean to harm you.

We must forgive, not for their good (most won't even be aware of their transgression against you), but for our own health and well-being. I do not believe for a second that Jesus wants us to forgive others because what they did was no big deal. He was too worldly wise to believe that nonsense. Again, I think this is the primary reason: Hold on to that anger, that unredemptive shadow thumos, and you will be manufacturing a form of soul poison. You'll be harming yourself, shriveling your soul, and misspending your courageous spirit on a fruitless venture.

Notes

1. Marilyn Manson with Neil Strauss, *The Long Hard Road Out of Hell* (New York: HarperEntertainment, 1999), 23.

2. David Seamands in Ken Blue, *Healing Spiritual Abuse: How to Break Free From Bad Church Experiences* (Downers Grove, IL: InterVarsity, 1993), 26.

3. Manson and Strauss, *The Long Hard Road*.

4. Ibid., 58.

5. Ibid.

6. David Hawking in Paul T. Coughlin, *Secrets, Plots & Hidden Agendas: What You Don't Know About Conspiracy Theories* (Downers Grove, IL: InterVarsity, 1999), 141.

7. See Francis A. Schaeffer, *The Mark of the Christian* (Downers Grove, IL: InterVarsity, 1970) and *The God Who Is There* (Downers Grove, IL: InterVarsity, 1968).

8. Matthew 23:5

9. Blue, *Healing Spiritual Abuse*, 18.

10. David Seamands in Blue, *Healing Spiritual Abuse*, 26.

11. Fyodor Dostoevsky, *The Brothers Karamazov: A Novel in Four Parts and an Epilogue* (New York: Penguin Classics, 1880).

12. See Psalm 8.

13. See John 4.

14. Matthew 15:14

15. See Acts 7.

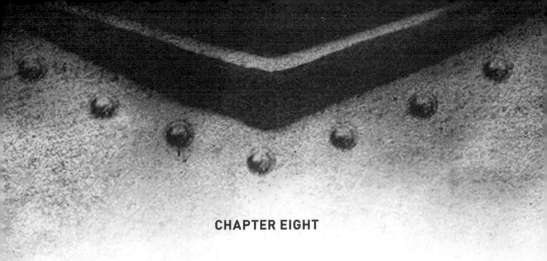

CHAPTER EIGHT

MATERIALISM:
THUMOS-NUMBING

Esteemed friend, citizen of Athens,
the greatest city in the world,
so outstanding in both intelligence and power,
aren't you ashamed
to care so much to make all the money you can,
and to advance your reputation and prestige—
while for truth and wisdom and the improvement
of your soul you have no care or worry?
(SOCRATES)[1]

Money doesn't talk—it swears.
(BOB DYLAN)[2]

It is preoccupation with possessions,
more than anything else,
that prevents us from living freely and nobly.
(BERTRAND RUSSELL)[3]

A friend of mine was going through a tough time when I called him. Business was slow, frighteningly slow; he felt that trapped-under-the-stone-like pressure throughout his day and then especially at night, when he didn't sleep more than a few fitful hours. He'd wake suddenly, then either lie in place or go watch television till sunrise. This pressure attacked and tightened his chest, making it hard to breathe.

"It's not working," he told me flatly from his cell phone; he was driving his Mercedes to work in Southern California. "I need more money," he said in a trance-like voice. Then—and to this day I'm not sure if he even realized he verbalized it—he went on: "I'd be better off dead. The insurance money . . . they would get that." He was saying it would be best for him, his wife, and their two children if he took his own life. That way they wouldn't have to face the shame of lacking money, the number one form of disgrace under our current brutal reign of materialism.

It is employment, not God, that is the fount of all blessings today, and you are an odd person inside or outside the church if you believe (and actually live) otherwise. Joblessness and job-related failure are the real standards by which we're measured. The corporate ladder has replaced Jacob's; wrestling with your boss or your "career arch" is now much more holy than wrestling with God. *Most of us do far more fear and trembling at work than we do working out our own salvation.* We spend more energy reaching for the approval of our colleagues than seeking the love of our Creator; we strive to give more love to our shareholders than we offer our spouse.

What I'm talking about here isn't our legitimate need to make a living, to provide for our family, to put something aside and eventually retire, if that is what one chooses. I'm talking about loving possessions and acquisitions with all of our heart, mind, and thumos. I'm talking about pouring more and more of who we are into stockpiling more and more luxuries that are inevitably empty, designed to impress.

Doesn't it seem to go without saying that this pursuit is far more in line with what the world values than what God values? The calamity my friend was experiencing is a good example. He and his wonderful family live in a beautiful home—a mansion, by historic standards.

And did I tell you he used to be a missionary? He wasn't considering suicide so his kids could eat. They have been, are, and will be fine. He was contemplating killing himself to avoid one of today's most utterly dreaded feelings: not being abandoned and divorced, not the tragic death of a loved one, not falling into egregious moral failure, not having abused one's own children, but *the shame of not being seen by peers as a successful man of industry*. Somehow this has become our all-consuming arena, the coliseum in which we soil and bloody ourselves to slay "lions."

Materialism (consumerism) is synonymous with covetousness, which is flat-out sin. It's lusting for stuff so as to experience more and more comfort and also to gain the envy of others. You don't have to be wealthy to be materialistic. Anyone can be covetous, regardless of their current levels of material inventory.

For some, consumerism causes them to possess a dangerously inflated view of self. This is another ugly example of sin's insidious nature—sin isn't creative or original, but rather it takes something good, like self-worth, and exploits it into something bad, in this case, arrogance and hubris. Sadly, materialism delivers at least some of what it promises—a level of admiration (though rarely to the degree that's desired).

Materialism is like drinking salt water: No matter how much you gulp, you're still thirsty. There's no end because there can't be an end; consumerism leads only to increased consumerism and escalating *dis*contentment. It's a terrible progression: Refusal to turn from consumption that doesn't satisfy brings the loss of hope; loss of hope blinds our eyes to wonder; hope and wonder are two crucial components to building godly thumos.

Consumerism deadens our thumos, because although growing wealth requires a tolerance for risk, it does *not* necessitate courage. Let's be clear: Noble thumos is sacrificial—it spurs us to give something up without expecting something greater in return. Therefore, in order to amass more and more goodies without admitting and facing our inner misery, we often learn to handle and manipulate cognitive dissonance, the feeling of stress (also guilt and shame) people suffer when their beliefs do not line up with their actions.

We can extract a pretty good paycheck from cognitive dissonance when we learn to sear our emotions and numb the vocal cords of our conscience. However, this contributes to the Great Numbness I described earlier, where we (especially men) go emotionally flat, unable to experience a range of feelings that give life flavor, richness, and purpose. It's the old Faustian bargain—barter for something (material goods) and trade away something far more valuable (honesty, emotional range, nobility, humanity and family connections).

Due to the seductive nature of materialism, some people gradually become fonder of stockpiling wealth than maintaining integrity. For instance, many authors start out with power and conviction, aiming to change the world. (And some do!) But after building what the industry calls their "platform," the area of a writer's life where he or she is known by others, some slip. Once they and their publisher know that anything they write already has a built-in audience, their writing goes flat, losing its edge and passion. Yet they keep writing as long as the money keeps coming.

Some likewise let their personal life become a shambles, and instead of being accountable and addressing their issues, they project an inauthentic reality and conceal themselves behind their notoriety. I'm sad to say that in Christian publishing and entertainment alone, I learn of several such examples every year. Those who write books and stand on stages with the intention of persuading and inspiring us to be better men and women are going to have trouble truly ministering when behind the scenes they're walking away from their spouse and flirting with their new public relations manager. Or when they're secretly and deliberately manipulating their audience. The marketing director of one of the industry's biggest names told a friend of mine, in regard to marriage conferences, "We have to make the men feel like dirt" in order to get them to come. Then, in case he hadn't made his point, he said it again.

As you can tell and have probably experienced, all of this does tremendous harm to our souls. We follow the lead of our lower nature instead of our higher calling when we make work our God and materialism our idol. The damage goes deeper than we initially realize. Sam Keen asks questions of himself that every working person should ask as well:

> In working so much have I done violence to my being? How often, doing work that is good, have I betrayed what is better in myself and abandoned what is best for those I love? How many hours would have been better spent walking in silence in the woods or wrestling with my children? Two decades ago, near the end of what was a good but troubled marriage, my wife asked me: "Would you be willing to be less efficient?" The question haunts me.[4]

Ground Zero: Christmas

There's one time of the year where the evil of materialism overplays its hand with particular horridness, when the crush of unnecessary acquisitions becomes apparent even to people normally cozy with consumer-mania. We see the problem—finding a solution is another problem. Like sheep without a shepherd, collectively we don't know what to do; we don't have a vision for a better way, for a better life.

A recent Gallup poll shows that a whopping 85 percent of adults believe Christmas is too commercial. And while more than 80 percent of Americans want to put an end to our December Derangement, they say they don't know where to begin—and they don't want to go it alone. There's an overwhelming desire to tear down the current construction of this so-called holiday, but no one wants to look like a freak doing it.

Jesus said the Sabbath was given to serve man, not the other way around.[5] He might say the same about the day we've designated to commemorate his birth: that it should be about loving God and others more deeply. As it's currently "celebrated," though, an amazing 84 percent of us resent the holiday season. We know that material consumption is out of control and that harried hurriedness is not good for our souls. We long for a kind of consensus, a movement that gives us permission to get this cultural monkey off our backs. We want a unifying campaign that injects genuine peace, goodwill, and remembrance of God's love into this wintry time.

Studies show that there is a tipping point at which we no longer feel happier but rather become unhappier within the barter economy of "giving something away to get more." In wealthy nations like ours, we "give away" social and family ties. To obtain and maintain more and more possessions, we shift time and energy toward accumulation and upkeep while shifting time and energy away from cultivating our relationships. This is the insanity of Affluenza. And, absurdly, there is no bigger monument to Affluenza than Christmas.

December *should* provide an ideal opportunity to model healthy spirituality for our children and to bring our families closer together. According to the children surveyed, this isn't happening—at Christmastime or otherwise. Though more than 90 percent say family and friends are more important than gifts, only 32 percent say they spend a lot of time with family. Only 13 percent of kids say they wish their parents made more money so they could receive more gifts.

Let me remind you that the word *Protestant* comes from a tradition of *protest*. It's time to protest again. Currently the holiday season is far more of a burden than a blessing; we endure it far more than we enjoy it. Speak your concerns about Christmas in public a few times and you're likely to start hearing amens. (Strangers may even hug you.)

Most of us are careful not to complain for fear of being called a Grinch. Pollsters hear how we really feel because they're a kind of secular priest with whom we're willing to share our hopes, fears, and dreams. What we've been confessing about Christmas is remarkable.

According to Gallup, 75 percent of Americans think the holiday isn't religious enough. This number climbs to 86 percent among those who attend church regularly. Says Carla Barnhill, former editor of *Christian Parenting Today*: "The only difference between Christians and non-Christians this time of year is that Christians go to church."[6]

When I've delivered presents to the needy children of prison inmates, as part of Project Angel Tree, I haven't always had enough presents for each child to receive one. That's partly because we spend more money on Christmas gifts for our pets than on these forgotten children. An estimated 140 million pet owners spend between $50 and $100 at Christmas on their pets. (Gucci sells goat-hair dog beds for more than $2,000.)

Though we *talk* about giving to those in need, the facts show that most of us don't share our wealth or goodwill with the disenfranchised. Economist and journalist James S. Henry writes,

> Most gift-giving takes place within the family or the same social class, and doesn't reach the people who really need our help. Christmas most certainly reduces our capacity for

charity by draining us of wealth that we might otherwise give to the needy, and of our charitable impulses. This is hardly what the person for whom the holiday is named had in mind.[7]

Critics of Western Christianity widely contend that our faith has been commercialized, hijacked by a consumer culture, and robbed of its redemptive power. Without question, Christmas is their Exhibit A.

In December 1957, C. S. Lewis got downright cranky in an essay about Christmas.

> It gives on the whole much more pain than pleasure . . . the thing is a nightmare. [Imagine what he'd say now!] Long before December 25th everyone is worn out. . . . They look far more as if there had been a long illness in the house.[8]

Presents, he lamented, are all too often a form of "blackmail."

> Have we really no better use for materials and for human skill and time than to spend them on all this rubbish? [Christmas is a time] in which everyone lives by persuading everyone else to buy things. I don't know the way out.[9]

Says columnist Cal Thomas,

> I'm not sure it's worth keeping Christmas anymore. Why participate any longer in this charade where the focal point of worship has shifted from a babe in a manger to a babe in the Victoria's Secret window?[10]

What we do this time of year is sometimes obscene. A woman who went shopping at Wal-Mart in Florida was trampled and knocked unconscious by her fellow shoppers. They weren't rushing to put money in the Salvation Army bucket, either; the mob "walked all over [my sister] like a herd of elephants" to get first shot at the booty of specially priced DVD players.[11] Peace on Earth, and *Good Will Hunting* to man.

More Stuff, Less Happiness

I think Robert Lynd said it best all the way back in 1915:

There are some people who want to throw their arms round you simply because it is Christmas; there are other people who want to strangle you simply because it is Christmas.[12]

We don't need some gray-haired Swiss scientist on PBS to tell us our family and community bonds are unraveling. Daily life confirms it. If we're honest, we'll admit that our wedding vows often apply more to our jobs than to our spouses. The average person spends much more time at work, thinking about work, getting ready for work, commuting to work, trying to make work happy, or working at home than they do with their family. Some have no choice. But many have plenty of choices that materialism steals.

Here are some facts about increased affluence that Madison Avenue won't tell you. In a study of one thousand lottery winners, a surprisingly high number were *less* happy six months later. Many had turned to drugs, and even more suffered a sense of isolation.

The average size of a home fifty years ago—when families were bigger—was the size of today's three-car garage, around nine hundred square feet. The average home by 2000 was almost three times larger. Furthermore, family incomes have increased 85 percent since the 1950s, yet polls show Americans overwhelmingly were happier fifty years ago.

Today, put an average family in a nine-hundred-square-foot home and they likely will think they are children of a lesser god. They may be tempted to sit in ashes, tear their clothes, and denounce their faith in the real God. But it's not like he hasn't warned us about the devastating results of having full coffers and an empty soul. In the parable of the rich landowner, the Lord calls him a fool; his soul is harvested that same night.

> Beware! Be on your guard against greed of every kind, for even when a man has more than enough, his wealth does not give him life. God said to him, "You fool, this very night you must surrender your life. . . ." That is how it is with the man who amasses wealth for himself and remains a pauper in the sight of God.[13]

Sometimes Jesus said things that require some figuring out. But on the destructive ills of consumerism his message is streamlined and crystal clear: *We can't serve God and money at the same time.*[14] His clear admonition to us? *Choose.*

The apostle Paul is just as no-nonsense on this topic:

> The love of money is the root of all evil things, and there are some who in reaching for it have wandered from the faith and spiked themselves on many thorny griefs.[15]

Hear this, though, as well: We don't want to transpose the mistake and glorify poverty for poverty's sake. There's a balancing act of sorts in regard to possessions:

> Give me neither poverty nor wealth,
>   Provide me only with the food I need.
> If I have too much, I shall deny thee and say, 'Who is the
>   Lord?'
> If I am reduced to poverty, I shall steal and blacken
>   the name of my God.[16]

We could paraphase this passage: "Don't make me so poor, Lord, that I resent you. And don't make me so rich that I forget you."

People in nations that are developing, moving out of widespread impoverishment, usually say they are happier with increased wealth. No surprises there, for poverty brings burdens that can crush a spirit. However, so can the weight of excess, and in a more seductive way.

Glenn Stanton, Director of Social Research and Cultural Affairs for Focus on the Family, pinpoints what this does to families. "Affluenza, the unnecessary accumulation of possessions, is about misplaced priorities. It sends the message loud and clear that life is about stuff, not people."

The word *home* is among the most powerful and richest terms—and realities—that we possess.

> It makes us think of a nest, a place that protects, comforts, supports, and nurtures. But Affluenza provides none of these things. It's about grasping and desiring. It's inhumane, and it's one of the greatest contributors to our destructive divorce rate since it inhibits us from connecting with our families and others. But forming and keeping healthy relationships can be hard. It's much easier to buy people things instead.[17]

Affluenza disintegrates spiritual vitality, and as Stanton notes, Christians somehow aren't much different than non-Christians when it comes to the insatiable desire for what's newer, bigger—and unnecessary.

> It's no coincidence that Christ did not possess a lot. He was telling us something with his life. We don't think Christianly about material possessions. We seek comfort from them instead. Christians don't like to think this way because materialism is one of their biggest blind spots.[18]

The Wrong Kind of Animation

Materialism, the will toward pleasure, not purpose, does far more than disconnect us from transcendent causes, which provide true meaning and real peace. Materialism is not passive—it's aggressive and pernicious, and it actively opposes such a connection. It's a seductive, attractive form of infidelity, a kind of fatal attraction. Materialism stops us from building our marriages, from playing with our kids, from providing for widows and orphans. Materialism seduces us to keep our mouths shut when we see clear injustice and heinous cruelty.

Our situation is worse when we realize that contemporary life is set up for a cautious man, not a courageous one. Culturally we define a good man as one who "makes the right moves" throughout life; the thrones and pedestals on which we place such apparently superior men often lead to behind-the-scenes compromises of integrity that slice into their already deflating or deflated thumos. Harvey Mansfield, professor of Government at Harvard, vividly details Affluenza's destruction of muscular thumos:

> Commerce is unmanly because it is materialistic, willing to settle for gain rather than victory, for trade-offs rather than justice. The commercial life rejects sacrifice and rests on calculation of advantage. The most famous defense of manly chivalry is an attack on modern calculation.[19]

Modern liberalism, he writes, is the largest external cause of the failure to exercise noble thumos, because it prescribes assertiveness for selfish reasons. We have replaced the manly man with the safe company man: "Professionals treat each other with 'professional courtesy' but never with chivalry."[20] They want longer and more trouble-free lives instead of potentially shorter or more difficult lives with substantially greater accomplishments and purpose.

And as G. K. Chesterton showed, materialism gradually destroys humanity: "I do not mean only kindness, I mean *hope, courage*, poetry, *initiative*, all that is human."[21] Note: Hope, courage, and initiative are all attributes of thumos.

While in Nazi concentration camps, Viktor Frankl saw grim examples of the deathly distortion caused by materialism's will-to-pleasure.

> [There were those who, one morning] at five, refused to get up and go to work and instead stayed in the hut, on the straw wet with urine and feces. Nothing—neither warnings or threats—could induce them to change their minds. And then something typical occurred: they took out a cigarette from deep down in a pocket where they had hidden it and started smoking. At that moment we knew that for the next forty-eight hours or so we would watch them dying. Meaning orientation had subsided, and consequently the seeking of immediate pleasure had taken over. Is this not reminiscent of another parallel, a parallel that confronts us day by day?[22]

Materialism is somewhat like the most addictive drug in history. Nicotine relaxes and stimulates at the same time; it brings "calmness" that by masking anxiety seems to invigorate, allowing for productivity and even clarity. And materialism does animate us, but in the wrong (selfish) direction and with the wrong (selfish) will, and so it's squarely in the category of shadow thumos. Materialism marries our affections to the immediate and the temporal, not the eternal, and certainly not the transcendent.

Every major philosopher and theologian worth his salt has told us this. We can ignore it if we want; we also must realize that the words *ignore* and *ignorant* come from the same linguistic root. Conversely, we become people of courageous faith when we measure ourselves against factors far more significant and substantial than the standards and endeavors of time and place. Right now, both inside and outside the church, the standard and the endeavor is materialism.

In light of the pharmaceutical industry's explosive push toward society-wide use of anti-depressants and all manner of related medication (that market is estimated at $23 billion annually), consider the following observation from Douglas Coupland about the connection between consumerism and depression:

> My friends are all either married, boring, and depressed; single, bored and depressed; or moved out of town to avoid boredom and depression. And some of them have bought houses, which has to be [the] kiss of death, personality-wise. When someone tells you they've just bought a house, they might as well tell you they no longer have a personality. You can immediately assume so many things: that they're locked into jobs they hate; that they're broke; that they spend every night watching videos; that they're fifteen pounds overweight; that they no longer listen to new ideas. It's profoundly depressing. And the worst part of it is that people in their houses don't even like where they're living. What few happy moments they possess are those gleaned from dreams of upgrading.[23]

I'm a product of the American Dream. My parents, as you may know, were Irish immigrants. Opportunity is the close cousin of freedom, and freedom is a blessing. But see how opportunity has become obsession and what that's done to so many of us: We've become dehydrated people chasing down drinks that do not quench and, in fact, leave us more parched every time we imbibe.

I think Coupland nails this point when he uses the word *upgrading*. My wife, Sandy, and I had a recent talk in which we concluded that our imperfect house, the one my son and I painted ourselves, is enough. I'll probably slap on some new siding in the next few years, because of sun damage. We'll probably remodel the kitchen, which is wearing out. (We're down to one working burner.) But we don't need more, and we don't really want more. Amazingly, the mere notion that we aren't driven to upgrade makes us an oddity among our peers.

Depression is increasingly common among middle-aged men who are financially affluent and high-achieving. A Gallup poll revealed that 66 percent of physicians say depression is the most common emotional health problem among men at midlife. I'm convinced we have good reason to believe that this connection has been around a long time.

Wrote Alexis de Tocqueville more than one hundred seventy-five years ago:

> In America, I have seen the freest and best educated of men in circumstances the happiest to be found in the world; yet it seemed to me that a cloud habitually hung on their brow, and they seemed serious and almost sad even in their pleasures.[24]

Their source of dis-ease? Americans, he concluded, "never stop thinking of the good things they have not got."

Neurasthenia. That's the name Dr. George Beard gave to what he called "American nervousness," in 1881, to describe the prevalent physical and mental state he observed.[25] Americans—especially young and well-educated, and privileged Americans, were and are emotionally fatigued and physically exhausted. Both of those states pillage our thumos—mostly for the untenable aspiration to acquire *more stuff*.

One last warning about materialism: Many who are infected with it don't know it. You *will* appear weird when you withdraw from it and begin to stand against it. Doing so will be among your most worthwhile achievements, and our collective thumos—our courageous faith and our integrity—depends on it.

As for the opposition and estrangement that inevitably awaits, an estrangement your thumos will need to help you fight and reject, David Awbrey cautions:

> No shopping-mall economy wants people to stop satisfying themselves, to start pondering the timeless questions of life, and to struggle with their personal share of an often shameful, sinful human nature. No way. Sin supplies much of the U.S. gross domestic product and suffuses popular culture. The country would be bankrupt without it. Avarice alone accounts for billions of consumer dollars. Imagine restaurants or liquor stores without gluttony; the fashion and movie industries without lust; television sports without couch-bound, remote-controlled sloth; celebrity tabloids without envy; law firms and car-repair shops without anger; politics, universities, the arts, and journalism without pride. . . .
>
> In wealthy and technological societies, the local deities for many people are health, wealth, youth, beauty, popularity, fame, power and accumulating stuff. In the brokenness of the world it is worth noticing that if you are suffering or experiencing frustration, failure or loss, these deities spit on you and turn away.[26]

Materialism, consumerism, Affluenza, love of money—this poison goes by several names. It's a disease that not only attacks noble thumos but also breeds shadow thumos. It's evil, for it provides the illusion that we are the self-contained captains of our own souls, and, in defiance of God himself, its foundational premise is that we must be preserved instead of redeemed.

Notes

1. Gregory Vlastos and Daniel W. Graham, "The Paradox of Socrates," in *Studies in Greek Philosophy* (Princeton, NJ: Princeton University Press, 1995), 7.

2. From Bob Dylan, "It's Alright, Ma (I'm Only Bleeding)."

3. Bertrand Russell, F.R.S., *Principles of Social Reconstruction* (London: G. Allen & Unwin Ltd., 1916).

4. Sam Keen, *Fire in the Belly: On Being a Man* (New York: Bantam, 1991), 67.

5. See Mark 2:27.

6. Conversation with author.

7. James S. Henry, from "Why I Hate Christmas (The Grinch Has It Right)," The New Republic, as quoted in David Comfort, *Just Say Noel! A History of Christmas From the Nativity to the Nineties* (New York: Simon & Schuster, 1995), 216.

8. C. S. Lewis, "What Christmas Means to Me" in *God in the Dock: Essays on Theology and Ethics* (Grand Rapids: Eerdmans, 1996), 304–05.

9. Ibid.

10. See at *www.beliefnet.com/story/137/story_13795_1.html*

11. From *http://elise.blogs.com/eliseblogscom/2003/12/december_1_2003.html*

12. Quoted in Ann Spangler, *She Who Laughs, Lasts!* (Grand Rapids: Zondervan, 2000), 205.

13. Luke 12:15, 20–21 NEB

14. For example, see Matthew 6:24; Luke 16:13.

15. 1 Timothy 6:10 NEB

16. Proverbs 30:8–9 NEB

17. Conversation with author.

18. Ibid.

19. Harvey Mansfield, *Manliness* (New Haven, CT: Yale University Press, 2006), 233.

20. Ibid., 232.

21. G. K. Chesterton, *Orthodoxy: The Romance of Faith* (Whitefish, MT: Kessinger, 2005), 14, emphasis added.

22. Viktor Frankl, *Man's Search for Meaning* (Boston: Beacon Press, 1946), 141.

23. In Keyes, *Seeing Through Cynicism*, 67.

24. Alexis de Tocqueville, *Democracy in America* (New York: Penguin Classics, 2003).

25. George Beard, *American Nervousness, Its Causes and Consequences* (New York: n.p., 1881).

26. In Keyes, *Seeing Through Cynicism*, 144, 178.

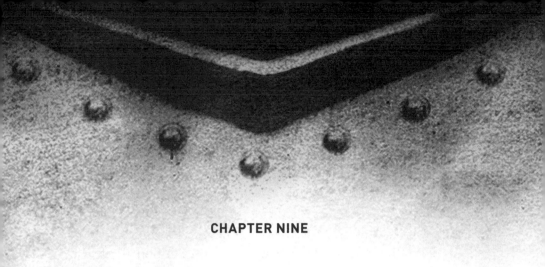

CHAPTER NINE

CYNICISM: THUMOS-FREEZING

We enjoy an irony that does not seek resolution,
because it supports our desire
to be invulnerable observers rather
than participants at risk.
We are spectators of our own lives,
free from the strain of drama
and the uncertainty of a story in which
our souls are at stake.
(R. R. Reno)[1]

If I am saved from cynicism at all
it is by some sense of personal loyalty
to the spirit and genius of Jesus.
(Reinhold Niebuhr)[2]

Cynicism is one of my guilty pleasures. I have a sharp tongue and can quickly turn a phrase. Within a sentence or two I can drain life from another person with a cutting jest. My Irish ancestors should raise a pint in my honor.

No one but me knows what's on the edge of my tongue that would prop me up loftily while making another person—my "subject"—the object of ridicule. I've worked hard to restrain this slice-and-dice propensity. I've learned (and am still learning) not to let the wrong thoughts become unleashed comments, though for much of my life doing so was one of my strongest features and most regular actions. I came to realize that using this ability that way is destructive to thumos—both other people's and my own.

So today I avoid media that are steeped in cynicism (*Rolling Stone* magazine being just one example). If I don't, a native voice soon beckons me, calling forth a cocksure and musky disposition that ascends an almighty throne, places a scepter in my right hand, and pronounces judgment upon all of God's creation. It comes so naturally; I rapidly find myself writing, in my head, with a crowd-pleasing flair. Through cynicism, I somehow can get several times too big for my britches.

During my cynical years, I cursed the darkness around me but didn't have the thumos to step out and try to shine some light. Now, having been on the battlefield awhile, I find myself the target of cynicism from others, usually younger men boozed up on ideology, just let loose from chilly academia. They're calling or writing to rain down the fire of cynical judgment from their ivory towers; I've discovered that they tend to assign motives to me about which they could not possibly know.

I used to contact some of them so I could tell them to get off their blessed assurance and go do something useful, but now, fortunately, I have neither the time nor the interest. I also hear from men who have become cynical about having been burned by organized religion; sometimes they accuse me of being a mindless parrot. Yet traditional church leaders along with aging hippies are among my loudest critics. Even as I actively endeavor to turn from it and tame it, cynicism has me coming and going.

Over time I've come to see that cursing the darkness was better than going through life not even seeing or acknowledging it. But not much better. Pointing my finger at those I deemed naïve, gullible, and hyper-spiritual didn't bring about anything good—it didn't create any light, love, or hope. As I've done many times, I mistook the quarrel for the battle. At some point, this happens to most everyone who has a fighting spirit, so if it's happened or is happening with you, don't beat yourself up about it. You do want to learn how to sidestep this mistake, but not at the cost of laying down your weapons for fear of using them imperfectly. Resolve to keep going, being aware that those with thumos spirit usually misspend it.

Cynics are made, not born, and the main sources of cynicism are common to our human experience, like dashed hopes, unmet expectations, and discovering no benefit from "playing by all the rules." To keep growing and strengthening our thumos, we need to expose cynicism's fundamental weaknesses. What we want in place of cynicism *and* its opposite, naïveté, is what I call healthy suspicion, which historical Christianity has embraced but which is undernourished today. (For instance, think of all the teachings you've heard that have exhorted you to embrace innocence [of a dove] without emphasizing or even mentioning also becoming shrewd [as a snake].[3])

Sources of Cynicism

Cynics are frustrated idealists who sense or intuit how the world should be and are grieved and angered by how it is currently. But they have mishandled their grief: Instead of insulating its heated energy (as with a Thermos) and then funneling it toward noble ends, they let it fly or fire it off in either bitterness or rage. Indignation is a God-given capacity, one we're commanded to exercise;[4] instead of allowing it to spur them toward problem-solving, though, cynics fail to hold on to and focus it (picture a small child trying to manage a fire hose at full blast). This unfruitfulness makes matters even worse, for it drains others of courage by depleting us of both heroes and hope.

The vast chasm between what life is and what life should be is enough to stretch out and snap our thumos. For many it does, but the broken nature of the cynic's boldness often is well disguised because he makes it look muscular, sophisticated, and tough. This discrepancy, and the lack of honesty that it builds, causes further pain and disillusionment, which unfortunately causes the cynic to retreat like a turtle into his shell for solace and protection; the shell is comprised of his mind, and his mind alone. There he comes increasingly to mistake criticism for action and denouncements for animation.[5]

It's not that cynics aren't accurate in their criticisms—they often are. That's usually only part of the story, though; the issue is that their pronouncements overreach and are slanted by presuming to understand matters they cannot possibly know. In this manner, cynicism really is a form of cranky gossip, a safe place where we can look tough and in the know, a safe zone not too far from life's playing field that insulates its inhabitants from injury while being just close enough to give the impression of participation and involvement.

Study any important facet of life—faith, marriage, parenthood, friendship, civic duty—and there you will find scores of cynics who once believed in that arena but were somehow hurt in it. Their hearts and visions have been broken; people need heart and vision to grow thumos. Among the saddest examples are those who speak in harsh or bitter or dismissive tones about the very institutions that bring vitality and healing to so many (for example, wounded divorcees, in regard to marriage).

Churches that emphasize ever-lengthening lists of rules and prohibitions are a Petri dish for spiritual cynicism. There's always another piety hill to climb, so there's no rest, and there's no peace that connects people. Likewise, formulaic churches—"Pray, then X and Y will happen"—are cynic factories because they consistently create, inflate, and then shatter hopes and expectations.

According to many letters I receive, wealthy churches that spend millions on buildings and programs but fail to lift burdens through ministry also create cynics. I know one pastor who simply grew sick of it—his thumos rose up and said *Enough! What are we really doing?!* So his church contacted a nearby elementary school and said that they wanted to adopt it.

"What do you need?" he asked. "Computers, fresh paint, some ceilings fixed; stuff like that," he heard. That's what they're providing right now. In this very practical process, probably unknown to many, they're also providing a powerful antidote to spiritual cynicism by putting their faith and love into action.

Cynicism's Achilles' Heel

Cynicism has a fatal flaw that few have taken the time to analyze and expose. In *Seeing Through Cynicism*, the best work I'm aware of in unveiling its deceptive nature, Dick Keyes writes:

> The genius of cynicism is that it is a voice in your ear which does not usually hang around long enough to be interviewed, much less interrogated. It can move on, leaving an insinuation, a slur, a humiliation, an intimation and then changes the subject to start on something else.[6]

Cynicism protects us from having our hopes destroyed by not allowing us to have thumos-producing hope in the first place.

If we do not hope, we are not disappointed. Cynicism can seem very safe and also very enlightened and sophisticated. In a world filled with disillusionment, this is no small consolation.[7]

Douglas Coupland has coined two innovative terms that help to further illustrate the true flimsiness of cynicism.

Knee-jerk irony is the tendency to make flippant and ironic comments as a reflexive matter of course in everyday conversation.

Derision preemption is a lifestyle tactic, the refusal to go out on any sort of limb and thereby avoid mockery from peers. Derision preemption is the main goal of knee-jerk irony.[8]

Keyes emphasizes cynicism's deep-seated self-indulgence:

> If anyone is looking for a respectable excuse for not getting involved working against the suffering, injustice and falsehood in this world, cynicism is ideal. If you see urgent needs and you would like to help, but you really don't feel like going beyond your comfort zone to destabilize your life or the life [of] your family in this messy situation, then cynicism can seem attractive. . . . In fact, there is no cause that is quite worthy of the investment of your moral energy, time and resources. You can see through them all. . . . In short, cynicism enables you to do nothing but feel morally superior to those who are doing something good but imperfect in an imperfect world.[9]

I am trying more and more to be like David in Nick Hornby's novel *How to Be Good*. David begins to grow suspicious of his own cynicism; this is a courageous move when you keep company with fellow cynics. He's in a discussion about the nation's president when, in a bold stab at authentic living, he says something that astonishes his friend and may well undermine the relationship:

"I no longer want to condemn people whose lives I know nothing about."

His friend is dumbfounded. "But . . . that's the basis of all conversation!"

David replies, "I'm tired of it. We don't know anything about him."[10]

Dick Keyes summarizes: "An honest acknowledgment of our ignorance can debunk cynicism and threaten the social relationship dependent on it."[11]

Only one person on this earth has ever had perfectly pure motives, and he's now in heaven at his father's right hand. The intentions of everyone else are suspect, and yet even within healthy suspicion I've found many, many good and honorable motives. I've been fortunate enough to meet and serve with many ministers across this country, and we've teamed up to help men, marriages, and children, to do our part in helping them toward more abundant living. These leaders are screwed up, just like me and you; they don't minister perfectly. However, they're trying, they're doing good, and they're making tangible progress in tangibly loving others, imperfectly fulfilling (but fulfilling nonetheless) the good works put before them.

While here and now we aren't perfect, there are people who possess God-glorifying motives. Martin Luther King Jr. lived beyond self-interest and through his thumos fought for dignity, love, and justice in the Lord's name. Alexander Solzhenitsyn pushed past self-preservation, in part because his heated thumos could not stand the former Soviet Union's corruption and brutality. Former *Time* senior foreign correspondent David Aikman summarized him this way:

By turns sardonically funny, anguished or burning in slow fury, Solzhenitsyn accomplished something truly rare in all literature, the moral impaling of an entire political system with sustained literary power.[12]

Few descriptions of a man's accomplishments also describe in detail the value, power, and blessing of noble thumos.

Christianity: Not for Pollyanna People

That Christian faith embraces a suspicion toward the human condition is a fact we can't ignore. Christianity promotes blind trust in no one, maintaining that there's something profoundly wrong, spoiled, or stained in our nature and that there's no lasting way to crawl away from this mess on our own. We need help. *Everyone* must be rescued or else they're doomed.

Though we're imbued with tremendous worth, we also are mortally wounded. We're like those mirrors in a funhouse, so distorted that our image is both comical and frightening. Unlike cynicism, though, Christianity provides the way out, retaining a vital skepticism while also providing redemption, hope, and the courage and faith required to persevere. We are like the cracked Liberty Bell: The fault would have consumed the entire bell if someone hadn't drilled a hole just above it, drawing the fissure to the hole so it would stop. The crack has been halted and consumed; Jesus' atoning work on the cross is the hole. That event was God's drilling into time so that the destruction of our sin would be drawn to and consumed by him; we can be rescued as soon as we will humbly accept rescue.

The believer's suspicion toward humans and human motives isn't infinite. Jesus at times saw qualities in people that were good, and he praised them.

The same Jesus who "knew what was in everyone" called Nathanael "an Israelite in whom there is no deceit" (John 1:47). The one who could see through people was not saying that Nathanael was sinless but that he was a person of integrity; he was not trying to con anybody. Jesus later marveled at the faith of a Roman centurion whose servant he healed (Luke 7:9) and at the love of a prostitute who washed his feet with her hair, "She has shown great love" (Luke 7:47).[13]

Cynicism leads to bitterness; bitterness fuels shadow thumos, and frankly, bitterness makes us stupid. Asaph saw this in himself, as he described in Psalm 73, a powerful confession of anger, bitterness, envy, cynicism, and remarkably, resolve. He awakened from the self-soothing, self-congratulatory effects of soul-numbing cynicism when he better understood the real reality of "wicked prosperity."

> When my heart was embittered,
>   I felt the pangs of envy,
> I would not understand, so brutish was I.
>   I was a mere beast in thy sight, O God.
> Yet I am always with thee;
>   Thou holdest my right hand.[14]

Asaph saw that "cynicism was not the result of honest insight but of the clouded misunderstandings that had come with being deeply embittered."[15]

Without actual suspicion, however, we will misemploy and misapply our courageous faith. We will rush into conflicts where we don't belong (that's part of the definition of *rashness*). Some battles aren't worthy of us; some are worthy and yet we don't (or don't yet) possess the power, weaponry, or wisdom for them. It's best not to enter such battles, or at least not to enter them very deeply. We need a healthy level of suspicion to ensure that we aren't sucked into someone else's self-interest cloaked in "the good fight." This takes maturity and usually a few rounds with B-level deception to figure out. Life provides plenty of opportunities to experience such deception and practice discernment, but there are few guides to help us learn well from them.

Suspicion does not turn away from life's dark side—naïveté does. Suspicion sees it and learns from it. At its best, too, suspicion provides tremendous clarity during times of confusion: "Suspicion itself should not be seen as some sort of moral failing but as an honest and realistic precaution for broken people functioning in a broken world."[16] All the same, realize that although suspicion is necessary, it's also dangerous. Overly suspicious people do not extend love. They are closed systems—transmitters, not receivers—and their transmission of courage is mighty low.

> Surely he scorneth the scorners:
> But he giveth grace unto the lowly.
> The wise shall inherit glory:
> But shame shall be the promotion of fools.[17]

The biblical terms most closely corresponding to *cynic* usually are translated "mocker," "scoffer," or "scorner." As Keyes points out, we hear the final word to the scorner by referring directly to God's response to the cynic.

> Here is the ultimate sting for the cynic. God sees through, unmasks, and scorns the cynic's cynicism. This is the greatest irony of all—and so something that is rarely imagined—that the transcendent God laughs at cynicism, not with the laughter of glee but of pity and sadness at its grandiose pretentions. When he who knows everything is not cynical, and we who know so little claim cynical insight, we appear ridiculous in his eyes.[18]

In order to stem the influence of cynicism that hampers us—generally, more so with men than with women—we need to accept and understand the paradoxes that surround us and to live within the tension they create. Additionally, we need to learn how to best bridge what appear to us as gaps. We do this in part by realizing that we live simultaneously in disparate worlds. One does not value what should be valued, a fact that's abundantly clear to most cynics. By and large we humans value power, influence, and control. That's the world of man. The world God made us for, the kingdom of heaven, the eternal reality, values love in every one of its facets and dimensions. The two worlds don't mix well.

Most of us have been trained to believe we must completely shun the world of man, the world of power. I disagree. We need to understand this world—how it functions and what it represents—and then, rather than emulating it, we are to bring redemption to it. Otherwise we become like the well-intentioned but innocuous Christians that Theodore Roosevelt denounced.

Roosevelt is a great example of a man who went through childhood with an ailing thumos but grew it to abundance in his adult life. Roosevelt observed that Christians of his day "were very nice, very refined, who shook their heads over political corruption and discussed it in drawing rooms and parlors, but who were wholly unable to grapple with real men in real life."[19] Of how many believers is this accurate still today? *Pleasantries and positivity do not usher in truth, justice, and mercy.*

If we don't comprehend how this world really works, then it's true: We can't "grapple with real men in real life." Jesus told us we are to live in the world without being of it;[20] this includes our not succumbing to cynicism, which has its home base fully in the world's camp. This is a worldview that sees our existence only in terms of force and power—the realm of kill or be killed.

By contrast, spiritual naïveté spends too much time in hyper-spiritual camps. There, "love" tends to be exceedingly saccharine, and most everything gets presented and accepted in terms of manners and moral judgment. The broad idea is that if you just embrace sweetness, niceness, and innocence, and embrace the harmlessness of a dove, then God's wellspring of goodness will pour over you in a cascade of amazing grace and favor.

There's a third way: again, we must live in both worlds (camps). If we hide from and avoid and ignore everyone and everything that isn't loving, we quickly become cloistered and irrelevant, having no clue how to overcome the obstacles to love. Reinhold Niebuhr, echoing Jesus' words,[21] understood this dynamic well:

> The children of light must be armed with the wisdom of the children of darkness but remain free from their malice. They must know that power of self-interest in human society without giving it moral justification. They must have this wisdom in order that they may beguile, deflect, harness and restrain self-interest, individual and collective, for the sake of the community.[22]

By understanding the nature of these two worlds, we can enter and remain in both of them with realistic expectations instead of having our hopes, ideals, and dreams dashed—the very maladies that foster cynicism in the first place.

I'm most cynical when I'm fatigued, disappointed, discouraged, and afraid. Each is kryptonite to our thumos; we need regular encouragement through God's Word and from others who care for us to combat them. When I'm experiencing an internal (philosophical) crisis, which leads to a drop in thumos, I read Job, the Psalms, and the Prophets (like Jeremiah). And when I'm experiencing a more gut-level beating of my thumos, I turn to the rugged life of Christ (the gospel of Mark is a good place to start) as well as to Paul's writing—for example, his letters to the Corinthians, where he admits his drops in courage and tells of how he ministered with fear and trembling anyway.

Like young, single pastors who feel compelled to preach on marriage and who almost always unfairly come down on men and think they're doing marriage a favor, cynicism attempts to explain too much that it doesn't understand. Writes Michael Kinsley,

> The cheap pleasures of cynicism are always in plentiful supply. Abandoning them is like going on a diet or giving up smoking. Hope, in other words, is the thing that takes work.[23]

To grow our thumos, then, we need to overcome both cynicism and naïveté while embracing a form of suspicion that's accurate in regard to the nature and state of others and ourselves. By walking this road we avoid the deflation of our thumos and at the same time help to ensure that it's deployed at the right time and in the right venues. This keeps hope alive—hope that is not ignorant and uninformed but instead genuine, love-extending, and life-giving. In this way we will let our "light shine before others, so that they may see [our] good works and give glory to [our] Father in heaven."[24]

Ultimately, what matters most regarding cynicism and its relationship to thumos is that in the end, cynicism blocks the animated and spirited form of love we're angling toward. This is especially sorrowful to me when I think of the most cynical people in my life. Most are well-educated. Most could help love others in tangible ways through their insights and incomes. They possess skills that could help others become freer, happier. They could, with humility, self-examination, and suspicion toward their own motives and behavior, help others find that zone between healthy suspicion and courage-crushing cynicism. But they don't. They remain on the sidelines, safe from the battle.

If you listen closely, you will hear how cynicism is the language of disguised grievances without redemptive power or a plan to facilitate something beneficial. You could say cynicism is gossip with hair on its chest. And it's also the language of resignation. In regard to thumos, a workingman's response is "Why try?"

Cynicism is more than just the language of self-preservation; it's also an undisclosed belief that one is powerless and impotent. I don't think this is the case for all cynics, but I know it is for some: Like Asaph and me, at times people feel trapped and helpless, and their panicked frustration often blasts out in the form of rage, like a wild animal caught in a snare. This too places cynicism in the category of shadow thumos—animation, will, and desire, in the wrong direction.

God warns us against swearing for similar reasons. He doesn't want us to watch what we say because he wants us to be good little boys who always please their mommas. He warns us about its corruptive nature because it sucks hope from our air. Swearing can also be an expression of powerlessness and impotency, and like an odor, it lingers.

A cynic is often a frustrated, wounded, and fearful idealist—frequently someone who tried to play by the rules they were given and then found that toeing the line did not deliver. The anger has turned into bitterness that's driven them to another camp and into the seat of the all-knowing scoffer, the one who weighs and pronounces judgment over right and wrong—all the while never moving from his comfortable perch to give to or help anyone. Seeing the horridness of this fate must remind us to turn from cynicism and instead to generate the hope-creating fuel we need to stay faithful, animated, engaged, and aware.

Notes

1. Keyes, *Seeing Through Cynicism*, 80.

2. Ibid., 134.

3. See Matthew 10.

4. See Ephesians 4:26 KJV.

5. Like the loop of fear—phobologic—that Spartans were expected to surmount, cynics possess their own destructive loop. It is a fear of exposure that causes them to abandon the battlefield, which is a far less noticeable desertion than raw cowardice.

6. Keyes, *Seeing Through Cynicism*, 78.

7. Ibid., 81.

8. Ibid., 82.

9. Ibid., 83.

10. Nick Hornby, *How to Be Good* (New York: Riverhead Books, 2001).

11. Keyes, *Seeing Through Cynicism*, 87–88.

12. David Aikman, *Great Souls: Six Who Changed a Century* (Idaho Falls: Lexington Books, 2003), 177.

13. Keyes, *Seeing Through Cynicism*, 159.

14. Psalm 73:21–23 NEB

15. Keyes, *Seeing Through Cynicism*, 111.

16. Ibid., 155.

17. Proverbs 3:34–35 KJV

18. Keyes, *Seeing Through Cynicism*, 163.

19. Theodore Roosevelt, *Theodore Roosevelt: An Autobiography* (New York: Macmillan, 1913), 96.

20. For instance, see John 17.

21. See Luke 16.

22. Keyes, *Seeing Through Cynicism*, 211.

23. Michael Kinsley, "Visiting a Place Called Hope." See at *www.time .com/time/magazine/article/0,9171,978294,00/html*

24. Matthew 5:13-16

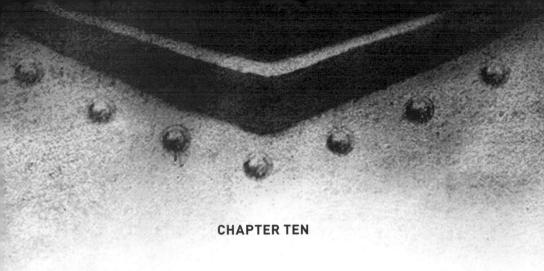

CHAPTER TEN

LESSONS FROM THE RESCUERS: THUMOS-ENCOURAGEMENT

I detest the masculine point of view.
I am bored by his heroism, virtue, and honour.
(VIRGINIA WOOLF)[1]

Courage is not an emotion.
Courage consists of doing what you said you would do
even when you don't want to.
In the face of danger you have a choice
to be the delegate of either your commitments
or your feelings.
(NICHOLAS LORE)

Asked to speak to a boys-only Sunday school class, I gave a short talk about bullying and emphasized the importance of caring for the weak and the oppressed, especially the physically and mentally challenged, whom bullies often target.

I told the boys that God made them male for a reason. I said that with this reason come certain responsibilities: namely, most males have greater physical strength than most females, and God wants us to use this strength justly and courageously, so we can be loving toward and protective of others.

I explained how the Greeks thought that the ideal man is a courageous man, someone who sacrifices for others, and how this belief should be embraced by Christians as well. I illustrated how without courage, our lives will be miserable, and at best our faith will be weak. I gave them a new word to savor: *thumos*.

As I talked more and more about the gift of courage and how we can be truly heroic through our loving strength, the kids literally leaned forward in their chairs. I don't think even one broke eye contact with me. I asked them questions, and they responded with fervor.

One boy, with no small amount of shame, admitted to the group that he had been bullied for a long time. Another boy admitted to being a bully. The whole class came alive when I told them God has given them special abilities to protect others, that among these gifts is a certain kind of courage he has placed in their souls, courage that needs to come out. I told them that the group of kids who "run" most schools—who set the moral thermostat for good or for ill—are male athletes. If they bully, the whole school tends to bully, but if they use their power justly, the school is a better place to be.

The boys *loved* this thumos talk.

But the Christian men in the room, the ones whose duty it is to stimulate and direct the boys' spiritual growth, couldn't have been more bored. One fell asleep. One kept giving me sleepy-cow eyes. Another had a bemused look on his face, like, "What planet are you from? This isn't what we had in mind." One stared at me with a sort of muted horror, as if I were teaching these young guys something sinful.

I was reminded of what Robert Baden-Powell said: "Manliness can only be taught by men, not by those who are half men, half old women."[2] I thought of C. S. Lewis's view of courage as "not simply one of the virtues but the form of every virtue at the testing point, which means at the point of highest reality."[3] If I had spoken these words aloud to the men in the room, I think they would have fallen pretty much on deaf ears. On the whole, courage, boldness, heated vitality—thumos—has little or nothing to do with how we're spiritually training our kids.

In fact, we're training them in contradiction. The "ideal Christian kid" (in today's culture), boy or girl, is what I defined earlier: pusillanimous (lacking courage and manly strength), having the character and nature of a small animal, small-souled. More than *90 percent* of kids witness bullying. Of that group, almost all say that they want to help the other person. Yet a measly *11 percent* intervene.

I'm not talking about bullies with knives or other weapons. I'm talking everyday, garden-variety bullying—young kids who verbally express contempt and disdain, which comprises 80 percent of all bullying. The majority does nothing about it even though they are urged from within to do something, and this includes all the kids who went to Sunday school that week. Statistically, most give in to cowardice, and most are doing exactly as they are being taught.

Conversely, we must *learn* to be courageous—for most people it does not come naturally. A great place to start is by realizing that our understanding of how we can encourage another person is tremendously incomplete, even inaccurate. One biblical word for encouragement, *protrepo*, means to "urge forward, persuade to stimulate another to discharge their ordinary duties of life." *Encouragement* can also include a component of comfort and/or consolation, but unfortunately this is almost exclusively the whole meaning of the word as we use it today, part of our anemic Official Script.

Consoling someone is only part of what's necessary for the growth of courage. We also encourage others by stimulating, invigorating, inspiring, and *persuading them to keep going.* Encouragement says, "You can do it." "Keep the faith."

"You're not alone." "Don't give up." And "You have what it takes!"

The author of the epistle to the Hebrews fuels a superior form of encouragement when he reminds his readers about the multitude of faith-inspiring witnesses who have gone before them.[4] *You're not alone and you can do great things as well.* He then reminds them of what these titans of faith actually accomplished: the overthrowing of kingdoms, establishment of justice, escapes from death, and growing strong in war and routing foreign armies, among others. This courageous faith helped turn their weaknesses into strengths.[5]

Then the author, who Martin Luther thought was the eloquent Apollos, writes something very un-evangelical. Banishing "worm theology," where believers are supposed to think of themselves as worthless and without dignity, he writes that those faith giants who endured death, poverty, distress, and misery were "too good for a world like this."[6] Therefore, he wants us to conclude,

> Since we are surrounded by such a great cloud of witnesses, let us throw off everything that hinders and the sin that so easily entangles, and let us run with *perseverance* the race marked out for us.[7]

Perseverance is one of the most nutrient-rich fruits of thumotic courage, born from faith but also coming up from somewhere else within us that joins with this faith and then acts.

Courage is contagious, but one must be willing to be infected. Better minds than mine have gone back and forth on the essence of courage: Some say we're born with it, others that we're not. I think we're born with the potential for courage, and that from there, the hard part starts: We either learn how to draw it out of ourselves or we don't. Furthermore, I believe that the quality of our life expands or shrinks based upon this decision and guidance (or lack of guidance). As Maya Angelou has said: "Without courage, we cannot practice any other virtue with consistency. We can't be kind, true, merciful, generous, or honest."

We've seen that cowardice, born from fearful self-interest and self-preservation, is the enemy of courage. We noted how cowardice makes us feel sludge-like, eroding our integrity and our dignity, mortifying our souls with guilt and shame and actually *diminishing* our self-regard. Isn't it at least intriguing, then, that we wouldn't already be focusing on this during an age in which self-esteem is perhaps *the* most untouchable sacred cow?

The U.S. military defines cowardice as "misbehavior before the enemy." It includes running away in the face of an enemy and willfully failing to do all within one's power to fight or defend when it's one's duty to do so. Militarily, cowardice's maximum punishment is death, and a part of our soul likewise goes dark when we give in to cowardice—we become vulnerable to a level of self-loathing that's unequal to what follows any other behavior. Remember how Martin Luther wrote that avoiding spiritual battles due to cowardice is a form of spiritual treason? We sense this truth but don't have words to describe it, the willingness to confess it (in order to be healed), or the training to fight for it.

Incredibly, Christians need permission to be morally courageous again, as when they battled to abolish slavery, as when they've warred against fascism, as when they've struggled for equal civil rights, and when they've rallied to love and care for children, born and unborn. People of faith need permission to be *good* again—to exercise moral courage in civic life. Will the church grant it?

The admonishments from Scripture couldn't be clearer.

*Be strong and courageous. . . . The Lord himself goes before
you and will be with you; he will never leave you nor forsake you. Do not be afraid; do not be discouraged.*[8]

*Be strong and courageous, and do the work. Do not be
afraid or discouraged, for the Lord God, my God, is with
you.*[9]

Be men of courage; be strong.[10]

The word *courage* was once reserved for the kind of
behavior requiring sacrifice and suffering on behalf of a person for the common good. This is part of the definition of
righteousness that's found in the Bible. We've discarded this
meaning, though, for a more inclusive, less demanding, and
me-centered understanding; our souls have been badly dam-
aged by this reduction.

Senator John McCain says courage is:

[that] rare moment of unity between conscience, fear, and
action, when something deep within us strikes the flint
of love, of honor, of duty. . . . It is an acute awareness of
danger, the sensation of fear it produces, and the will to
act in spite of it. I think it is the highest quality of life
attainable by human beings. . . . I think God meant us to
be courageous so that we could know better how to live,
how to love what, and as, He commands us to love. It is
not enough to be honest and just and demand that we be
treated honestly and justly by others. We must learn to love
honesty and justice for themselves, not just for their effect
on our personal circumstances, but for their effect on the
world, on the whole of human experience.[11]

One of our largest misunderstandings about courage
is that it's basically synonymous with suffering. Enduring
something painful that you think is inescapable is admirable,

yes, but it's not courage. Courage is when you have a choice about whether or not to suffer, and you choose the suffering in order to help bring about a greater good.

Lessons From the Rescuers

One of my heroes is Fritz Graebe, an unsung Oskar Schindler. With thumos, and through tremendous wiles, shrewdness, cunning (all behaviors deemed unchristian by many), he helped save the lives of hundreds of Jews from the Nazis.

In order to build courage in my children, I read to them about the lives of courageous people. My son Elliot was so moved by Graebe's heroism that he opted to portray him in a school program called "Night of the Notables." He dressed up like Graebe and told the assembled students, teachers, and parents about how he put his own life at risk to save others.

Justice Moshe Bejski of the Israeli Supreme Court, chairman of the Commission for the Designation of the Righteous, asked a question, in 1974, that indicated an urgent new direction of inquiry by Holocaust survivors and, by extension, anyone who cares deeply about love, truth, justice, and righteousness:

> Why was it that in approximately twenty states under Nazi occupation or influence, which had the combined population of hundreds of millions, there were relatively so few persons who were prepared to help those who were in such urgent need of relief during that period?[12]

Many others asked various forms of that question as well. Thankfully, the lives of Fritz Graebe and other Holocaust rescuers have been studied at great length and in great detail. The cumulative results of that examination are answers to

Bejski's haunting question, and they give us a thumos lesson unlike any other.

I wrote about this study in *No More Jellyfish, Chickens, or Wimps*, a book for parents who want to raise courageous children. Now I want to look at these findings from a more adult perspective, especially as it relates to the creation of thumos.

Jesus said there is no greater love than that someone lay down his life for another.[13] Fritz Graebe did this repeatedly during a time in his life when he was well off. He was a comfortable professional who had no reason to become involved. He wasn't Jewish, nor was anyone in his family. However, while his own flesh was safe, Graebe had a more humane definition of what *flesh* means. He held unyielding convictions that drew him into battle against the sophisticated machinery and insidious mindset of the fascist murderers.

Graebe and other rescuers exhibited three common traits that aided the development of courage:

- An adventurous spirit that's humane and purposeful—not to be confused with much of today's outdoor adventure pursuits, which are usually self-centered and reckless for the sake of recklessness.
- Identification with a morally strong parent or morally strong heroic figure.
- An ability to identify with socially marginal people, along with a willingness to break with tradition and to withstand persecution when pursuing justice and truth.

Those who value courage also examined and exalted other predominant character traits in Graebe. He cultivated an empathetic imagination that placed him in the shoes of others. He saw people as fully human *and* prized their innate dignity, and he reinforced this through an ultra-practical expression of his Christian faith.

He fostered the ability to present himself as in control of a critical situation even when experiencing profound doubt. He'd work himself into an indignant fever when fighting on behalf of others (another similarity to the life of Martin Luther). He talked to himself, inflating his thumos, before embarking on important missions. He learned how to project strength even when he felt powerless.

Fritz Graebe believed that life is meaningful and that his life was purposeful. Unlike many Christians who are misled by bad theology, Graebe didn't accept wormish worthlessness but was convinced that he mattered—that *we matter.* Noble thumos drives a person to embrace God-given value without spilling into hubris. It compels people not only to believe in but also to become and to do the heroic. Graebe believed in the core of his being that his actions mattered, that ultimately they would determine who he truly was.

He also possessed the ability to be both proactive and pro-social. His mother instilled in him the foundational principles of right and wrong. He wasn't one to just sit back and let life happen to him and others while calling himself "a gentle spirit." He acted; he exerted himself; he got things done. For example, as a young man he suffered from stuttering, but instead of giving in or "just praying about it," he studied the problem and strove to overcome it. (He did.) He wasn't mild or lukewarm—he possessed a sword of willingness and he used it. Just as God told David, and as Solomon obeyed David, Fritz Graebe *did the work.*

He had experience with suffering and death. He had experience with the loathsome, fearsome side of life, and I think this experience extracted some of the natural human fear of darkness, or as Paul sarcastically put it, "Where, O death, is your sting?"[14] Much of the darkness we see around us is real, but it's also overblown—it's often nowhere near as powerful as it presents itself to be. I think the piercing of this falsehood early in his life freed Graebe to be more like Jesus Christ.

As a German engineer for Siemens Corporation, Fritz Graebe had the ability to confront and manage prejudice and fear while in the midst of the enemy. In Europe prejudice against Jews was widespread, and they often were objects of ridicule and scorn. Those were behaviors Graebe's mother would not tolerate, and he learned not to accept them either.

Graebe would lick his emotional wounds after, not during, his confrontations with authorities. The Spartans called this shedding of fear *hesmu phobou*, part of what they called *phobologia*, the science of fear. After battle, if a Spartan would weep and shake uncontrollably, his fellow soldiers would honor his fear shedding by providing comfort without shame.

Once, while riding my mountain bike off Roxy Anne Peak in Medford, Oregon, just a few miles from home, I came down the peak on a road I'd never taken before. It almost cost me my life. And I learned something profound about the connection between comfort and courage growth.

It was a gray winter evening. The sun was almost down. I had a lot of what we call southern Oregon gumbo—clay mud—on my tires, so I was trying for as much speed as possible in order to have it fling off. I was thinking of home, of the dinner Sandy had waiting, and of the hot tub afterward, when suddenly in front of me was a low-lying metal cable stretched across the road, about two feet off the ground at the sagging middle, the kind of cable used to close a rural road. In other words, a very cheap and hard-to-spot gate.

I was on a collision course with a thin cord of metal restraints. I slammed on my disc brakes—I can still smell the burning rubber when I think about that day—and laid the bike down on its left side. The bike and my lower body were able to slide just under the cable, but my upper body couldn't. The cable caught me under my right arm, right on my ribs. Instantly I felt like a very large letter *U* where my hands and my toes touched.

And then, thank God, the cable snapped. I flailed in the air like a rag doll a few feet above the blacktop. My back and head hit the ground first. Then I must have kept sliding downhill another twenty feet or so.

I came to on my back. With my knees in the air, I tried to will my body into breathing again, but I couldn't—I felt like I was drowning on land. Though I could move, I couldn't get up. I was covered in sweat, and now the sweat and the shock were conspiring against me, for the air temp was only a few degrees above freezing. No one was around. I tried to yell for help. I couldn't. My chest and lungs felt paralyzed. I could only lie there, shaking like an old man trying to lift heavy weights.

I got my right hand over to my left ribs, thinking for sure I would find a gap, or something sticking out, or worse, something sticking *in*. I was shaking more and more from the pain and the cold and also from the fear that I had internal bleeding. I thought that this could be it for me, a family man with three kids, dying while on a mountain bike just a few miles from home. Some bikers die from being attacked by a cougar. Now that would be exceptional—there's a story in it. But being done in by a thin little cable I should have seen coming? *That's Darwin Award material*, I thought. *Shame in the making.*

Mercifully, though, at last three high school students glimpsed me from down the hill and came running.

When they arrived, I tried to explain what happened but could barely talk. The muscles in my neck kept misfiring. I couldn't control them or stop them from cramping. So I gagged my way through the attempt, and I still could barely breathe.

Then the young lady with the thin face and blond hair did something I didn't expect.

She held my left hand.

I felt as if she reached through a portal—of strength to weakness. It was as if a very pleasant form of electricity poured through her hand and into my body, like I was being filled with life-voltage mixed with warm butter. I stopped shaking. I got my breath back, finally. My mind stopped reeling. Her strength kick-started mine. I felt hope again, and with it a fighting spirit.

The Greeks taught that no mortal can be courageous in isolation. I was no longer alone.

Keep in mind that nothing else changed. It wasn't as if I'd been wrapped in warm wool blankets, or told that an ambulance was about to arrive, or was seeing an angel overhead commanding me to "Fear not, O weak one!" Only one thing changed: Someone with strength reached across gender and age, from clean clothes to sweaty grime, from health to shock-sickness, from strength to weakness. In a very real way, this healed me of the fear and pain I was feeling. Her compassion, like that of one Spartan soldier to another, from one friend to another (as with Graebe), got my courage flowing again.

Thumos people know how to maintain a courageous front—that is, they can project courage when they feel they have none. Fritz Graebe pulled a gun on a Nazi soldier though he had no intention of using it. When the courageous feel fear beginning to freeze them, they lean *into* fear. The way they push fear back with their bodies and their thoughts separates them from other people.

Athletes keep their thumos flowing by moving around before competing, and many public speakers and entertainers move around before performing as well. They know that fear can paralyze them, and they don't let it happen. These are people with a plan, people who have wrestled with fear and have found its weaknesses.

Graebe developed a community of compassion and support among other courageous souls. Acknowledging the unlikelihood of courageousness in isolation, he did not go it alone—he surrounded himself with others who encouraged him—pushed him forward instead of giving him excuses to quit. Research shows that this capacity to provide compassion and support increases with age. Courage is socially contagious, so if you want more courage, hang out with courageous people.

And finally, Fritz Graebe was a hospitable man—he received visitors and Holocaust strangers as well. Most rescuers had an active church role at some point and were aware of the biblical texts on hospitable acts and lifestyle. Their most frequently quoted passage was that of the Good Samaritan,[15] and they emphasized that Jesus tells us to identify with those in need (which could mean imprisoned, naked, sick, hungry, thirsty, foreign, and so on).

Graebe had a big heart, and by marrying that heart to the God-honoring convictions in his mind, he created acts of justice, love, and mercy that the world could not and cannot ignore. He is one of the greatest people of the twentieth century.

Like so many people of godly thumos action, he was hated by his peers for his good deeds. He provided both powerful and horrifying testimony against his fellow countrymen during one of the subsequent Nuremburg Trials. He moved his family to San Francisco to escape the hostility, where he died in 1986. Through Graebe, we see once again how the burden of noble thumos makes us heroes to those with larger souls, and enemies among the petty and small. There is usually no way around this fact for those who are too good for a world like ours.

Douglas Huneke, the man who compiled so many of these facts about the Holocaust rescuers, ended his study with this important observation:

> These common traits of the rescuers are skills that can be taught and learned. As people learn and practice them, others who are in distress are more likely to be the recipients of direct, meaningful intervention. These skill-related traits do not develop out of nothing or come to a person accidentally. They must be rehearsed and affirmed in a way that insures their continued refining and practice.[16]

In other words, thumos courage can be learned when it's understood and valued and trained.

Research into the creation of courage shows other needful components as well. Another is openness to experience and creativity. People are more courageous when they see they have options, which is one reason why depressed and negative people often are not courageous. Ways to increase this capacity include journaling and idea spiders, where you write a goal in the middle of a board or page and then draw lines to related goals and ideas. In time you may well observe connections and options you didn't notice before.

Our world was given a shining example of creativity's connection to courage in the life of Pope John Paul II, who will likely be the most memorable pontiff of my lifetime. Karol Jozef Wojtyla was a poet and a lover of poetry. He also was an actor who wanted to use theater to expose the atrocities of Nazi brutality to all peoples they attempted to conquer, especially those of his beloved Poland. He joined the resistance against the Nazis, and then, as pope, the resistance against Soviet occupation of Poland. He broke with tradition when he believed doing so was necessary to spread God's love, peace, and mercy. Even people who were not fans of organized religion, including my own father, could not help but speak highly of him.

He was the first non-Italian chosen to lead the Catholic Church in more than four centuries, in part for his popularity among the young, his loving heart, his fertile mind (he spoke eight languages), and his infectious sense of humor. But he was also known for his thumos-courage, which made him stand out among his peers, especially through his charisma.

The connection between courage and charisma—the hard-to-define x-factor that some possess—is obvious to our senses. The pope's courage bolstered his charisma, his magnetism, his persuasiveness, his eloquence, his vision, and his ability to pull others to his side and join his causes. Courage can bolster your charismatic x-factor as well.

Less than eight months after his inauguration, in 1978, John Paul II returned to his homeland for nine days. Adoring crowds met him wherever he went and were a source of acute embarrassment to the communist government. Officially, the country was atheistic, and it suffered food shortages. The pope added to the authorities' discomfort by reminding his fellow Poles of their God-given nature. "You are men. You have dignity. Don't crawl on your bellies," he told them.[17] And from there, the Soviet Union began to lose its grip on Poland.

A common expression about John Paul II by his peers that helped to explain his popularity was that "he was a man before he was a pope." Please don't miss what this actually means. What people noticed about him, what made him more courageous, bigger and better than those around him, was that unlike many spiritual leaders today, he possessed vitality of both soul and spirit.

When I say he was soulful, I mean that he was connected to the realities of life without being so "easily entangled" by its sinful side.[18] He was world-savvy, wise, courageous, and virile, *and* he was connected to the invisible, mysterious reality of divine energy and will. This dual connectedness gave him uncommon power, perception, and proportion regarding what really matters to people. It gave him a bottom-up orientation to life instead of today's prevalent top-down orientation. As with Fritz Graebe, his intimate encounters with wickedness and evil likewise propelled him in forging thumotic strength.

I think this helps to explain in part the power behind C. S. Lewis's writing as well. Yes, he was brilliant and gifted beyond the norm. He also came to Christ after a lot of wrestling in the soul-world of academia and its demanding intellectual rigors. He brought this soul power, life-wisdom, and virility into his Christian life—he didn't discard it—and decades later the world continues to be fascinated by this unique and rare melding.

I think about Pope John Paul II also as the leader who pardoned the man who tried to murder him, who visited him in prison, praying for his would-be assassin and requesting the same in return. I think about his courage in standing up for religious freedom and human dignity throughout the world. Then I compare it to the sermons I've heard from men trying to convince us that the papacy will usher in the satanic New World Order of apocalyptic lore. I think about the hours of convoluted sermons I was not brave enough to stand up and walk out on—today I wish I'd made public displays of disapproval.

I envision the better me standing up slowly and calmly as people do in movies. I give my pastor a long, pensive stare—a form of steady courage and an acknowledgment that I will not be party to this message—then I turn to my wife and quietly say, "Let's go," and we slowly traverse the aisle as if part of a wedding procession, heads up, eyes straight forward. But I'm left with the heavy stickiness of my cowardice instead.

I think about the members of the large charismatic denomination that has pounded out these worthless conspiracy theories, and I ask myself, "What would they have done in Poland if they'd seen people butchered in the streets and then later seen many others crushed under military occupation?" I'm pretty sure I know what they'd have done: nothing. They wouldn't have resisted for the good of those around them. Instead they would have done what evangelicals are prone toward doing: they would have made islands. They would have built their churches and colleges and, by and large, they would have gone along to get along, actually providing fuel for the antagonists of our faith.

They wouldn't have possessed the kind of thumos that enters the real world, as Roosevelt said, to wrestle with real men and real issues. They would not have been capable of such greatness and heroics in part because their theological training and their church culture wouldn't have allowed it. They'd even have called such behavior "worldly." They should be ashamed of themselves for attacking John Paul II, a man of such courage, but I assure you they are not, and neither will those who comprise this denomination require their leaders to renounce their bigotry, character assassination, and false witness.

Wonder and Mystery

Closely related to creativity are mystery and wonder. D. H. Lawrence wrote that a sense of wonder is our sixth sense, "and it is the natural religious sense."[19] Mystery and wonder give us a keen spiritual edge, helping us to see life with increased enthusiasm, animation, and gratitude. They fill us with an awareness of possibility and compel us to fight off spiritual boredom and claustrophobia.

Wonder and mystery fill the chest and lungs—we breathe more deeply when in their presence. I am no longer amazed but am humored when I hear formerly pacifistic friends of mine declare upon the birth of their child that they would fight to defend him or her. Children awaken thumos in us like nothing else, and while it's upsetting that they didn't carry this conviction about *other* children before, at least they've joined the company of the courageous. I feel like giving them a certificate and a gift card.

Mothers get their thumos going in the protection of the child's body, mind, and soul. Fathers do as well (there's always overlap), but their thumos tends to focus on the macro, the world "out there" that the child someday will enter. This is one reason that at a dinner party, most of the time, the men will talk mostly about civic life and the women will talk mostly about family. I'm not saying this is the way it should be, that it shouldn't change, but that it's the way it is. This is why most reformers and revolutionaries are men and always will be men—it's the world "out there" that tends to most fully capture their thumos.

It's because children are the universal language of life and culture that they draw out of us the better side of our thumos. Writes International Justice Mission's Gary Haugen, in his excellent work *Just Courage,*

> Over time, I have found a nearly universal point of con-
> tact—and that's the experience of being a parent. Parenting
> seems to be the great leveling experience among human
> beings—especially in the unique sense of vulnerability
> that mysteriously accompanies parents of all places. . . .
> We love so much and can control so little.[20]

There is nothing more repulsive and grief-producing than witnessing the abuse of a child at the hands of an oppressor. Coming in a close second is witnessing adults who do nothing when it's within their power to thumos-act on behalf of a child. We are hardwired to be repulsed by cowardice so that we will be animated to love when duty calls us to love and protect.

But it's more than protection of the weak and innocent that spurs our courage regarding children. It's the wonder of birth and of family, this "mini-civilization" that we create, the possibility of our children surpassing us in good deeds, joy, and fulfillment. There's the wonder of watching their personalities unfold, seeing how the flesh of our flesh is like us but not like us.

As a parent, you feel and know that you're part of something bigger and better than you, and the wonder of it makes you feel alive and humble. It takes the pressure off, and somehow, in a way I can't well describe, it depletes fear.

God's wondrous, mysterious spirit and will, seen in his actions supernaturally and his creation naturally, also animate us toward the right orientation in life because they give to us the experience of his active presence among his people.

I remember as a teenager being very troubled while trying to sleep. I remember praying that God would protect me and help me, and that he would send his angels to minister to me. Right after that prayer our dog, Shilo, who was sitting by the side of my bed, looked up at the ceiling. And he kept looking, for a very long time. Like hours, in dog time. To the human eye there was nothing that should have grabbed and held his attention. No spiders, no flies, nothing unusual, nothing moving. I lay there with a sense of awe that was frightening at first but later settled into a confident assurance that I was loved and protected. I was emboldened and invigorated through wonder, mystery, and awe.

Socrates told us that wonder precedes vision, and thumos needs vision, a bone to gnaw on. When we have vision without wonder, it's almost always mechanical, cold, and too "efficient" to include the work of God's Spirit.

Mystery and wonder scared me during the early years of my spiritual walk. I was attracted only to what was "concrete" in God, and on some levels this was necessary, though I see now how it created some unfortunate rigidity, an inability to experience joy, and an undercutting of my courage.

I speak for many men when I say that in order for our faith to remain alive and vibrant, for us to play our part in taking the courageous steps necessary to imitate Christ, we don't need six more rules about our spiritual walk. We need six fresh mysteries—mystery animates us and stirs our thumos, making us cheerful fighters. True, we need comfort like anyone else. But we also need strangeness: We need to be spiritually jabbed, shocked, disturbed by wonder and weirdness. Yet most of Jesus' unfamiliar, startling, sarcastic, and pugnacious comments and behavior get washed out of most sermons, books, and songs.

G. K. Chesterton called the mixture of the familiar with the unfamiliar "romance" with God,[21] and it's no coincidence that it's a Catholic, not a Protestant, who reminds us of this. Our Catholic brothers and sisters are far ahead of us in regard to handling the mysteries of faith and living within the blessed tension that mystery creates. They are not as prone to try to release this tension, which provides adventure, spiritedness, vitality, and enthusiasm for the divine realities in our lives. This is a muscular romance that's intrinsic to heroism and chivalry—both attributes of thumos.

As Christians, we should use words that explain, but we should also use them to "evoke, to set us to dreaming as well as thinking, to use words at their most prophetic and truthful. The prophets used them to stir in us memories and longings and intuitions that we starve for without knowing that we starve."[22] That, starving modern man, is what we long for, what intuition tells us is mystery, the inspirer of courage.

For some strange reason that I cannot fully explain, these mysteries fill me with a rugged form of hope. "If you lose hope," warned Martin Luther King Jr., "somehow you lose the vitality that keeps life moving, you lose that courage to be, that quality that helps you go on in spite of it all. And so today I still have a dream."[23]

The most mentally healthy people, said Scott Peck, are those with a "great taste for mystery and . . . profound curiosity."[24] Peck found that one attribute characterizing the least mentally healthy is a *lack* of mystery and curiosity.

> What bothers me the most when I visit a psychiatric hospital is not the insanity, not the rage or the fear or the anger or the depression, but the apathy. Sometimes it is drug-induced, but a terrible apathy often characterizes the mentally disordered.[25]

I relieved the tension I felt while writing this book by dipping in our hot tub. At night I would listen to the wind stir the pine and fir trees behind me, and every so often, forty-five minutes or so after dusk, a large white owl would fly silently and directly over me, perch, and give me an almost contemptuous glare, as if to convey, "Did I say you could stare?" That bird of prey filled me with awe—that piercing combination of fear and wonder, among the most animating feelings humans can possess.

After a while, all I felt was wonder. Perhaps that's what awesome experiences are designed to do: condition us against fear so we can feel wonder all the more. I live in the city, so such an experience is pretty improbable. I've asked around the neighborhood and no one else has seen the owl. I like to think that God was gracing me with his own special kind of weird airmail.

Notes

1. Alex Zwerdling, *Virginia Woolf and the Real World* (Berkeley: University of California Press), 298.
2. Robert Baden-Powell, *Scouting for Boys* (New York: Oxford University Press, 2005 edition), xxxiv.

3. C. S. Lewis, from *The Screwtape Letters* in *The Complete C. S. Lewis Signature Classics* (New York: HarperCollins, 2007), 184.

4. See Hebrews 12:1.

5. See Hebrews 11:32–34.

6. Hebrews 11:38 NEB

7. Hebrews 12:1

8. Deuteronomy 31:7–8

9. 1 Chronicles 28:20

10. 1 Corinthians 16:13

11. John McCain and Marshall Salter, *Why Courage Matters: The Way to a Braver Life* (New York: Random House, 2004), 200.

12. Moshe Bejski, "The 'Righteous Among the Nations' and Their Part in the Rescue of Jews" (Shoah Resource Center, *The International School for Holocaust Studies*, 1989), 1.

13. See John 15:13.

14. 1 Corinthians 15:55

15. See Luke 10.

16. Douglas K. Huneke, *The Moses of Rovno*, (New York: Random House, Ballantine Books, 1985), 186–187.

17. See *www.cnn.com/SPECIALS/1999/pope/bio/papal/*

18. Cross reference Hebrews 12:1.

19. In Annegreth Horatschek, *Alterität und Stereotyp* (Tübingen: Gunter Narr Verlag, 1989), 662.

20. Gary A. Haugen, *Just Courage: God's Great Expedition for the Restless Christian* (Downer's Grove, IL: InterVarsity, 2008), 91–93.

21. See G. K. Chesterton, *Orthodoxy: The Romance of Faith* (Whitefish, MT: Kessinger, 2005).

22. Buechner, *Telling the Truth*, 23–24.

23. Sondra Myers and Benjamin R. Barber, *The Interdependence Handbook: Looking Back, Living the Present, Choosing the Future* (IDEA, 2004), 40.

24. M. Scott Peck, *Further Along the Road Less Traveled: The Unending Journey Toward Spiritual Growth* (New York: Touchstone, 1998), 76.

25. Ibid.

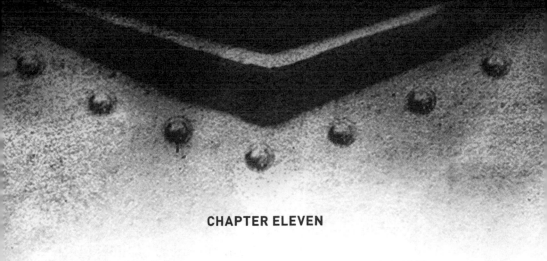

CHAPTER ELEVEN

GRIEF-WORK, FELLOWSHIP, AND FAITH: THUMOS-CREATION

We live in a cowardly, death-denying culture. . . .
We cannot live with courage and confidence
until we can have a relationship with our own death.
Indeed, we cannot live fully unless there is something
that we are willing to die for.
(M. Scott Peck)[1]

Then said Mr. Holy-Man,
"There are two things that they
have need to be in possession of,
that go in pilgrimage; courage and an unspotted life.
If they have not courage
they can never hold on their way."
(John Bunyan)[2]

Grief is our sometimes-complicated response to loss. It can be the loss of a spouse, a dog, a job, or all that is familiar through relocation. Those who function in life's more philosophical sphere feel grief when they ponder their mortality and relatively short lifespan. And contrary to the suggestions of popular culture, the loss of our innocence, such as virginity and sobriety, also produces a unique form of existential grief. Our response to grief-producing loss, if not handled well or honestly, undercuts our thumotic eagerness for living.

We tend to go wrong two ways with grief—overreacting and underreacting. We sometimes respond to our loss like a trapped animal, spewing rage, pointing fingers, harboring resentment, clinging to bitterness, reserving the right to a good amount of self-pity. Like for ancient Asaph, this tends to get us quickly in trouble in all major areas of life: faith, work, marriage, and parenthood. It pushes most everyone away from us, even the people we love, which only increases our loss and intensifies our grief.

We've all known people like this. We try to reason with them, to talk them down off their ledges. We warn that "you're just making things worse for yourself," and we see within them a growing cynicism toward life in general. Though they don't see it, their response to loss is like a worm that's been stepped on: coiled up and rolling around in pain. It's a natural response, but one that often leads to more pain and social isolation when prolonged.

All the same, it's *under*reacting that's more common today, especially in men: We choose not to feel the pain of grieving the loss. Again, our ability to submerge our emotions and "soldier on" is both a gift and a curse; if applied too often and for too long, this survival skill can make us two-dimensional and boring, it can alienate us from others, especially the women and children in our lives, and it's the largest contributor to "the Great Numbness."

A friend of mine just lost his mother. He says that when he thinks about her for too long, when the grief starts to flow, he "just turns the channel." That's not on the TV—it's in his heart. He switches off his emotions, and in doing so, without knowing it, he takes bite after bite out of his humanity and depletes himself of the emotional vitality he needs to be a courageous father and husband. *Courage—which is so much more than emotion—requires emotions to fuel it.*

Currently I'm reading *Letters to a Bullied Girl: Messages of Hope and Healing*. It's about two sisters, Emily and Sarah Buder, who learned that a girl they didn't even know, Olivia Gardner of northern California, was being bullied. These bright, compassionate, and courageous sisters wrote to Olivia, encouraging her to remain strong through her ordeal.

This emotionally packed volume, which is dedicated to the memory of Corinne Sides—bullied for months until she committed bullycide at age thirteen—is a collection of letters written to Olivia from people across the country: targets, former bullies, and bystanders. Many are from adults now ashamed of their behavior as adolescents.

Through this book you learn that bullying is not about anger or about conflict resolution. Bullies have no real interest in resolution—it's mostly about *contempt*, a powerful feeling of superiority and a blatant destruction of another's dignity and value. More and more studies show that bullies do not suffer from low self-esteem, which has been a common assumption. Rather they make others suffer out of their excessive self-esteem. Most bullies are enamored with themselves, and they're surprised and contemptuous when others aren't.

Ultimately, bullies are a tolerated group of supremacists, a living and breathing example of megalothymia (the desire to be recognized as superior to others—described in chapter 6). They are shadow thumites, animated people willing to take great risk in the direction and cultivation of wickedness and evil.

"I truly believe," says Corinne's mother, Rochelle, "that if other classmates or children her age had shown her kindness and compassion, she would not have felt so alone and desperate and would still be here today."[3] Courage is missing from that list of virtues, the very virtue they needed in order to *act* lovingly.

I am filled with grief from what I witness between the covers of *Letters to a Bullied Girl*. It's from this grief that my thumos is stoked. I increase my efforts and my prayers against this scourge by which, due to Mello-Yello Christianity, many of my brothers and sisters still are mostly unmoved. I work to build a team, then an army, to throw against it, to change our orientation from cowardly to courageous. There's a place for you in this battle right now.

I write a portion of each book while in some some kind of recreational vehicle. Recently, while working on this one, I was in my 1986 VW Westfalia, camping at Steward State Park in southern Oregon. While out for a walk between chapters, I came across an American Clipper motor home—and my heart instantly sank.

When I was a child, I accompanied my father on a trip to an RV dealership in Southern California. We looked at many RVs, inspecting different floor plans, and I can still remember that new RV smell mixed with his Old Spice cologne. He settled on an American Clipper for our family—until he heard the price. I saw him wrestling in his mind, *Can we afford it?*

It's risky, Tom. You've got six mouths to feed, his eyes seemed to say. He told the salesperson that he couldn't swing the payment, and we walked toward our International Travel-All to drive away. And then he did something I cannot forget. He stopped, turned quickly back toward the dealership, and I saw a look in his eye that to this day fills me with great sadness.

My quiet and charming father, a man who for most of his life wouldn't have complained if you dipped him in coal oil and set him ablaze, *wanted* that travel trailer. He longed for it with a degree of intensity and a boyish enthusiasm that was not common for him to express. His emotions were on his sleeve, a rare occurrence, this from a man who worked very hard providing for our family. He deserved that trailer. He earned it, and he didn't get it for noble reasons; he had a family to keep afloat.

If he were alive today, I tell you, I would buy him a fleet of those trailers, one for each day of the week! When I see one, I remember that look in his eye, hope dashed by disappointment borne from the burden of being a family man. And it fills me with a kind of grief that's hard to fully explain.

I used to run from these feelings, you know, "turn the channel." I can do it as well as anybody else. But I also know now that it's bad for my courage and damaging to a loving orientation toward others. So I didn't run from the grief that filled me while on that walk; I honored it. Here's an insight that really takes the worry out of grief: Don't try to fix what happened. I let myself feel its weight—I didn't change the emotional channel, and I didn't try to clean up all the emotional mess.

And we must do something with it—otherwise it will swamp us or numb us. So I gave that grief to God—not in a coward's way of avoiding pain, but in trying to redeem it for something valuable. I thanked the Lord that I had such a father to mourn, for many guys do not or did not. I thanked him for my capacity to mourn. I thanked him for caring about how I feel, and I thanked him that nothing can separate me from his love.

On the other side of mourning and grief, I find gratitude. I care more afterward. I'm more alive, animated, eager to do what's right.

To me, honoring grief goes something like this: I wish things had turned out differently. I really do. But they didn't, and there's no meaningful way that I can make things better— or else I would, or at least I would try. So I'm going to feel this pain, and I'm going to breathe deeply through it; and, God, I'm going to ask you to help me through it. I'm going to try to learn something from it and see if there's something I can be grateful for as well.

In doing so, I discover something Jesus told us: "How blest are the sorrowful; they will find consolation."[4] Consolation makes me more flexible in a soulful way, and I have a renewed energy and animation as well. In many ways it's similar to how we feel after a good physical workout: keener, stronger, yet with greater peace.

If we don't bring this deep grief to God, we will expect others to drain it for us—and this almost always will include a woman who loves us. And though she can help us part of the way, she just doesn't have the capacity to consume all of it, to redeem it. God knows some will bravely and lovingly try to consume our grief for us—but it won't work. It can't work, and it's cruel to expect a woman of goodwill to accomplish this for us.

Porn, drink, pot, meth, work—they numb our grief, which feeds the Great Numbness that kills our thumos courage. Grief always produces a scar, and these scars contain wisdom that points us back to health and healing. We need to go through the grief to get to the wisdom, health, and healing.

We need to feel our grief because we need feelings, but not just feelings, to get us moving—active, doing, present in love. Our lives are like combustible engines, which need three things to run: gas, air, and fire. Thumos is the animating fire-spark that moves the pistons up and down. Otherwise there's no reaction, no movement.

After my mother died, I asked my father about how they met. I already knew most of the facts because when your parents are immigrants and you don't have contact with other relatives the way most Americans do, you pepper your parents for information like a *60 Minutes* investigator. I wanted to go deeper into their pivotal story, hoping that my questions might make him feel better by remembering better times.

I knew they met at a dance hall in downtown Dublin, not far from the River Lithy. But what I didn't know until that talk with my father was that a man wasn't allowed to dance unless he wore suspenders. And I didn't know they stayed out nearly all night even though my dad had to work the next day, something I also did many times while dating.

My dad mentioned a man named Joe Loss. After some searching, I found a CD of his music and surprised my father.

I fibbed and said, "Dad, I picked up an old CD and was hoping you'd help me figure out who it is."

"Sure."

We put the CD in his bedroom stereo system, and within a few notes he recognized Joe Loss. He was transported back fifty years or so within just a few seconds. His eyes went someplace else. It was as if his petite date, my mother, were standing in the room with her sultry Elizabeth Taylor eyes, cigarette and all. Mom could stop traffic back then. Dad's heart must have fluttered. He stopped talking, turned to his bedroom window, and leaned heavily on the sill. His shoulders shook. I feared what I had done.

I left him alone in that room, with that music and with memories of more vital times. Times when he was trying to win the heart of a beautiful woman, before his heart attack and his triple bypass surgery. Before the inevitable loss and death that life deals us all.

Grief can be like a fever, and I watched some of it break later that day. He felt her loss that evening in a deep way that he'd had yet to do. Then and only then were his body and his mind in an enjoyable state of repose. My father played Joe Loss music until he died about two years later, basking in memories of more sure and virile times. He played them loud while he fixed up his new home, even sanding cabinet doors by hand, just one block away from mine. Sometimes he played them so loud he couldn't hear me knocking on his door.

That aptly named musician didn't bring total healing to my father. If the loss is substantial enough, then the grief never fully goes away. I doubt there ever is such a thing as complete "closure" to life-altering loss. Many today doubt that there are even stages of grief that everyone goes through.

The theory originally promoted by psychiatrist Elisabeth Kübler-Ross includes the five stages of denial, anger, bargaining, depression, and acceptance. Over the past forty years, our understanding of grief has improved, so this cycle of grief theory has been challenged as being too simplistic, too one-size-fits-all. Others have added to the dynamic of grief the tendency to feel shock and numbness (there's that word again), yearning and searching, disorganization and despair, and reorganization.

I have been unable to "get over" my father's passing, and I don't even try anymore. I don't try to "fix" this loss within me. The loss of him is something I neither clutch nor avoid. It comes and goes like the weather, and it would be as foolish to try to control these feelings as it would be to command the weather.

My father didn't know about the nuances of grief or the importance of feeling it in order to live a better life. If I'd talked to him about the stages of grief, he would have sat there politely and believed hardly a word of it. So I tricked him, not so he would feel grief but so he would feel relief, which came through grieving.

Like a lot of men, he didn't have a strong understanding of feelings. But it's significant that in order to feel grief and be liberated from its molasses-like control over life, he didn't have to collapse on the floor like some opera singer clutching a dead lover. Feeling grief for him did not mean a complete breakdown or wild mood swings. But it did mean feeling it, something he hadn't been willing to do but that snuck past him through the evocation of music, which like humor, has a way of bypassing our defenses.

We're afraid of painful emotions. They tend to give us a panicky feeling because they make us feel out of control. We like control, even when it brings us into a comfortable numbness. We like control even when it ruins our life.

I'm told by a pilot friend that if John F. Kennedy Jr. had just taken his hands off the controls, the plane would have corrected itself and flown straight and level. Instead, thinking he knew what he was doing, he kept his hands on the wheel, insisting on control while unable to discern land from sea and then corkscrewing the plane into the ocean, ending three lives. There are times we need to cease clutching so tightly and have faith that God's goodness will see us through to the other side of our grief.

If we don't do this "grief-work," then our losses will marry us to our past and we will never really be present in the present. We all know people like this. They can't have a meaningful conversation because part of them is still "back there." The lights are on but no one's home. They are wedded to the weakness that the loss produced, and they just aren't going to step up to the plate of life and partake in a more muscular form of faith and love while in that state of suspended animation. We need to feel our grief because on the other side of that experience is empathy, and empathy— the creative ability to put oneself in another's shoes and feel their suffering as if it were one's own—is a fundamental ingredient in the creation of courage.

One practice that's helpful to me in getting to the noble-thumos side of grief is looking at old pictures of my parents. As I have mentioned, my mother was both loving and troubled, and her trouble troubled me. She was phobic, and while visiting relatives in Ireland I was given a photo of her that helped me see this fact in a new light. It was taken while she was a pretty young woman, near Grafton Street in downtown Dublin during World War II.

She was well dressed, clutching her bag to her chest, and the look on her face was very suspicious and somewhat anxious. I had seen that look many times as a child. She was at times haunted by thoughts that weren't grounded in reality— a gracious way of saying she was a little crazy at times.

In seeing this picture, I felt sorrow for her. No one wants to live that way. What a burden it must have been for her. Overarching fear chews people up and spits them out. My compassion rose for her and so did my ability to love those around me. I didn't thirst for apologies from her and her sometimes sinister ways, and I didn't try to fix the problem either (another male strength/weakness.) I felt . . . relief.

While we're looking at the importance of well-handled grief, I need to bring back another topic I've been beating up on pretty hard throughout these pages. I've been hammering the Happiness Mentality because it stops us from getting to a more muscular approach toward life. So appealing, so popular, yet so damaging.

This happiness-in-perpetuity spirituality that's part of the "victorious Christian life" denies us a pathway through our grief and to noble animated spiritedness. "It prohibits the rich experience of living through painful situations, or fully feeling and being in the sadness, grief, and fear that are natural parts of human existence."[5]

I think this is one of the reasons why our conferences can strike such a deep chord: These gatherings are honest about grief. I don't stamp a smiley face where one does not belong. Men share their grief with other men—not in the feral, shadow thumos way, but in an authentic way that eventually leads to freedom and vigor. I try to give men permission to be human again.

Grief is unavoidable. "To weep at tragedy as Jesus wept is to weep at that which is inevitable. Given the vulnerability of man and the pitiless storm of the world, tragedy is bound to happen. Given the sinfulness of man and the temptation of the world to sin, tragedy is bound to happen. 'Man is born to trouble as the sparks fly upward,' Job says, and there is inevitability in the tears we shed over it. They are part of what it means to be human."[6]

Fellowship and Brotherhood

As said before, courage is not forged in isolation, and though throughout our lives we've seen this dynamic play out over and over, for some reason we miss it. Jesus sent his disciples out in twos. Marines are rarely sent out in fewer than twos. Mormon missionaries knock on our door in pairs. New York's Guardian Angels, of subway fame, patrol in no fewer than twos. Joshua and Caleb were able to hold off popular disdain and keep their courage flowing because they leaned on each other.

Isolation, eventually, makes us low on courage. If you don't think you need other people to lean on, you're pretending, and you're not in the battle. Thumos has its fans—and its enemies. We need a band of brothers if we're serious about a courageous faith.

Unfortunately, to their own peril, Christian men have rejected fellowship, partly because they have been expected to practice it the way women do, instead of the more earthy way men prefer. I saw this in a small group I was asked to join a few years ago. The guys were mostly in their forties and fifties, and they'd done fellowship groups before. If this one was going to be like all the others, they wanted no part of it. They expressed anger toward and disdain for some of their past groups, citing a phoniness that made them feel they simply were wasting their time.

These men also didn't like it when someone tapped as the official leader felt free to preach at them while at the same time revealing nothing meaningful about his own life and struggles. They didn't want another expectation of pasting a grin onto their lives and pretending everything was okay when it wasn't. They wanted it to "be real," which is what a *fellowship* group should be in the first place.

Having traveled the country now for many years in ministry, I can tell you that churches with a pastor who expresses noble thumos have more men in attendance. Noble thumos calls to other guys. It's like a high-pitched frequency to dogs: they can hear it, and they respond to it. It's a kind of porch light to summer bugs; they're attracted to it in a visceral way.

Intuition tells me that guys are attracted to thumos ministers because they know on some level they speak similar languages. And they sense that their nature will be appreciated, not condemned. They know on some level that this guy, unlike others they've known, can be trusted and that he will love them in a non-smothering way. Such a man will care about them and uphold their dignity and grant some level of autonomy, which so often gets mistaken for pride. *We need autonomy (the result of a functioning will) to stand against a crowd and for what God values.*

I'm convinced this is one reason Jesus did not have a hard time attracting male followers. He actually had to turn some away from his inner circle. I think about how he honored the thumos of two men in particular—James and his brother John—by giving them the name *Boanerges*, which means "Sons of Thunder."[7] We don't know for certain what Jesus was angling at here, but we have reason to believe he was celebrating their animated and intense character. I suspect that such a nickname put the other disciples at ease as they realized their thumos would be handled well also.

As I speak at different churches I keep a close eye on how they're trying to reach men. Within a half hour or so, I usually have a pretty good sense for the health of a men's group. The healthy ones are where guys are animated, loving, and free to express what they think, to disagree with each other without the world falling apart in the process. You see iron sharpening iron during these moments, and I'm filled with a great sense of gratitude when I see it. And I also get to hear from men about what they would like to see regarding fellowship but don't get to experience. So here are some thoughts.

The more fruitful men's gatherings I've been part of are places where deep and robust laughter is heard. C. S. Lewis recognized this powerful soul glue: "There's no sound I like better than adult male laughter."[8] Robust laughter not only draws guys together, but women are attracted to male laughter and humor as well. In fact, while it's not in the top three attributes men look for in a woman, a good sense of humor consistently is in the top three reasons a woman will be attracted to a man.

I've mentioned that men yearn to do fellowship differently than women. Though you might think that should warrant the Most Obvious Statement of the Year award, this commonsense reality isn't recognized in many churches or para-church organizations.

For example, many of us aren't crazy about touching one another, especially if we don't know the guy we're being forced to touch. This doesn't mean we've "repressed our emotional development." It doesn't mean we don't care about each other.

At the beginning of most men's conferences, I put the entire group at ease when I say, "At no time during this presentation am I going to ask you to hold the hand of the man next to you, especially the kind where you interlock your fingers!" Men laugh and clap with appreciation because they just don't like doing it—and that's okay. We shake each other's hands, not hold them (unless we've been shot in combat or are having a colonoscopy).

I can't really speak for our sisters when they get together, but I know that when women are present during male fellowship, men aren't honest. They become painfully difficult to reach as they stiffen up and start thinking they have to give the "right" answer—that is, what the women deem right and appropriate. Men don't come clean, and they sure don't feel safe expressing grief. Suppressing it keeps them emotionally numb and often cowardly.

More Earthiness

Men also gravitate toward music that has some bite to the lyrics and the beat. I remember one conference where between my sessions the ministry leaders played Amy Grant music. And what was remarkable to me was that I had to go upstairs to the control booth and point this out.

"It's a men's conference—do you have any other music you could play? Do you have any U2?"

The sound guy was bewildered. He didn't grasp why Amy Grant wouldn't be a great music choice. I wish I were making this up. We've got a long way to go.

Most men like earthiness, an attribute of thumos. We prefer stone to vinyl. We prefer to be outside rather than inside. I want to spend more money on outdoor furniture and landscaping than my wife does. I would rather buy extra camping equipment than another leather couch.

When God first created man, he named him for the dust of the ground, *adamah*.[9] Women were created from the bone of man. This could have something to do with why guys prefer to be closer to what is earthy. Men are more repelled by sermons and services that are perfect, clean, and scripted. We like to sweat more, cleave wood more, touch brick more.

Some male earthiness is vulgar and raunchy. Some of it isn't, even though it's often mistaken for what's sinful. A great example is the preaching of Chuck Swindoll, one of my radio favorites, because he speaks to men in ways other preachers don't.

Once, referring to the sons of Issachar, Swindoll said, "[General] Patton would say they had guts. You'd say at work, they had balls." He was speaking at a men's conference, and the talk was broadcast during his national radio show.

That same year he talked about his prostate exam, and he drew a lot of laughter. "Got through prostate, checked out great. I bragged about that to Cynthia about three hours. 'I've got a great prostate.' She said, 'Get a life, honey.' "

Swindoll was removed from one large network that had a hard time with his earthiness. They wrote, regarding the "sons of Issachar" comment, that it was language "unbecoming of a pastor," that it was "crude and vulgar." Regarding his exam, they said they found it "unacceptable to broadcast Chuck Swindoll's recounting of the length of the finger of his doctor and describing it in his body while checking his prostate. This is both crude and offensive." (I'm waiting for Christian radio to give us "Christian Weather Updates," where every day is sunny and 75 degrees, with a light wind out of the north that carries a hint of honeysuckle.)

But most men outside of professional ministry don't think Swindoll was offensive. Most men think he's being real, and they're drawn to him for it. I listen to him and the few who are like him *because* of the earthiness, which is soul-feeding insight for living.

Many Christians seem to have the spiritual gift of being easily offended by common male standards. They must have a terrible time when God and his chosen servants use graphic and earthy language in the Bible. For instance:

You stupid Galatians! You must have been bewitched. . . . Can it be that you are so stupid?[10]

Why don't these agitators, obsessive as they are about circumcision, go all the way and castrate themselves![11]

How *dare* Paul express anger in this manner?

I feel Chuck Swindoll's pain. While speaking at a men's retreat, I described an act of bullying that I witnessed in high school. A healthy young man was throwing things and speaking cruelly to a young man with Down's syndrome. While the healthy guy tormented him, the mentally challenged guy was naked and dripping wet, so angry and fearful that all he could do was moan loudly. It makes me sick when I think about it today, and I tell this story to help get men to play their part against adolescent bullying.

In describing this situation at the retreat, I said, "That poor kid was going through hell." And I later was criticized by the "spiritually mature men" in the group for using the "language of the people." They were—grab a hankie—offended.

Spiritually mature? I think thumos-dead would be more accurate. The word *hell* described what that young man was going through, which is easy to ignore when it's not you enduring the torment. And what's more telling to me about these men's "spiritual maturity" is the word *hell* being more bothersome and memorable and grief-producing than other words I used, such as:

- On average, 160,000 American kids a day stay home from school due to bullying.
- Eighty-five percent of school shooters interviewed said they brought a gun to school and murdered indiscriminately due to being bullied, sometimes for years.
- We now have a new word in our vocabulary to contemplate and mourn—*bullycide*, which is suicide in response to bullying that happens across the globe.
- One of the main bullied groups is physically and mentally challenged kids—and the church has made no formal effort to help such children until now.
- Children who are bullied are more likely to suffer from depression and related mental problems later in life.

Nearly two years later, I have not heard from one of these "spiritually mature" men about being part of the solution to this problem. They haven't even offered to join our Protectors Prayer Partners to pray for the kids whose parents contact us, seeking our help and God's help to rescue their child from the anguish of bullying.

I think spiritual maturity is found, in part, through an active approach toward love, toward self-extension and sacrifice for others. I don't think it's in finding offense wherever offense can possibly be found. People who are so easily offended—the ones frequently held up by the church as being so wise and mature, the ones who "live by all the rules"—really, *what do they do?*

I grew up among such men. Some do hardly anything meaningful or truly redemptive, but my, how they follow the rules. The rules mean everything, even when they lead to spiritual death, cowardice, and arrogance in the keepers. Their sons and daughters can't wait to get away from their faith, yet these fathers can't understand why.

Men, I can tell you why: Your faith is lifeless. It's boring. It's ugly and twisted and unloving. It's the jerky gyrations of a misspent life, of needless worry and heavy burdens that wear out our spiritual knees. It overlooks or rejects the truly important things while majoring on the minors, and the people you call heathen see this deception better than you.

How's that for irony? But I know you—I used to be one of you. You will not listen until some kind of two-by-four cracks you across the head. That will be God's grace in disguise, and even then some of you will never see it, will never change.

Your gnat-straining drives people, especially men, from the church. You will let your minds get caught on one accurate, powerful, and righteous word yet completely ignore much weightier matters such as "justice and mercy"—this is exactly what Jesus condemned with the strongest of language. Your actions, and even more your *inaction*, make it plain that you don't care about establishing justice and mercy, and so you miss out on the joy of helping others.

You won't open your wallet to help little kids who are being bullied, and you won't pray for them, but on a dime you're ready to point your finger and call down judgment upon the ones with some courage and on the ones who with fear and trembling are seeking to give and to serve lovingly. How spiritual you must feel, you mighty warriors.

Who do you think you are? Why do you expect people to "clean up their act" around you? Get over yourself! What's wrong with using "the language of the people," anyway—aren't they the ones we're trying to reach?

I agree with Billy Sunday on this one:

> What do I care if some puffy-eyed little dibbly-dibbly preacher goes tibbly-tibblying around because I use plain Anglo-Saxon words? I want people to know what I mean and that's why I try to get down to where they live.[12]

It's pathetic that petty little rules manage to keep people on the sidelines of life. This is another big reason men in particular aren't crazy about church culture: We define our spirituality and faithfulness by what we don't do instead of by what we actually do. What are evangelical men known for? They *don't* swear (except in private), they *don't* drink (except on vacation, away from other church people who might tattle), they *don't* get angry (except at home or in the car), they *don't* see bad movies (except online or in hotel rooms).

What are we known for *doing*? Other than pointing toward heaven after a touchdown, a goal, or a home run, not very much. Aside from the don'ts, it's not the things we do that we're known for but the things we say.

Why are we known for what we don't do? Because what we *don't* do comprises 80 percent or more of our messages. We are caught today just like the Pharisees were, in a personal piety trap. Again, defensive spirituality is so much easier than offensive spirituality. In the former, you measure your spiritual growth by what you don't do. But even the heathen can do that—it's just a matter of where people decide to set the bar.

Muscular love, offensive and disruptive, is seen in what we do. In sports, defense destroys while offense creates, which is why as a coach I spend far more time working on offense. It takes thumos to go on the offensive; the rules aren't as clear, and it's more conspicuous, so there's more criticism. A lot of offense is figuring it out as you go, while still moving forward—very much like vibrant faith and love.

We need spirituality with some earth under its nails in order for imperfect fellowship and brotherhood to grow. We need our spirituality to be connected to the full spectrum of our existence, which isn't happening right now, largely because of the Happiness Requirement. This taskmaster says the tone of our lives should be and remain *happy*, and if it's not, then there's something wrong with us. If we're unhappy, we need to work double time to get ourselves back to a happy place.

I'm no fan of pain, and I usually don't go out of my way to bring it into my life, but I've learned that prohibiting pain, and stuffing dark emotions, and pretending I'm not having grieving thoughts . . . all of this prevents me from living a richer life and from connecting deeply to others.

People who don't allow themselves to visit the dark side of life may appear happy but aren't soulful. They aren't creative, which is essential to courageous living, because through creativity we find a place for will to flow. Insisting on constant happiness (no matter how fake) stops us from being both sensitive and receptive to the suffering of others—it halts courageous and loving faith.

For church to be a place where courage is grown, it needs to become a place where pain and grief are expressed. Not just from those who go there, but also as expressed in the Bible, and as expressed in music. It needs to be a place where we know we can bring our sorrows, and we will know this from the songs we sing, the sermons we hear, and even from the décor and architecture that surrounds us.

Mike Ellis, a pioneer in men's ministry, sent me some ideas for ministers that help create authentic fellowship for men:

- Be real. Let people see the actual human being inside you. Most times that will occur through your personal stories.
- Talk like normal people talk. I didn't grow up in the church, so I don't understand when you talk with a Christian accent.
- Use humor. If you don't make me laugh, I'm probably going to tune you out. By the way, the best humor is revealed through your everyday life.
- Don't tell me what to think. Lead me on the journey toward truth, but let me reach my own conclusions. In other words, don't try to sell it.
- Be honest. If I think you're credible, there's a better chance I'll think your message is credible.
- Avoid being too polished. In fact, I love it when you leave your prepared statements and share anything off the cuff.
- Reveal your weaknesses. As silly as it may seem, it makes me smile when I hear about your mistakes. It helps me to respect the areas where you are gifted.
- Be brief. Shorter is better. I'm probably only going to remember one or, at the most, two things that you say.
- Make me smart. I don't care how smart you are, but I like it when you make me feel smart. That's easier when

you use small words and make it easy for me to apply what you're teaching.

- Tell me why I should care. Help me understand why I should listen. If you don't help me understand why it's relevant to my life, I'll be thinking about my next blog post or my next tee time or my favorite '80s slow-dance songs.

Fellow ministers, let's avoid the sinful temptation to clean up life's innate rough edges. Don't try to explain too much. Leave some mystery. Jesus directly answered three questions out of more than one hundred seventy posed to him as recorded in the four Gospels. Why do we feel so compelled to respond exhaustively to every query?

Mix the familiar with the odd. Authenticity and earthiness bring spirituality back to reality, back to our soul-side, where thumos lives as well. They enhance and help explain the ironies of life and keep us from the profane enticement to release life's tensions, the ones that keep us from spinning into heresy and insanity. We need paradox in our faith in order for it to compel us, to feed our thumos.

Courage and Faith

That courage is inseparable from faith wasn't always news to ministers and leaders. Past generations had a better handle on this than we do today. To quote John Bunyan again in *Pilgrim's Progress*: "There are two things that they have need to be in possession of, that go in pilgrimage; courage and an unspotted life. If they have not courage they can never hold on their way."[13]

"You of little faith," Jesus said to Peter. "Why did you doubt?"[14] He said this while standing on and walking on water at night. He said this just after Peter walked on water for a few miraculous steps. He said this while Peter was sinking into the water, after he cried, "Lord, save me!"[15] Peter likely knew how to swim. He probably could have saved himself. But fear has a way of clouding our thinking just as it can kill our faith and our courage.

In all the turmoil of this scene, we forget the answer to the question Jesus poses—he already said it a few verses earlier. We should also note that while he's asking this question of Peter, in general, he asks of us all: *Why do you doubt me in light of all I've done, all I can do?*

We all lack faith. Let's take a closer look at why.

Peter sees a Savior Man walking toward him on the water. He thinks it's a ghost, and the group cries out in terror. Their minds (a miracle is taking place before my eyes, it's true) and their hearts (this is frightening, this is scary) were engaged. Then Peter, uniquely showing a tremendous display of thumos, says, "Lord, if that's you, tell me to come to you on the water." Jesus says to come, and he does.

But why does Peter lose his faith and in the process start to sink? I think the answer is found in the first words Jesus tells the boatload of frightened men: "Take courage! It is I. Don't be afraid."[16]

He doesn't say take *my* courage. He means for them to stoke their God-given capacity for flexing this pivotal virtue.

Peter takes courage, which bolsters his faith. But then he remembers the wind and the waves and becomes afraid again. Fear suddenly buries his courage and swamps his faith.

Not only can fear and cowardice drain faith, they can also steal it away completely. Jesus, in his parable of the sower,[17] said that certain people just don't have a "rootedness" or "staying power," and they walk away from their faith when the going gets tough. Some people have nothing within them to help them stand firm, to grip and hold on to what's essential to their spiritual growth, to keep them from being pushed over. Courage is a nonnegotiable ingredient in the terra firma of our faith, part of the structure that gives it mooring, footing, and action.

Think about the manner in which Jesus died, and I'm not just talking about the crucifixion. I'm talking about how it came about. He chose the twelve disciples knowing full well that one would betray him—with the feigned affection of a kiss. And he did it anyway. And in Gethsemane he was abandoned by his friends, who fell asleep on him. Twice.[18]

Have you ever had your friends abandon you during a tough time, while you took a controversial stand? I have, and it's gut-wrenching. It tears your chest out. You feel like the walking dead. It's bewildering, and at times it's like there's literally nothing under your feet when you walk. It's hard to breathe. Your throat chokes up. You feel utterly alone—no one anywhere. It's terror-producing, and I'm convinced that it somehow shortens our lives.

Yet in Gethsemane, where Jesus admits to those closest to him that horror and dismay were engulfing him ("My heart is ready to break with grief"), he still persevered. Not because he followed his heart—which clearly failed him, by his own admission—but because of an inner heat and a higher calling, a cause that transcended him: his Father's will.[19]

In Gethsemane, utterly alone, isolated from others to help build his courage, and feeling so distant from his Abba, he forged ahead, alone. We mortals are just not capable of such lone-courage living. We need others. We need fellowship. An isolated man is not a courageous man, at least for very long, and especially not while on an important mission.

Skeptics ask: Why are all those miracles from Jesus so important to you? When it comes to thumos courage and free will, they mean everything. Jesus *chose* the cross. Again, suffering in and of itself is not courageous. It's electing to suffer that puts Jesus' death in the pantheon of deaths. It's the manner in which he died—his choosing not to slay his murderers through whatever miracle he could have performed—that haunts history. Unlike most prisoners of war, Jesus had a choice. With supernatural power and free will in play, the manner of his death is inexpressibly miraculous.

It's important to point out once more that there are about two dozen examples of cowardice in the Bible and about two dozen examples of courage, including instances of personal bravery—from Deborah in leading Israel's armies,[20] from Jael in killing Sisera,[21] and from Esther, in convincing the king to save her people.[22] The word for *courage* itself appears at least ten times in the New Testament, and there is no reference among them to God reaching into people's lives and *giving them courage*. We *are* told three times to take courage[23] and we're told three times to keep up or hold on to our courage.[24] Paul even says he hopes that he will have sufficient courage so that "now as always Christ will be exalted in my body, whether by life or by death."[25]

I have longed to find a New Testament example of an anointing of courage, a time and a place where God intervened and turned a coward, like I can sometimes be, into a real champ. I haven't found it. There isn't one, unless my understanding of an anointing is wrong.

One definition of *anointing* is to "equip for service."[26] Courage, I've concluded, is a virtue that we are called to exercise, as seen in the life of Joshua. In fact, the Bible shows us people known for courage acting cowardly, such as Saul and David. This gives me hope, which gives me courage.

Perhaps it comes down to this: Similar to other virtues and through the power of the Holy Spirit, we can choose to be courageous—or not. I *have* prayed for courage in my own life, and I've prayed that God would give the people I love courage as well. Of the times when I've felt more courageous after praying, I think one reason why is that through prayer I've found a comforter, an advocate, and I'm reminded of how someone truly loves me. And then I'm also reminded of the times when Jesus went forward with boldness and courage, which frees and ignites me to do the same.

After I'd spoken at a church in Oregon, a woman came up to me and said my message on being courageous was about her. She said friends have told her for years that she was more courageous than your average Joan, and that she had banished the word *nice* from her vocabulary. "I don't like that word," she said with a powerful grin and happy eyes.

But then something remarkable happened. This strong woman teared up. She shed similar tears to those I've wept when I've come across someone else who sees what I see, who confirms both my conclusion and the antidote to our lack of courageous faith. She had been wandering in the wilderness for a long time, and my talk confirmed within her that she wasn't alone and that she wasn't crazy. Because that's what happens, eventually: Thumos people think they're just plain nuts sometimes. You feel like the odd one out, a pilgrim without a homeland, because frankly, you aren't welcomed by the keepers of the Script.

It's the men and women of thumos—the malcontents, misfits, visionaries, prophets, those wielders of double-bladed axioms—who always have and always will be the ones who shake the world's foundation by their faith in action. And during their brief appearance on this poorly lit stage with many trapdoors, this better breed is among the most widely reviled and misunderstood—even toward one another. Later, upon their passing, after the ripples of their disruptive faith have been absorbed, they're adored—irony of ironics.

They are, as the author of Hebrews put it, "too good for a world like this,"[27] exactly like their fierce and disruptive hero, the best-kept secret of the Bible, Jesus Christ.

Notes

1. Peck, *Further Along the Road Less Traveled*, 50–52.
2. John Bunyan, *Pilgrim's Progress*, W. R. Owens, ed. (Oxford University Press, Oxford's World Classics, 2003).
3. Olivia Gardner, with Emily and Sarah Buder, *Letters to a Bullied Girl: Messages of Healing and Hope* (New York: Harper Paperbacks, 2008).
4. Matthew 5:4 NEB
5. Gerald G. May, *Will and Spirit: A Contemplative Psychology* (New York: HarperOne, 1982),14.
6. Buechner, *Telling the Truth*, 56.
7. Mark 3:17
8. Walter Hooper, "IX: The Inklings" in *C. S. Lewis: A Complete Guide to His Life and Works* (New York: HarperCollins, 1996), 16.
9. See Genesis 2:7.
10. Galatians 3:1–3 NEB
11. Galatians 5:12 MESSAGE
12. In Clifford Putney, *Muscular Christianity: Manhood and Sports in Protestant America*, 1880–1920 (Cambridge, MA: Harvard University Press, 2001), 60.
13. Bunyan, *Pilgrim's Progress*.
14. Matthew 14:31
15. Matthew 14:30
16. Matthew 14:27
17. See Matthew 13; Mark 4; Luke 8.
18. See Matthew 26; Mark 14.
19. For example, see Mark 14:36.
20. See Judges 4.
21. See Judges 4:18–22.
22. See Esther 4.
23. Matthew 14:27; Mark 6:50; Acts 23:11
24. Acts 27:22, 25; Hebrews 3:6
25. Philippians 1:20
26. For example, see Acts 10:38.
27. Hebrews 11:38 NEB

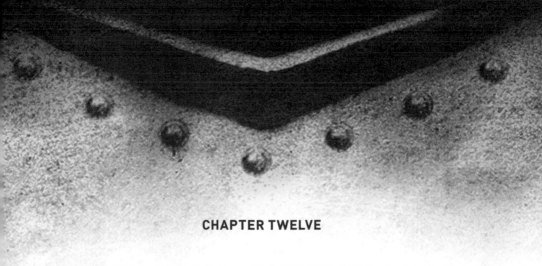

CHAPTER TWELVE

START SMALL, BUT TAKE A HILL

*Where are they now who represented
genius, valor, self-sacrifice,
the invisible heavenly world to these? Are they dead?
Has the high ideal died out of them?
Will it be better with the new generation?*
(RALPH WALDO EMERSON)[1]

*Christian brethren, this is life:
temptation, trial, struggle, conflict, possible victory—
the strenuous life. You cannot cowardly give it up.*
(HENRY C. KING)

We've long been taught about the necessities of a renewed mind[2] and a sincere heart.[3] My hope with this book is that we will also discover how essential is a noble, adventurous, abundant-living, hope-growing, God-glorifying, joy-producing *thumos*, which helps launch both our changed minds and regenerated hearts into courageous action.

The main purpose of this book has been to help us do our part to forge and then unfetter a more courageous faith—which frees and empowers us to get to the good deeds the apostle James and others exhort us to complete—and to extol greater depth, strength, and staying power through this virtue that underpins all others. Faith divorced from deeds is as lifeless as a corpse.[4] True religion is *not* found *only* in what we don't do.[5]

We've observed that James reminds us of a justice mandate to our faith: We are to help those who are weak, those who are being exploited by the strong. This requires boldness of will, a capacity that most everyone possesses but which must be trained, seasoned, and maintained. We ignore this command at our own peril. For example, Isaiah told us God is displeased with worship that does not include the work of justice.[6] Through Amos, the Lord is even more direct:

> Take away from Me the noise of your songs;
> I will not even listen to the sound of your harps.
> But let justice roll down like waters
> And righteousness like an ever-flowing stream.[7]

Writes Buechner: "Any preacher who does not speak [these particular truths] in his own right, naming names, including his own name; any religious person who does not heave them at the injustice and unrighteousness of his own time and of himself, runs the risk of being irrelevant, sentimental, a bag of wind."[8]

Have you ever heard the topic of justice mentioned during a worship service? I haven't, and I have tried to envision what would happen if it were.

Imagine around thirty minutes into worship, as only the violins continue, the well-dressed leader points to the huge screen behind her and says:

> This girl on the screen, her name is Maya. Maya's been a sex slave in Thailand for more than four years. She's only fourteen.
>
> Maya was stolen soon after her parents died. At the brothel she is threatened with beatings and even death if she tries to escape. She's forced to take drugs that numb her soul. She now has multiple diseases.

We have a chance tonight to help Maya and others like her. There are people ready and able to courageously rescue her and others from her prison. . . .

What do you think the response would be as the strings gently weep, as God's pretty people sway back and forth? Since I've never experienced such a biblical approach, I'm left with only a guess. But it's an educated one.

I suspect most would say to themselves or to the person next to them, "What's this? *Rescue?* Who are these people, liberals? I came here to worship the *Lord*." Putting Maya's world on the big screen is too jarring for low-thumos people like us. We'd probably have to offer counseling in the sanctuary wings for those who'd just had their "peace in the Lord" stolen by the Lord.

Seriously, can we not hear what God says? If there's no justice, then all the shiny staging and lighting, all the glossy lyrics and lipstick aren't only displeasing—they're *appalling* to him. Our lack of intervention on behalf of those who need justice amounts to false sincerity. A lie.[9]

Yet at the same time, I know that this approach to worship *could* take off like wild fire. The potential *is* there—it just needs to be called out through courageous leadership, through a more muscular understanding of what it means to be pastoral. We need a band of the bold, the company of the courageous, to take this hill. Stand against the Script and put courage back on our radar.

The worship leaders I know and the worship leaders I meet are chafing. Our lack of faith in action is driving them nuts. Most of the people who physically stand and raise their hands to the music remain soulfully seated. They are like Fourth of July sparklers: They give the appearance of heat and animation, but they're nothing more than pretty. They burn, but they don't keep you warm and they make horrible guide lamps. All sizzle, no substance.

Courage to Say No

It's a pivotal day when those of us who are low on courage admit it. There's no shame in this admission, but instead liberation, purpose, and joy. What would be shameful, indeed sinful, is if we allowed ourselves to stay in that state of soul. Our lives provide ample opportunities to express courageous faith, and one of the best ways to begin this journey is learning to say no.

An inability to say no is mere submission. Jesus submitted to the will of his Father, but not to the will of those around him. Although we've been trained to believe otherwise, submission to others is not always servanthood. It doesn't make us loving—it makes us weak and ineffective.

Without a viable ability to say no, we cannot be strong and courageous. Thinking everything has to be yes makes us avoid people—avoid life—and this is cowardice in disguise. Eventually, failure to say no on behalf of ourselves and others leads to abdication, resentment, and cynicism, all of which undercut the production of thumotic action.

One of the underreported reasons why many people cannot produce a courageous *no* is that they do not yet possess a strong sense of self, which is vitally connected to the understanding of soul emphasized throughout these pages. They don't have enough soul—an authenticity of living that's tied to the real world, with real vision, clarity, and grit— from which to draw courage, the kind that Jesus wanted his disciples to pull out of themselves on the choppy Sea of Galilee.

They also have the wrong image of themselves, the most notable being that they're "really nice people," which, they've been told, is the pinnacle of Christian virtue. They have a false image of God in human form. Despite the mountain of evidence to the contrary, they still contend that Jesus did not quarrel, disagree, speak bluntly, create firm boundaries, or otherwise disrupt the world around him.

They somehow believe that Jesus was a wave-free zone, and people who don't roil the water don't say no. For many of us, not being seen as "nice" feels like a death blow—that's one of the reasons we've created this fictitious Jesus. If he didn't have to go through the suffering and live with the heat that follows forging a courageous no, then we don't have to either.

The sooner we retrain ourselves, the more we will grow spiritually, which will further fortify our ability to say no when saying no is the right thing to do. I think the ability to say no on behalf of others is one of the more distinctive traits of male love. Men like the incisive nature of a redemptive *no*, which is why on the whole we're more attracted to martial occupations. This is a big part of what might be described as kingly energy.

From the male perspective, the masculine expression of love at its best is supportive and nurturing but without absorption of another into our self. It keeps boundaries clear and visible while it cleaves and cuts. This is why men are more prone to respect the autonomy, the individuality, of another person, and sometimes this respect is mistaken for lack of care. Male love says to another person, while saying no: "You need help, and I'm here to give it, but I respect you as an individual. I don't expect you to be like me. Remain who you are as you accept my help. I have no intention of absorbing you. (In fact I can't even stomach the thought.)"

So when a man helps another man, he'll put his arm around a shoulder or his hand on a shoulder—supportive but not smothering. This is different from many feminine styles of love, and it has nothing to do with right and wrong. They are complementary.

The ability to say no without feeling woozy leads to the issue of ownership. Who are you? Who owns you? If you think your parents or church or culture owns you, then eventually you'll end up carrying out their will and living by their definition of you. They usually will lay claims upon you that override your will with theirs. If the church is authentically asking you to adopt God's will instead of your own, then that's a different story. But the church can often ask you to take on the will of its leaders disguised as God's. Sometimes this is done out of ignorance, and sometimes it can be a thumos-crushing form of spiritual dissimulation.

Again, *God* owns you, and he gives this ownership back to you along with his love and guidance. This dual stewardship, so to speak, creates a solid level of responsibility that's essential to courageous faith. No one else is responsible for your life, and the sooner we come to this sobering conclusion, the sooner we become our whole selves. And the sooner we become whole selves, the sooner our capacity for courage increases.

Keeping ownership between yourself and God leads to the realization that you are valuable, that you matter, and that you are needed right now, today. Without this rugged understanding of the gift of your life (being, existence) and the gift of living (animation, spiritedness), you won't take your life and the lives of others as seriously as you should. It is the seriousness of life—the "drama," as Scott Peck put it—that causes us to embrace and celebrate the miracle of living, which in turn feeds and fires our thumos courage.

I've been told that the number one event that turns a non-voting citizen into a voting one is home ownership. Such people now feel they have something to lose, some flesh in the fight. This causes them to take action, to become more animated and involved. Likewise, when we take ownership of our lives, we're prone to greater vitality. Having something valuable at stake brings an accompanying vigor, and herein we also start to see the value of others more clearly, and so our capacity for courageous faith and love increases.

Saying no is a discipline of the courageous. But like most new things, it will feel odd at first, usually bringing a vague sense of being ill at ease. Warns Henry T. Close:

> I will feel guilty, anxious, uneasy, frightened, as though in some strange way I have betrayed something or someone. If I understand in advance that this will happen, it will make it easier to handle. . . . I will need lots of practice in small areas, making sure that I do not invite people to take advantage of me. . . . Every time I succeed, I will feel better and stronger, and it will be a bit easier the next time. All of this will be difficult at first, in the little things as well as the big ones, but in a sense my whole life is at stake. . . . I regard people who say No as more real than people who don't—and I like real people.[10]

There's that word again, *real*. We don't like people who aren't authentic because the soul deficiency we sense within them makes them less trustworthy, powerful, and redemptive.

But What About Our Weaknesses?

If you're like me, something has been bugging you while reading this book. It's a topic that's very dear to (if not an obsession for) many evangelicals. It's *weakness*.

If you're unfamiliar with evangelical culture, let me fill you in on something. We talk a lot about weakness. We talk so much about it that around us you might feel like a pretty bad person if you don't feel weak all the time.

The reason we emphasize weakness is because the Bible emphasizes it. However, we've done something unusual to the paradox of being strong through weakness: We've largely redefined what it means, and as is often the case when we don't understand or appreciate paradox, we've overemphasized weakness at the expense of traits like boldness and courage.

We receive this view from Paul, who writes that he asked God to take away a physical thorn in his flesh. Three times he asked and was refused.

> [God said,] "My grace is sufficient for you, for my power is made perfect in weakness." Therefore I [Paul] will boast all the more gladly about my weaknesses, so that Christ's power may rest on me.[11]

In a startling revelation, Paul even says he finds joy and pride in his weakness.

We all have struggles that others don't. For example, have you ever heard someone pray about a problem that doesn't hinder you? I remember hearing one man pray about an issue with a co-worker. It wasn't a big one—just the garden variety that pops up in most every workplace. I said to him, "Why don't you have a talk with the guy; you know, don't yell or anything, just talk with him. Tell him you don't like what he's doing, that it hurts your ability to do your job."

He replied that he couldn't, that he wasn't strong enough to have such a straightforward conversation. And then, remarkably, he said it was good he was weak in this way, because he would be kept humble while God would be seen as strong in the situation. He never actually did have the conversation with the person hindering his work. His weakness remained weak, and he continued to hold that condition as a badge of spiritual honor. Would you want such a man as your boss? Your attorney? Your spouse? Your pastor?

Most of the time such an interaction is within my capacity. I can do it. I'm not crazy about potentially tense conversations, but I can handle them. It's a strength I have that this guy didn't, and my attempts to help him through a weakness and into strength fell on deaf ears.

So how can I reconcile the Bible's clarion call to greater strength and loving courage toward others with Paul's words about boasting in weakness so that Christ's power can rest upon us? Being a believer can't mean I have to pretend I'm weak when I'm not. I'm not going to pretend I don't have strengths when I do—that's just a churchy way of lying.

These strengths are helpful to me and to those I care about and minister to—*should* I actually abandon things I do well? Some Christians think they should.

Gary Haugen says this about it:

> Do I have to let go of my sources of strength—my gifts, my passions, my training, my expertise? No. . . . Those are good things from God. I think [God] simply wants us to take them on a more demanding climb, where we will actually need his help, and where he delights to grant it.[12]

We need to embrace our strengths, to be bold and courageous while at the same time thrusting ourselves into situations where we know we will face our weakness. We need to reach beyond what we're currently capable of doing, trusting that God's grace will be with us when we do and that his power will come to rest upon us. This opens doors to him in our lives.

Just as I'm stronger in some ways than others, I'm weaker in some ways as well. I don't have to pray for strength to talk to a troubling colleague, but I would need to pray for strength if I had to lead people into war. And if our campaign were successful, I could boast only in having received power come to rest upon me as a gift.

I know a man who mentors juvenile delinquents. They have problems he cannot fully comprehend and burdens he cannot remove. He's weak in that way, as most of us are. So he prays that God will strengthen him and give him the right words to say or not say. God has helped him be strong, bold, and courageous as he extends himself in love for others. His weakness is not an excuse to stop but a reminder to bow and to press forward.

Courage in Little Things

I am very proud of my friend Bob Just, founder of Concerned Fathers Against Crime (C-FAC), which helps single men, fathers, and their sons patrol their neighborhood with cell phones, flashlights, and a tangible concern for others. They don't carry guns, and they don't get out of their cars if they see something suspicious. They call the police and let them handle it.

Bob started C-FAC fourteen years ago, and he's worked hard to fine-tune his unique program, a movement really, in order to bring justice and mercy and order to his community. One of my sons and I have been on patrol with C-FAC, driving up and down the streets of Grants Pass, Oregon. At first I was fearful of being a bridge person, of standing in the gap between righteousness and lawlessness. I didn't want to do it, but the men I went with gave me the courage to lean into this gap and then eventually, surprisingly, enjoy it. That's what brotherhood was meant to do. I felt the martial spirit grow within me, and I found the experience exhilarating—I wanted more of this noble-thumos work.

Bob knows a lot about finding courage, and so I asked him to share his insights into what hinders people, especially men, from bringing courage into faith and civic life: "Despite the pressing crime issues in our community, developing and launching Concerned Fathers Against Crime (C-FAC) wasn't easy. One of the biggest problems we faced was simply getting large numbers of men to commit to the task at hand. It didn't seem to matter that we were only asking them for a few nights of patrolling a year. They still held back. Over time we discovered the reason: Fear. I'm not referring to fear of bodily harm—a minimal risk during a cell phone patrol—but to the more subtle fears we all experience, like the fear of adding one more responsibility to our busy schedule. Or simply that ever-present fear of the unknown.

"It's strange to observe this in men who would without hesitation give their lives for their wives and children. This is not about cowardice. It's about things that we fear will get in the way of our larger responsibilities—like a missed moment to play catch with our ten-year-old son because we took work home from the office. Stress and worry too often block us from the life we want to live.

"The greatest of these kinds of fears in my experience is the one that says we have no time to spare. That single fear can become a powerful stronghold, blocking God's guidance to actions that could change our lives. Most men share this kind of fear due to the pressures to provide for their families and to protect them from unforeseen danger, including spiritual danger. There's a reason we have traditionally accepted life's priorities as God, country, family: because without God, both country and family are lost, and without country our families are set adrift in a chaotic and dangerous world.

"On a much smaller scale, men know they should not let their communities be taken over by gangs and drugs. They know law enforcement is overwhelmed. They know they should do something but they don't know what, and they're not sure the time they could invest would make any real difference. So the C-FAC board's first battle against fear rested on convincing men that if each one gave a little of his time, the accumulated team impact would be real and lasting. In other words, that they could make a difference.

"The concept of a 'band of brothers' digs deep in our souls. Our hearts yearn for a team to join and a righteous fight to win. However, these days most men are loners out of necessity rather than choice. Mature men don't have many opportunities to be on a real team. We are busy with our family lives and our careers. Still, our warrior instinct knows battles are won the same way football games are won—with a self-sacrificial team effort. For victory to be achieved, we know we must all pull our weight.

"Unit cohesion is the force that finally defeats fear. As a C-FAC team bonds and actually becomes a 'band of brothers,' all those fears of being too busy melt away. The shared experience of protecting the community builds team morale, and soon the men actually like the challenge and look forward to 'the hunt.' Thus a man's decision to commit to the mission is complete, and that fear that keeps us all in our armchairs is defeated. We come to see that the true mission is not one particular patrol night or other; the mission is men gathering together to protect their community, to minister to one another, and to demonstrate to younger men and boys what it means to be a community father."

More Soul, Less Superstition

For thumos-love to grow through tangible expressions like C-FAC, many of us will need to pour into our lives more soul than we've previously been trained to do. This will connect us to the world as it really is, not so we can be conformed to it but so that we can do our part to redeem it. For many of us during this unique time in church history, this will mean that we walk away from hyper-spirituality and especially superstitious beliefs about God. For some of us, we must learn to pray less and do more, just as those who are big on soul but small of spirit need to pray more and do less.

In the actualization of this essential balance, we will bring to our lives and the lives of those around us more time-proven life principles with which we'll be better able to carry out God's will on earth. We'll be better prepared to play our dynamic part in a world that really needs us. We will, as Roosevelt rightfully challenged, be better able to wrestle with real life and real people in real time.

What does this look like? A recent experience with The Protectors gives a solid example.

A friend of mine was bullied from kindergarten to his senior year in high school. He hated school, he felt horrible about himself, and he found himself in the world of illicit drug use for nearly twenty years. He cried numerous times while reading *No More Jellyfish, Chickens, or Wimps*—especially the parts where I call upon adults and peers to take a muscular stand against bullying.

I explained to him how this is a pivotal time in our ministry: The Protectors needs greater financial support and prayer support in order to begin meeting the vast current needs. And this man, who truly believes in our unique ministry, and who has the power right now to lift many children out of bullying—a netherworld of horror in which he's felt tormented for much of his own life—said to me, "Well, if God wants it to happen, it will happen." His statement was gargantuan on spirit-talk, diminutive on soul-doing.

It was also very superstitious and presumptuous. Though God is capable of miraculous and direct intervention, he mostly chooses to move in other ways. God usually works through his people. Through his hyper-spiritual view of life, though, my evangelical friend washed his hands of any personal responsibility to help lift the burdens of others. As I've said throughout this book, too, I no longer believe this kind of redirection to be accidental. It's a deliberate (though sometimes subconscious) attempt to hide cowardice behind pious language.

I continue to be amazed, confused, mystified, and angered by this kind of response from people who *know* the hell of bullying and yet somehow have brought themselves to think God is now going to reach down like a fairy godmother and magically grant the wishes of the millions of children who need practical help. Again, God works primarily through his people in whom resides his Spirit, and the Spirit spurs our souls to action but does not override our will. We need co-willingness.

This work is to be born in part from our soul-doing region—it won't get done through wishful thinking born of spiritual superstition. We must have a thumotic willingness to join up and serve with what rests in us—not God, our neighbor, spouse, parent, minister, but *in us*. In order for my friend to better emulate the love of Christ, he, like me, needs greater courage and deeper care for others. Cultivating and growing this courage and care requires that we invest more in tending and fortifying our souls.

Close the Gap

John Renken, a friend of mine and a pastor in Clarksville, Tennessee, is a hand-to-hand combat instructor in the army who at one time also held the world record for fastest knockout in full-contact fighting—eleven seconds, in Tokyo. I have watched the video, and it's impressive. His opponent was much bigger and stronger, but John kept his courage stoked. Instead of defaulting to a defensive orientation, he attacked with a left foot to the head. Footage shows that his highly focused opponent—perhaps drunk with hubris, a fruit of shadow thumos—didn't even see it coming.

John trains military personnel to defend themselves with their bare hands, and he says there's one thing he cannot really teach another person. It's up to them to do it, or not, and that makes all the difference: "One of the main and most difficult objectives of this training is instilling in our soldiers the courage necessary to close the gap and engage the enemy in hand-to-hand combat. I agree with the Army in their definition of Warrior Ethos, which in many ways is the exercise of *thumos*: 'The defining characteristic of a Warrior is the willingness to draw close to the enemy.'"

Draw close to the smaller fears in your life. Close those gaps—they're rarely as powerful as they appear. You don't have to be macho to do it. You can be tiny, frail, timid, even weak in body, spirit, and soul. It's not a fatal condition! The growth of courage is found in the doing.

One of history's most notable examples of *thumos* transformation is that of former U.S. President Theodore Roosevelt. He was a sickly and cowardly child, but through faith in God and through his own blood, sweat, and tears, he grew into a thumotic marvel.

Upon his death in 1919, the Boy Scouts of America spoke of Roosevelt in terms befitting a messiah:

> He was frail; he made himself a tower of strength. He was timid; he made himself a lion of courage. He was a dreamer; he became one of the great doers of all time. . . . He broke a nation's slumber with his cry, and it rose up. He touched the eyes of blind men with a flame and gave them vision. Souls became swords through him, swords became servants of God.[13]

Disruption

While working on this book, I kept stumbling upon one of the defining fruits of *thumos*: disruption. And while thinking about this aspect, I was reminded of my own youth and of the stories parents tell me, and of the stories from fathers in particular. I have held this observation to the end of this book in order to give it the emphasis it deserves.

"My son is expected to behave like a little girl in school, at church, and at home," dads tell me. This complaint comes from college grads, professors, executives, and guys we would consider metrosexual. They're not men brimming with machismo.

Jeff, a caller into our radio program, was taught by nuns at his Catholic elementary school. He's in full-time counseling now because he thinks he's "worthless and stupid," the same script the nuns handed him because they found him hard to handle. Like so many Christian men neutered from their thumos, he thinks he's the world's doormat instead of a righteous and powerful door, a healthy boundary maker.

"Hard to handle?" I asked. "How?"

"I was always hyperactive . . ."

I stopped him. "Jeff, I don't know you very well, and I wasn't there when those nuns beat up on your soul, but my guess is that you weren't hyperactive, you were just a boy being a boy. Some people appreciate that and many don't. Don't buy their definition of you—it's too expensive. You will have to fight the lies they told you about yourself."

Jeff feels toward church the way someone who was almost hung might feel about rope. He has a lot of soulwork to do, and he's doing it, but he has an uphill climb. Imagine the outcry if male teachers across the country started criticizing little girls for being "hyper-compliant"? Every one would lose his job.

Men possess more animating thumotic spiritedness, which is found unacceptably disruptive by society, and so it is driven out of boys and men through motherly shame, through pulpit brow-beatings, and now through excessive medication. But it's not only opposed by certain women. I know male coaches who will not coach boys they find "too hard to handle" (that is, they don't want disruption). I also sometimes find boys "too hard to handle"—yet I also find in their company a zest for life that's unique, penetrating, enlivening, and *necessary*. Sure, sometimes they wear me out, but most of the time they energize me.

I emphasize this because I think most of us, if we're honest, have seen this trait more in boys than in girls. It's so noticeable that *Thymos* is the name of the academic *Journal* of *Boyhood Studies*.[14] We can't deny it, and accordingly we can't deny that *thumos* indwells us both, albeit in different ways and to different degrees.

And I point this out not to shame anyone but to illuminate a remarkable opportunity we all have to season this potentially noble gift to humankind. If we are honest about our want and need for courageous faith, then people who want to work with boys and young men should be required to demonstrate their love for this characteristic. Let's seek applicants who favor and foster it.

Right now our slouching spine is our Achilles' heel, a form of cowardice that we mistake for gentleness. We're experts at spotting and denouncing raw aggression and pride, and amateurs at spotting raw cowardice and fear, a sweaty second to pride by way of destruction. If we are serious about *integrity*—among the largest buzzwords in men's ministry today—then we must learn to become more serious about spotting cowardice, confessing it to one another as the sin it is, then bolstering our God-given capacity for courageous faith. Where there is no courage, there is no integrity.

In order for our feet to be put upon this firmer foundation, we will have to do more than fight our inner demons. We, brothers and sisters of thumos, will have to fight and rewrite the Official Script. Change the plot, change your role. Scrap the tragic ending and, with God's grace, create a more redemptive one. The cast of the courageous may never be as large as you think it should be. It has always been this way. Fight anyway.

Blessed are those who become the courageous, animated people God created them to be. Blessed are the malcontents too unsatisfied to remain harmless to the thieving prince of this world, and too genuine and trustworthy to be restrained by falsehoods wherever they may hide.

Notes

1. Ralph Waldo Emerson, in David Josiah Brewer, Edward Archibald Allen, and William Schuyler, *The World's Best Orations: From the Earliest Period to the Present Time* (Cambridge, MA: Harvard University Press, 1901), 2540.

2. See Romans 12:2.

3. See Hebrews 10:22.

4. James 2:26 THE MESSAGE

5. See James 1:27.

6. See Isaiah 58:6.

7. Amos 5:23–24 NASB

8. Buechner, *Telling the Truth*, 18.

9. For instance, see Isaiah 59:15–16.

10. Henry T. Close, "On Saying No to People: A Pastoral Letter," originally published in *The Journal of Pastoral Care* (1974, 28[2]): 92–98.

11. 2 Corinthians 12:9

12. Gary Haugen, *Just Courage: God's Great Expedition for the Restless Christian* (Downers Grove, IL: InterVarsity, 2008), 18.

13. Clifford Putney, *Muscular Christianity: Manhood and Sports in Protestant America, 1880–1920* (Cambridge, MA: Harvard University Press), 35.

14. *www.boyhoodstudies.com/thymos.htm*

TWELVE-LESSON DISCUSSION GUIDE

Chapter One: When a Dog Is More Manly

1. There are dogs—then there are *dogs*. Think about the dogs in your life that you've respected the most. What are the top three attributes you admire in them?

2. If you're part of a mixed group, separate the attributes that women list and men list. If there are differences, discuss them—what do you think they point to? If you're part of a men-only study, what attributes do your lists have in common?

3. In which area of life would it be best, for you and for those you love, if you began to emulate the noble behavior of dogs? What positive changes might take place?

4. Think of times when you've seen bold and courageous people being mistreated by others, and share examples. What does the prevalence of such mistreatment tell us about human nature? What does it tell us about our view of courage?

5. Read Matthew 23:23–39, and discuss the role thumos played in Jesus' denunciation of the Pharisees. In what situations do you feel it would be right for a Christian to emulate Jesus' dealings with the Pharisees?

6. Before continuing with the book, list three ways you think thumotic courage is grown and three ways it is diminished. At book's end, revisit this by comparing the list to any changes you would make. Discuss your discoveries.

Chapter Two: MIA—A Martial Spirit

1. The English word *masculinity* is about a hundred years old, and our understanding of it has changed throughout the decades. Write down a one-sentence definition that comprises your understanding of the word or how you think society would define it today. Compare/contrast with this book's definition: *love bolstered by courage*. In what ways is your definition or society's similar or different? Share and discuss in your group.

2. If pastors' sons comprise the group of men most robbed of a martial spirit, and if this is intrinsic to soul-growth, we can see the potential ramifications for the church's future leadership. What do you suggest we do to begin helping to correct this travesty?

3. How do you see your life benefiting from a stronger martial spirit? Who else might benefit, and how?

4. Think about a time in your life when you could have benefited from another person's martial spirit, yet it was never exercised. How did this make you feel? How did it affect your thoughts or beliefs?

5. Think about a time when someone else would have benefited from your exercising a martial spirit, but you didn't. How did this make you feel? How do you wish you'd acted differently?

6. This chapter explores the concept of "blessed dissatisfaction," or "holy discontent." What tends to nudge *you* toward dissatisfaction? What makes you feel discontent? In what ways do you see the growth of spirited thumotic courage helping you to confront these factors?

Chapter Three: Soulful Manliness

1. Even though the "gentleman" concept does not appear in the Bible, Christian men are expected to conform to the definition's current standards. Write down four attributes you believe are included in our culture's understanding of being a gentleman. Then write down four attributes you would expect from a good police officer. Which list do you think is more accurate, and why?

2. Brad Miner says that "a true gentleman—a chivalrous man—is just a bit more savage than most people imagine. . . . A man who is not roused to combat evil is no gentleman." Compare his words to your first list of gentlemanly attributes—are there differences? Does your original definition include the ability and willingness to combat evil?

3. Think about how, in the sporting world, offense creates and defense destroys. Which approach better describes the way you have been living your life? What role has courage been playing, or not playing, in your decisions and actions?

4. A person's "inner sword" is a symbol of willingness to fight for what's right. When was the last time you used your inner sword? How did you use it? Who was critical of you as a result, and who praised you? What do you think Jesus would have said or done in the same situation?

5. All people possess life, but not all people are truly alive. Think about the people in your life who are more vital than others. What traits and behaviors do they have in common? What are two of their characteristics that you could build into your life? In what ways would your life improve?

6. Think about the times when you've been a coward. What emotion(s) did you feel? Have you asked for God's forgiveness? If your cowardice hurt another person, have you asked him or her to forgive you? Why do you think cowardice needs to be forgiven? What does this tell us about the importance of courage?

7. Think about a transcendent cause that seizes your affections and gets your blood pumping. Why do you think this grabs you more than other worthy causes? How do you think bolstering your courage could help you do your part for this cause?

Chapter Four: Courage of Substance, and of Shadow

1. This chapter explains the difference between shadow thumos and noble thumos. In the space below, list words, phrases, and related thoughts that represent what you see as examples of each.

2. If noble thumos dominates your life, what are ways you can share this blessing with others? And if shadow thumos dominates your life, what behaviors need to stop, and who can you trust to help you change?

3. Inner debates are a specialty of thumos. Our thoughts and emotions come together to debate and wrestle with our conscience. More than just "trying to figure something out," this happens when we're trying to strengthen our courage.

   What are some key words, phrases, and verses that you can say to yourself to bolster your courage during this pivotal time in your life?

4. One of the most helpful ways a person can grow courage is to remember times they've been successful in similar situations. Think about when you have been up against difficult odds and yet were successful. What happened? What role did you play? What role did God play? Is it reasonable to think such success could be yours again? Why or why not?

5. Head religion and heart religion are both prevalent in this age when thumos religion is hardly acknowledged. Of the three, which expression are you most familiar with? How do you think this kind of "religion" has helped or hurt your

faith? What can you do to bring greater balance and integrity to your faith?

6. List the differing attributes in a person who is *willful* ("My will be done") and a person who is *willing* ("Thy will be done").

7. What courses of action can you commit to today that will make you more willing than willful?

Chapter Five: Low on Living, Low on Life

1. Studies show that church is more attractive to people who tend toward passivity, and passive people tend to be low on vitality. With this in mind, think about the majority of sermons you hear in which Christians, especially men, are encouraged to embrace meekness and mildness. Is this the right spiritual prescription? Why or why not?

2. Low-thumos living is also low-energy living. If you were married to someone who didn't invest energy into your relationship, how would you feel? If you've been told that you're a low-energy spouse, what are three healthy changes you can implement over the next six weeks to address this situation?

3. There are those who can be accurately described as "hyper-spiritual," who have pat-answer "spiritual solutions" for virtually everything. Have you received counsel from such a person? If you've followed the advice, what have been the results?

4. Low-thumos folks do more than just hurt themselves—they can actually suck the life out of others. Is there anyone in your life who is negatively impacting your capacity for courage? How can you defend yourself against this corrupting influence?

5. Do you agree that women are attracted to men with thumotic heat? Why or why not?

6. This chapter explores the film *The Weather Man* as an example of someone who lacks thumotic energy and then finds it. (*Note:* The film contains vulgar behavior and language.) Consider watching the movie, and respond to the following questions:

   • Why is David Spritz so weak in the face of his troubles?

   • To which of David's problems can you specifically relate?

   • What helps David change into a better man?

   • How might you do something similar to improve the quality of your life and the strength of your faith?

- Why do you think God counts cowardice as sinful on a level with sorcery and sexual immorality?

- How is God courageous? Give examples.

Chapter Six: Training That Drains—A Script That Needs Rewriting

1. The prophet Isaiah tells us that God gives us a spirit of *power*, which can also be translated as *strength*, a derivative of courage. In what area of your life would this gifting be beneficial?

2. Think about courageous people you have known well. What similarities in upbringing did they have? For example, did they suffer particular episodes of difficulty? Similar seasons of challenge? What have such common experiences taught you?

3. Discuss the differences between peacemaking and peace-faking. What role does courage play in creating peace that is more than personal (peace that is communal)?

4. Machiavelli wrote that Christianity's sanctification of mild personalities has "rendered the world weak and handed it over as prey to wicked men." Would you feel safer going into physical battle with men from your church or with men from your workplace? Why? Discuss pros and cons.

5. If you think you'll receive resistance while helping to rewrite the Official Script, how can becoming as wise as a serpent help you in your efforts? Be as specific as possible.

6. The Official Script tells us to avoid behaviors that have the ability to reduce or remove our "joy" and "peace" in the Lord. Yet we see in Scripture Jesus living in a way that is not always joyful, peaceful, or contented—in fact, it is more often confrontational, frustrated, and indignant. Where does this seeming contradiction come from? How can it be resolved?

7. Jesus said that the greatest commandment is to love God with all your heart, soul [i.e., the seat of thumotic will and animation], and mind. Who comes to mind when you think of those who love through their soulfulness?

8. When was the last time you showed courage? Why did you do what you did? When was the last time you showed cowardice? Why did you do what you did? What happened after each instance? Thank God in prayer for the acts of courage. Ask his forgiveness for the sin of cowardice, and ask for individual and corporate strength to keep standing against it.

Chapter Seven: Spiritual Abuse: Thumos-Spilling

Cautionary Note: The topic of spiritual abuse can become combustive, so it's especially important to begin this section with shared prayer and a reminder that grace must be afforded to whomever is speaking.

1. If you've experienced spiritual abuse and find the courage to speak up about it during the discussion, know that others need to learn from your experience. Here's a bit of advice: Don't try to fix what happened to you. Just tell about it. Speak the facts and let them fall where they may. If at all possible, omit names so as to keep the conversation from getting personal or accusatory. Also realize there probably are people in your group who feel compelled to defend certain behaviors of spiritually abusive leaders. In the event that you are challenged in this way, a good response generally is "I am simply telling you my experience."

2. Francis Schaeffer coined the term *glorious ruins* to describe human nature, which is both vile and magnificent at the same time. It seems we Christians quickly spot the flaws in obsessing over our worth while ignoring or denying our sinfulness. What reasons can you give, then, for why we don't have a better ability to recognize the opposite error of wallowing in our imperfections while overlooking or rejecting the glory of God's image in us?

3. From this chapter's list of spiritually abusive characteristics, mark the ones you've experienced during your spiritual journey. As past events come to mind, write down ways in which these traits, and the way they've been acted out, have affected

your courage. (You could make this an ongoing exercise—it may take some time to comprehend the full impact of spiritually abusive teaching and thinking. Demonstrating courage today is so neglected that most of us aren't accustomed to focusing on it.)

4. Author Ken Blue asserts that spiritual abuse is a form of social evil. If this is true and if courage is essential to love, then is overlooking courage (or rejection of it) a form of spiritual neglect? Give reasons why you agree or disagree.

5. People under the scourge of spiritual abuse often need a rescuer, a deliverer—someone with the heated animation of thumotic courage. Who today might need the strength of your godly martial spirit? What specific needs could you meet?

6. Jesus clearly was not "happy" all the time—for instance, sometimes he was angry, and sometimes he was grief-stricken. What factors do you see that influence Christians to think they should be "happy" all the time? Are there compelling reasons to trust someone who always acts happy? Why or why not?

7. Is there anyone you need to forgive? In what ways can courage help you to live in a continual attitude and practice of forgiveness?

Chapter Eight: Materialism: Thumos-Numbing

1. For many of us, living more simply and humbly would give us far more time and energy, and money, to live more nobly. What redemptive act(s) could you embark upon with these additional resources?

2. What brings you to your knees in prayer more: personal/ national economic instability/uncertainty or social injustice/ impoverishment? Does your response indicate a need for soul-growth? If yes, explain.

3. If possessions are holding you captive, what three choices (changes to your perspective and your behavior) could you make to free yourself to live more nobly? What role will courage play in your decisions?

4. Think about recent Christmases: How much of your time and energy has gone into the remembrance and celebration of Christ, and how much into consumer-driven busyness? Are there changes you could implement this year to bring about peace, love, and thankfulness while also reducing frustration and anxiety?

5. The author writes that materialism is not passive or neutral but *actively opposes* our loving connection with others.

Consider specific relationships that you have: How might materialism damage or weaken them?

6. In what ways does materialism try to preserve us instead of redeem us?

Chapter Nine: Cynicism: Thumos-Freezing

1. This chapter was designed to help us avoid internal *and* external cynicism, which depletes us of thumotic courage, faith, and more muscular expressions of love. This is an important distinction, because even if you do not tend toward cynicism yourself, you are no doubt surrounded by it to some degree.

2. Think about the more cynical people in your life, past or present. In what ways did/do you see them helping others?

3. Have you noticed that, in general, men are more susceptible to cynicism than women? Do you have any ideas as to why? How does male cynicism relate to willingness, animation, and courage?

4. In what ways are you actively protecting yourself and those in your care from the eroding influence of cynicism? If you're starting now to defend yourself and others against cynicism, which friendships (without naming names) might be put in jeopardy as you take these steps? Are these generally people of courage?

5. The main sources of cynicism explored in this chapter are dashed hopes, unmet expectations, and discovering no benefit from playing by all the artificial rules. What are some other sources of cynicism? What can you do to guard against them or at least change your attitude about negative experiences that you have no control over?

6. Faith gives substance to our hopes, while cynicism keeps us from feeling our hopes being dashed. What are some ways we can keep hope alive through our faith and avoid cynical escape?

7. Think of a time in your life when you lacked "sufficient suspicion." What happened to you? What happens to others when they lack it? What messages in church have you heard that help people live abundant lives, in part, through healthy suspicion?

8. Theodore Roosevelt complained that the Christians of his time were "very nice, very refined . . . [yet] wholly unable to grapple with real men in real life." Is this true of the majority of believers you know? Why or why not? How could thumotic courage help us remedy this lack?

9. What do you think of Reinhold Niebuhr's observation that "the children of light must be armed with the wisdom of the children of darkness but remain free from their malice"? How might such "street-smart" wisdom help to forge courageous faith and stem cynicism?

Chapter Ten: Lessons From the Rescuers: Thumos-Encouragement

1. We're created with the capacity for courage, but we must be trained in how to activate it from our inner being. In what ways are today's children trained to grow their courage? In what ways can we start to improve their moral education?

2. More than comforting and consoling, *encouragement* means "to propel and urge" another person forward. In what ways has your spiritual training encouraged you to move forward with courage and boldness? In what ways was this neglected?

3. The courageous people who helped to rescue Jews from the Nazis shared three major characteristics:

   - An adventurous spirit that is humane and purposeful

   - Identification with a morally strong parent or morally strong heroic figure

   - An ability to identify with socially marginal people, along with a willingness to break with tradition and withstand persecution while pursuing justice and truth

   In what ways can you graft into your life these qualities? For example, if you didn't grow up with a morally strong parent, which heroic figure most energizes your thumos? What does this connection tell you about yourself and what the world needs today from you?

4. Recall a time when someone gave you the gift of comfort and it bolstered your courage. What did you do with this newfound courage? How can you give it to others?

5. One way to build courage is to be around people of courage. Name three people you consider to be courageous. Also name a courageous person (or two) with whom you could spend more time.

6. Pope John Paul II was a powerful combination of the spiritual (mystically and mysteriously connected to God) and the soulful (tangibly and pragmatically connected to this world). In what practical ways might your life benefit from a better balance of spiritual vitality and soulfulness?

7. Wonder and mystery animate our lives and jump-start our courage. What makes you wonder? What remains mysterious to you? What can you do to bring more wonder and mystery into your life?

Chapter Eleven: Grief-Work, Fellowship, and Faith: Thumos-Creation

1. When handling our grief, we tend to either overreact or under-react. Which are you more prone to do? What adjustments could help bring you back toward balance?

2. Although courage is not born from our emotions, it needs emotions—like empathy and indignation—to fuel it. What can you begin doing to increase your capacity for healthy emotional expression?

3. Do you have unresolved feelings toward your parents? In order to help bring resolution of grief, it sometimes helps to look at pictures of them when they were young, especially

before they were parents. Do you have access to such photos? If you do, study them. Look at their eyes and body language. What do you see and perceive? How does it affect you? Does this help or hinder your ability to forgive and, in the process, become more animated and alive?

4. The Bible tells us that cowardice is sinful. So if courage—along with spiritual growth and maturity—is instilled and built through the appropriate feelings of grief, compassion, and empathy, and if you find it hard to experience these emotions, would it be sinful if you didn't try? Why or why not?

5. Fellowship is so important to our thumos growth, but it needs to incorporate certain aspects in order to be both attractive and helpful to men. What are practical ways you can help bring more *humor and earthiness* into your fellowship and brotherhood?

6. The world has always been changed for the better by people with thumos. Make a list of the top five people who, in your lifetime, helped to make the world a better place. Note the ways you observed courage, animation, boldness, integrity—*life*—in them and from them.

Chapter Twelve: Start Small, but Take a Hill

1. Remember your original list of three ways thumotic courage is grown and three ways it's diminished? (See the last question in the section for chapter 1.) Take a look at that list now. Is there anything you would add, subtract, or revise, based on what you've read and discussed?

2. Thumos disrupts the status quo, and many people love the status quo, even when it's harming them and others. Some even hate the *people* who bring disruption into their lives. In what situations do you think it would be right to make this kind of enemy?

3. God requires justice as a part of our worship. What ideas can you think of for joining justice to worship—not only in services but also as a whole way of life? What changes can you make personally in order to help persuade others of the importance of this?

4. The ability and willingness to say no, creating firm boundaries on behalf of yourself and others, is essential to courageous faith in action. But in order to be able to do this, we must have a strong sense of self. What does it mean to have this and at the same time not be self-obsessed? And what does Jesus mean when he says we are to love our neighbor *as we love ourselves*?

5. Who or what do you need to say no to today? Are you willing to live with the consequences, whatever they may be?

6. What hill are you motivated to take right now? (*Hint:* This tends to be in line with what grieves you.) Write three sentences that explain the problem or difficulty and how you expect to solve it in a tangible way. Which two thumos-empowered people do you know who could help you, through God's grace, to take your hill? In what ways might your faith need to become more soulful and less "spiritual" in order to complete your task?

RAISING SECURE, ASSERTIVE
KIDS IN A TOUGH WORLD

HOPE FOR LIFE FROM
PAUL COUGHLIN
STRONGER CHILDREN. COURAGEOUS FAITH. BETTER MARRIAGES.

Coughlin Ministries equips everyone to live more hopeful, freer, assertive and proactive lives through unique resources and life-changing presentations.

Paul Coughlin, author of several books including the best-selling *No More Christian Nice Guy, Married But Not Engaged, No More Jellyfish, Chickens or Wimps*, and *Unleashing Courageous Faith*, is an international speaker, talk show host, and Founder of The Protectors, the faith-based solution to adolescent bullying. Paul has been interviewed by *Nightline, Newsweek, New York Times, LA Times, Focus on the Family, 700 Club*, and *C-SPAN*, among other national media.

Coughlin Ministries began and continues to equip men to live lives of deeper love and faith, increased strength, and greater freedom by

filtering through damaging stereotypes and addressing practical issues that each man faces. Coughlin Ministries helps men harness their God-given strengths in order to unleash a courageous faith that strengthens individual souls, families, and communities.

His life-changing presentations include: Promise Keepers Canada, Iron Sharpens Iron, No More Christian Nice Guy Conference, Married But Not Engaged Marriage Conference, How To Raise Courageous Kids in a Tough World Conference, and The Protectors Summit: The Faith-Based Solution to Adolescent Bullying. To invite Paul to speak at your next event, go to **www.paulcoughlin.net** and click on "Schedule an event."

He and his family of five live in southern Oregon where Paul, voted Coach of the Year, is a boys varsity soccer coach.

COUGHLIN MINISTRIES

P.O. Box 4457 • Medford, OR 97501-0174